FrontPage™ Web Publishing & Design for Dummies®

FRONTPAGE™ WEB PUBLISHING & DESIGN FOR DUMMIES®

by Asha Dornfest

IDG Books Worldwide, Inc.
An International Data Group Company

Foster City, CA ♦ Chicago, IL ♦ Indianapolis, IN ♦ Southlake, TX

FrontPage™ Web Publishing & Design For Dummies®

Published by
IDG Books Worldwide, Inc.
An International Data Group Company
919 E. Hillsdale Blvd.
Suite 400
Foster City, CA 94404
http://www.idgbooks.com (IDG Books Worldwide Web site)
http://www.dummies.com (Dummies Press Web site)

Library of Congress Catalog Card No.: 96-79276

ISBN: 0-7645-0057-0

Printed in the United States of America

10 9 8 7 6 5 4 3 2 1

1O/TQ/RS/ZW/IN

Distributed in the United States by IDG Books Worldwide, Inc.

Distributed by Macmillan Canada for Canada; by Transworld Publishers Limited in the United Kingdom and Europe; by WoodsLane Pty. Ltd. for Australia; by WoodsLane Enterprises Ltd. for New Zealand; by Longman Singapore Publishers Ltd. for Singapore, Malaysia, Thailand, and Indonesia; by Simron Pty. Ltd. for South Africa; by Toppan Company Ltd. for Japan; by Distribuidora Cuspide for Argentina; by Livraria Cultura for Brazil; by Ediciencia S.A. for Ecuador; by Addison-Wesley Publishing Company for Korea; by Ediciones ZETA S.C.R. Ltda. for Peru; by WS Computer Publishing Company, Inc., for the Philippines; by Unalis Corporation for Taiwan; by Contemporanea de Ediciones for Venezuela. Authorized Sales Agent: Anthony Rudkin Associates for the Middle East and North Africa.

For general information on IDG Books Worldwide's books in the U.S., please call our Consumer Customer Service department at 800-762-2974. For reseller information, including discounts and premium sales, please call our Reseller Customer Service department at 800-434-3422.

For information on where to purchase IDG Books Worldwide's books outside the U.S., please contact our International Sales department at 415-655-3172 or fax 415-655-3295.

For information on foreign language translations, please contact our Foreign & Subsidiary Rights department at 415-655-3021 or fax 415-655-3281.

For sales inquiries and special prices for bulk quantities, please contact our Sales department at 415-655-3200 or write to the address above.

For information on using IDG Books Worldwide's books in the classroom or for ordering examination copies, please contact our Educational Sales department at 800-434-2086 or fax 817-251-8174.

For press review copies, author interviews, or other publicity information, please contact our Public Relations department at 415-655-3000 or fax 415-655-3299.

For authorization to photocopy items for corporate, personal, or educational use, please contact Copyright Clearance Center, 222 Rosewood Drive, Danvers, MA 01923, or fax 508-750-4470.

 is a trademark under exclusive license to IDG Books Worldwide, Inc., from International Data Group, Inc.

About the Author

Asha Dornfest

On her first day of college, Asha Dornfest took a bold step: She replaced her broken typewriter with a PC.

Asha did not consider herself a geek; her computer was simply a tool to help her write papers and reports. But by her senior year, she had defended her clunky PC against so many insults from Mac-loving roommates, she came to regard her computer with a sense of kinship. (Okay, so that's a *little* geeky.)

After graduation, Asha trudged into the real world with a liberal arts degree and strong computer skills. (Which do you think got her a job?) She quickly realized that she enjoyed showing people how computers could simplify their lives (when the things weren't making life more difficult, that is).

In 1994, Asha discovered the Internet. Soon after, she and her husband started a Web design business in their dining room and began hawking their electronic wares. (Mind you, this venture began during the Web-publishing Stone Age; some people had never even *heard* of the World Wide Web.) A savvy friend quipped that …*For Dummies* books about Web publishing might one day hit the shelves. Asha laughed.

Today, Asha writes books and articles about Web publishing and other Internet-related topics. She welcomes visitors to her virtual home at `http://www.dnai.com/~asha`.

ABOUT IDG BOOKS WORLDWIDE

Welcome to the world of IDG Books Worldwide.

IDG Books Worldwide, Inc., is a subsidiary of International Data Group, the world's largest publisher of computer-related information and the leading global provider of information services on information technology. IDG was founded more than 25 years ago and now employs more than 8,500 people worldwide. IDG publishes more than 275 computer publications in over 75 countries (see listing below). More than 60 million people read one or more IDG publications each month.

Launched in 1990, IDG Books Worldwide is today the #1 publisher of best-selling computer books in the United States. We are proud to have received eight awards from the Computer Press Association in recognition of editorial excellence and three from *Computer Currents'* First Annual Readers' Choice Awards. Our best-selling *...For Dummies*® series has more than 30 million copies in print with translations in 30 languages. IDG Books Worldwide, through a joint venture with IDG's Hi-Tech Beijing, became the first U.S. publisher to publish a computer book in the People's Republic of China. In record time, IDG Books Worldwide has become the first choice for millions of readers around the world who want to learn how to better manage their businesses.

Our mission is simple: Every one of our books is designed to bring extra value and skill-building instructions to the reader. Our books are written by experts who understand and care about our readers. The knowledge base of our editorial staff comes from years of experience in publishing, education, and journalism — experience we use to produce books for the '90s. In short, we care about books, so we attract the best people. We devote special attention to details such as audience, interior design, use of icons, and illustrations. And because we use an efficient process of authoring, editing, and desktop publishing our books electronically, we can spend more time ensuring superior content and spend less time on the technicalities of making books.

You can count on our commitment to deliver high-quality books at competitive prices on topics you want to read about. At IDG Books Worldwide, we continue in the IDG tradition of delivering quality for more than 25 years. You'll find no better book on a subject than one from IDG Books Worldwide.

John Kilcullen
President and CEO
IDG Books Worldwide, Inc.

Eighth Annual
Computer Press
Awards ≥ 1992

Ninth Annual
Computer Press
Awards ≥ 1993

Tenth Annual
Computer Press
Awards ≥ 1994

Eleventh Annual
Computer Press
Awards ≥ 1995

IDG Books Worldwide, Inc., is a subsidiary of International Data Group, the world's largest publisher of computer-related information and the leading global provider of information services on information technology. International Data Group publishes over 275 computer publications in over 75 countries. Sixty million people read one or more International Data Group publications each month. International Data Group's publications include: **ARGENTINA:** Buyer's Guide, Computerworld Argentina, PC World Argentina; **AUSTRALIA:** Australian Macworld, Australian PC World, Australian Reseller News, Computerworld, IT Casebook, Network World, Publish, Webmaster; **AUSTRIA:** Computerwelt Osterreich, Networks Austria, PC Tip Austria; **BANGLADESH:** PC World Bangladesh; **BELARUS:** PC World Belarus; **BELGIUM:** Data News; **BRAZIL:** Annuário de Informática, Computerworld, Connections, Macworld, PC Player, PC World, Publish, Reseller News, Supergamepower; **BULGARIA:** Computerworld Bulgaria, Network World Bulgaria, PC & MacWorld Bulgaria; **CANADA:** CIO Canada, Client/Server World, ComputerWorld Canada, InfoWorld Canada, NetworkWorld Canada, WebWorld; **CHILE:** Computerworld Chile, PC World Chile; **COLOMBIA:** Computerworld Colombia, PC World Colombia; **COSTA RICA:** PC World Centro America; **THE CZECH AND SLOVAK REPUBLICS:** Computerworld Czechoslovakia, Macworld Czech Republic, PC World Czechoslovakia; **DENMARK:** Communications World Danmark, Computerworld Danmark, Macworld Danmark, PC World Danmark, Techworld Denmark; **DOMINICAN REPUBLIC:** PC World Republica Dominicana; **ECUADOR:** PC World Ecuador; **EGYPT:** Computerworld Middle East, PC World Middle East; **EL SALVADOR:** PC World Centro America; **FINLAND:** MikroPC, Tietoverkko, Tietoviikko; **FRANCE:** Distributique, Hebdo, Info PC, Le Monde Informatique, Macworld, Reseaux & Telecoms, WebMaster France; **GERMANY:** Computer Partner, Computerwoche, Computerwoche Extra, Computerwoche FOCUS, Global Online, Macwelt, PC Welt; **GREECE:** Amiga Computing, GamePro Greece, Multimedia World; **GUATEMALA:** PC World Centro America; **HONDURAS:** PC World Centro America; **HONG KONG:** Computerworld Hong Kong, PC World Hong Kong, Publish in Asia; **HUNGARY:** ABCD CD-ROM, Computerworld Szamitastechnika, Internetto online Magazine, PC World Hungary, PC-X Magazin Hungary; **ICELAND:** Tolvuheimur PC World Island; **INDIA:** Information Communications World, Information Systems Computerworld, PC World India, Publish in Asia; **INDONESIA:** InfoKomputer PC World, Komputek Computerworld, Publish in Asia; **IRELAND:** ComputerScope, PC Live!; **ISRAEL:** Macworld Israel, People & Computers/Computerworld; **ITALY:** Computerworld Italia, Macworld Italia, Networking Italia, PC World Italia; **JAPAN:** DTP World, Macworld Japan, Nikkei Personal Computing, OS/2 World Japan, SunWorld Japan, Windows NT World, Windows World Japan; **KENYA:** PC World East African; **KOREA:** Hi-Tech Information, Macworld Korea, PC World Korea; **MACEDONIA:** PC World Macedonia; **MALAYSIA:** Computerworld Malaysia, PC World Malaysia, Publish in Asia; **MALTA:** PC World Malta; **MEXICO:** Computerworld Mexico, PC World Mexico; **MYANMAR:** PC World Myanmar; **NETHERLANDS:** Computer! Totaal, LAN Internetworking Magazine, LAN World Buyers Guide, Macworld Netherlands, Net, WebWereld; **NEW ZEALAND:** Absolute Beginners Guide and Plain & Simple Series, Computer Buyer, Computer Industry Directory, Computerworld New Zealand, MTB, Network World, PC World New Zealand; **NICARAGUA:** PC World Centro America; **NORWAY:** Computerworld Norge, CW Rapport, Datamagasinet, Financial Rapport, Kursguide Norge, Macworld Norge, Multimediaworld Norge, PC World Ekspress Norge, PC World Nettverk, PC World Norge, PC World ProduktGuide Norge; **PAKISTAN:** Computerworld Pakistan; **PANAMA:** PC World Panama; **PEOPLE'S REPUBLIC OF CHINA:** China Computer Users, China Computerworld, China InfoWorld, China Telecom World Weekly, Computer & Communication, Electronic Design China, Electronics Today, Electronics Weekly, Game Software, PC World China, Popular Computer Week, Software Weekly, Software World, Telecom World; **PERU:** Computerworld Peru, PC World Profesional Peru, PC World SoHo Peru; **PHILIPPINES:** Click!, Computerworld Philippines, PC World Philippines, Publish in Asia; **POLAND:** Computerworld Poland, Computerworld Special Report Poland, Cyber, Macworld Poland, Networld Poland,-PC World Komputer; **PORTUGAL:** Cerebro/PC World, Computerworld/Correio Informático, Dealer World Portugal, Mac*In/PC*In Portugal, Multimedia World; **PUERTO RICO:** PC World Puerto Rico; **ROMANIA:** Computerworld Romania, PC World Romania, Telecom Romania; **RUSSIA:** Computerworld Russia, Mir PK, Publish, Seti; **SINGAPORE:** Computerworld Singapore, PC World Singapore, Publish in Asia; **SLOVENIA:** Monitor; **SOUTH AFRICA:** Computing SA, Network World SA, Software World SA; **SPAIN:** Communicaciones World España, Computerworld España, Dealer World España, Macworld España, PC World España; **SRI LANKA:** Infolink PC World; **SWEDEN:** CAP&Design, Computer Sweden, Corporate Computing Sweden, Internetworld Sweden, it.branschen, Macworld Sweden, MaxiData Sweden, MikroDatorn, Natverk & Kommunikation, PC World Sweden, PCaktiv, Windows World Sweden; **SWITZERLAND:** Computerworld Schweiz, Macworld Schweiz, PCtip; **TAIWAN:** Computerworld Taiwan, Macworld Taiwan, NEW ViSiON/Publish, PC World Taiwan, Windows World Taiwan; **THAILAND:** Publish in Asia, Thai Computerworld; **TURKEY:** Computerworld Turkiye, Macworld Turkiye, Network World Turkiye, PC World Turkiye; **UKRAINE:** Computerworld Kiev, Multimedia World Ukraine, PC World Ukraine; **UNITED KINGDOM:** Acorn User UK, Amiga Action UK, Amiga Computing UK, Apple Talk UK, Computing, Macworld, Parents and Computers UK, PC Advisor, PC Home, PSX Pro, The WEB; **UNITED STATES:** Cable in the Classroom, CIO Magazine, Computerworld, DOS World, Federal Computer Week, GamePro Magazine, InfoWorld, I-Way, Macworld, Network World, PC Games, PC World, Publish, Video Event, THE WEB Magazine, and WebMaster; online webzines: JavaWorld, NetscapeWorld, and SunWorld Online; **URUGUAY:** InfoWorld Uruguay; **VENEZUELA:** Computerworld Venezuela, PC World Venezuela; and **VIETNAM:** PC World Vietnam.

10/22/96

Dedication

This book is dedicated to my family — my husband, Rael, and my parents, Jagdish and Rosalyn Jirge, and Franklyn and Carol Dornfest — for their love, understanding, and encouragement.

Author's Acknowledgments

I'd like to thank the folks who made writing this book such a fun and exciting adventure.

My editorial team at IDG was top-notch. Kelly Ewing, my project editor, orchestrated the entire production process, from helping develop the initial outline to finalizing the wording on the cover. Her editorial skill, encouragement, and friendly disposition were a constant source of motivation.

My copy editor, William Barton, and my technical editor, Michael Lerch, sifted through each chapter. Not only did they make sure that the book is easy to read, technically accurate, and grammatically correct, they suggested tons of improvements as we went along. I thank them for their patience and excellent work.

I'd like to thank Gareth Hancock, Jim Sumser, Mary Bednarek, and Joyce Pepple for their assistance. I'd also like to thank Victor Engel, who generously allowed me to include his color palette on this book's CD. Very special thanks go to Brenda Kienan, who introduced me to the nice people at Dummies Press.

I am grateful to Akorn Access (`http://www.akorn.net`) for their excellent FrontPage Internet service. Kudos to Bill Fisher and Ed Selby for their technical expertise and willingness to go the extra mile to help customers. I'd also like to thank the helpful members of the Akorn FrontPage Mail Reflector, a peer-to-peer mailing list that detangles the most persistent FrontPage snarls.

Finally, I want to thank my husband, Rael, and the rest of my family and friends for sticking with me while I went into hiding to write this book. I couldn't have done it without you.

Publisher's Acknowledgments

We're proud of this book; please send us your comments about it by using the Reader Response Card at the back of the book or by e-mailing us at feedback/dummies@idgbooks.com. Some of the people who helped bring this book to market include the following:

Acquisitions, Development, & Editorial

Project Editor: Kelly Ewing

Assistant Acquisitions Editor: Gareth Hancock

Product Development Manager: Mary Bednarek

Media Development Manager: Joyce Pepple

Associate Technical Editor: Kevin Spencer

Copy Editor: William A. Barton

Technical Reviewer: Michael Lerch

Editorial Manager: Seta K. Frantz

Editorial Assistant: Michael D. Sullivan

Production

Associate Project Coordinator: Regina Snyder

Layout and Graphics: Cameron Booker, Linda M. Boyer, J. Tyler Connor, Dominique DeFelice, Maridee V. Ennis, Angela F. Hunckler, Todd Klemme, Jane Martin, Mark C. Owens, Brent Savage, Kate Snell

Proofreaders: Laura Bowman, Melissa D. Buddendeck, Nancy Price, Dwight Ramsey, Rob Springer, Carrie Voorhis, Karen York

Indexer: Sherry Massey

General & Administrative

IDG Books Worldwide, Inc.: John Kilcullen, CEO; Steven Berkowitz, President and Publisher

IDG Books Technology Publishing: Brenda McLaughlin, Senior Vice President and Group Publisher

Dummies Technology Press & Dummies Editorial: Diane Graves Steele, Vice President and Associate Publisher; Judith A. Taylor, Brand Manager; Kristin A. Cocks, Editorial Director

Dummies Trade Press: Kathleen A. Welton, Vice President & Publisher; Stacy S. Collins, Brand Manager

IDG Books Production for Dummies Press: Beth Jenkins, Production Director; Cindy L. Phipps, Supervisor of Project Coordination; Kathie S. Schutte, Supervisor of Page Layout; Shelley Lea, Supervisor of Graphics and Design; Debbie J. Gates, Production Systems Specialist; Tony Augsburger, Supervisor of Reprint and Bluelines; Leslie Popplewell, Media Archive Coordinator

Dummies Packaging & Book Design: Patti Sandez, Packaging Specialist; Kavish+Kavish, Cover Design

♦

The publisher would like to give special thanks to Patrick J. McGovern, without whom this book would not have been possible.

♦

Contents at a Glance

Cartoons at a Glance

By Rich Tennant • Fax: 508-546-7747 • E-mail: the5wave@tiac.net

Table of Contents

Chapter 13: Eye-Popping Extras: Multimedia, Components, and Scripts 237

Part III: Nifty Web Site Additions *257*

Chapter 14: Membership Has Its Privileges 259

Chapter 15: Can We Talk? 271

Introduction

● ●

A couple years ago, only geeks, academics, and soda-fueled computer jocks populated the Internet. Today, the proliferation of desktop computers, plus the advent of the World Wide Web, has thrown the Internet open to the world. Everyone, from CEOs to seventh-grade students to weekend technology fiends, wants to get online. And they don't just want to surf. Each person wants to carve out a unique personal space: They want a Web site.

Until recently, however, only the technically-gifted attempted to publish sites on the Web. Seemingly overnight, a new breed of computer consultant — the Web publisher — emerged to fill the huge demand for professional-looking sites. If you wanted to look good on the Web, you needed either techno-gusto or the bucks to commission someone who had it.

Not anymore. FrontPage 97, the newest member of the Microsoft Office dream team, brings Web publishing to the masses. Without any knowledge of HTML (*Hypertext Markup Language,* the language used to create Web pages), you can use FrontPage to build and manage a sophisticated Web site, complete with all the advanced features and nifty effects you see on those *other* sites.

The thing is, FrontPage is no wimpy one- or two-disk program. It's a hefty, powerful piece of software. And like a lot of powerful software, FrontPage is easy to use — *after* you discover what all those buttons and menu items do.

Enter *FrontPage Web Publishing & Design For Dummies.*

Why This Book Is For You

I show you how to use FrontPage, Microsoft's powerful Web publishing package. *FrontPage Web Publishing & Design For Dummies* demystifies the world of Web publishing and explains all of the capabilities of FrontPage in classic *...For Dummies* style: plain English, and with a big dose of fun.

FrontPage Web Publishing & Design For Dummies goes a giant step further than other books published on the subject. I don't just show you how to build a Web site with FrontPage — I tell you how to build a well-designed, attractive, easy-to-navigate Web site that will impress even the most jaded of your techie friends.

Web publishing is quickly graduating from a skill to an art, complete with its own set of unwritten rules and tricks of the trade. This book initiates you into the ways of the pros, giving you the nod on little secrets that other users stumbled over by sheer luck. I don't just show you how to build a Web site with FrontPage — I show you how to build a *good* Web site with FrontPage.

Who You Are and What You Already Know

FrontPage Web Publishing & Design For Dummies gets you up to speed with the workings of FrontPage so that you can get straight to creating a knockout Web site. I therefore make a few assumptions about who you are and what you already know how to do.

- ✔ **You've developed a cordial relationship with your computer and its associates: the mouse, keyboard, monitor, and modem.** You ask the computer nicely to do things by pressing keys and clicking the mouse button, and usually, it complies. You're comfortable with the basic capabilities of Windows 95, such as using the Start menu, double-clicking icons to launch programs, getting around the Windows 95 desktop, using the Windows 95 Explorer, and choosing commands from menu bars.

- ✔ **You have an Internet connection, and you've spent some time surfing the Web (your significant other calls it obsession, but the poor dear is prone to exaggeration, I know).** You don't necessarily understand how the Internet works, but you have a guru (an Internet service provider, company techie, or nerdy neighbor) to call when you have a problem.

- ✔ **You have FrontPage sitting in a box in a highly visible location on your desk so that passers-by will see it and comment upon how technically-savvy you are.** If you're brave, you've installed FrontPage on your computer.

- ✔ **You've never tried your hand at Web publishing.** If you've tried Web publishing, you've never done it with FrontPage. If you have worked with FrontPage, you were perplexed after fiddling with the program, rushed to the bookstore, and are reading this book right now.

What's Inside

FrontPage Web Publishing & Design For Dummies contains everything you need to create beautiful Web sites with FrontPage 97. FrontPage is actually several interconnected but distinct programs, each with its own area of expertise. FrontPage is no small topic, so I've divided the subject into easily chewable parts.

Part I: Getting Friendly with FrontPage

Part I introduces you to the stars of the show, the FrontPage Explorer and the FrontPage Editor. You use the FrontPage Explorer to create and administer Web sites. The FrontPage Editor is in charge of editing Web pages, the basic building blocks of Web sites.

Part II: Creating Web Pages That Make You Look Like a Genius

Part II familiarizes you with basic Web design and the FrontPage Editor page formatting and layout capabilities. You discover how to add and format text, create hyperlinks, insert graphics and clickable images, and build tables (the electronic kind, not the wooden kind). You also find out how to create an interactive form that lets your visitors communicate with you. You become acquainted with frames and how they can make your Web site easier to navigate. You get to know about WebBots, a unique FrontPage feature that lets you add exciting capabilities to your Web site. Finally, you find out about eye-popping extras, such as multimedia, ActiveX controls, Java applets, plug-ins, and scripts.

Part III: Nifty Web Site Additions

Part III shows you how to add special FrontPage features to your Web site: a visitor registration system and an interactive discussion forum.

Part IV: Taking Your Web Site to a New Level

Part IV puts you in touch with the FrontPage group features and publishing capabilities. If you are part of a site-building team, these features let you control access to the site, as well as keep a running To Do list of tasks. You also discover how to make your Web site visible on the World Wide Web.

Part V: The Part of Tens

The Part of Tens is full of fun, interesting, highly-useful-but-not-mandatory stuff. Read this part with your feet up on the desk and a tall, cool drink in your other hand. Find out about ten things you can do with your Web site, ten must-have free Internet tools, and ten Net spots you don't want to miss.

The Appendixes

FrontPage travels with an entourage: the Bonus Pack. These programs — the Microsoft Internet Explorer Web browser, Microsoft Image Composer, Microsoft Personal Web Server, and the Web Publishing Wizard — work with FrontPage to form a complete Web publishing suite. Appendix A introduces you to the basic workings of each program.

Read Appendix B if you haven't yet installed FrontPage, and you want more help than the documentation included in the box gives you. Appendix C shows you how to install and use all the stuff stored on the CD-ROM tucked away in the back of this book.

The Bonus CD!

The CD-ROM included with this book comes with all sorts of free software and other goodies. Here's an overview:

- **Custom-designed Web page templates:** I designed a set of custom templates that you can use to add pizzazz to your own Web pages.
- **Internet Launch Pad:** Throughout the book, I refer you to helpful and interesting sites on the Internet. The Internet Launch Pad — a Web page that you can open with any Web browser — contains hyperlinks to every site mentioned in the book and more.
- **Paint Shop Pro:** My favorite shareware image editing program.
- **NETCOLPC.GIF:** An image file that contains all the colors you can use in your Web graphics.
- **WS_FTP LE:** An easy-to-use FTP program you can use to publish your Web site.

How To Use This Book

Think of me as your FrontPage fairy godmother. I introduce you to the world of FrontPage, magically answer your questions, and stand aside, wand poised and ready, when you want to play with FrontPage on your own.

You don't need to start at Chapter 1; simply flip to the section of the book that tells you what you want to know.

If you're new to Web publishing, you may want to skim the book to get a sense of what building a Web site entails and then read the stuff that looks particularly interesting.

If you're the adventurous type, fire up FrontPage, push all the buttons, play with all the menu items, and refer to the book when you get stumped.

I use a few text conventions throughout the book:

- ✔ A notation like "Choose File⇨Open FrontPage Web" is a condensed version of "from the File menu, choose the command Open FrontPage Web."
- ✔ When I say "Press Ctrl+N," it means "while holding down the Ctrl key, press the letter N."
- ✔ Whenever I'd like you to type something, I indicate that something in **boldface,** like this: In the Name text box, type **Matilda**. Things I want you to type that appear in numbered steps are not bold.

Icons Used in this Book

Icon-studded notes and sidebars highlight special information.

This icon points out important details you don't want to forget.

Here, you find a time-saving FrontPage shortcut. Or you may receive a hot design tip that you can use to spiff up your Web site.

Don't worry, your computer doesn't explode when you see this icon. The icon is only a warning to alert you to a potential FrontPage or Web publishing sticky spot.

The information flagged with this icon is for those of you who want to dig a little deeper into the technical aspects of Web publishing. If you just want to get that Web site published, skip this stuff.

The Web is a veritable cornucopia of Web publishing and FrontPage information. Throughout the book, I point to Net sites that offer additional help, free software tools, and information about related topics. (The Internet Resources page included on the CD contains links to these sites.)

System Requirements

You may be tempted to skip this section, thinking, "I've got FrontPage, what else could I need?" Read it anyway. If you don't recognize something in this list, you may not have it.

- ✔ A personal computer with a 486 or higher processor
- ✔ Microsoft Windows 95 operating system, Microsoft Windows NT Workstation 3.51 Service Pack 5 or later operating system (FrontPage doesn't work with Windows 3.1.)
- ✔ Microsoft FrontPage 97
- ✔ 8MB of memory for use on Windows 95; 16MB of memory for use on Windows NT (16MB recommended for Microsoft Personal Web Server.)
- ✔ 30MB of available hard disk space (Get rid of those disk space-hogging financial records and tax documents to make room.)
- ✔ CD-ROM drive
- ✔ VGA or higher-resolution video monitor (SVGA 256-color is recommended.)
- ✔ A mouse or compatible pointing device (Your index finger doesn't count.)
- ✔ An account with an Internet service provider or access to a company Web server with at least 1MB of storage space for your Web site files. Preferably, your Web server supports FrontPage Server Extensions. (For information on what FrontPage Server Extensions are, flip to Chapter 18.)
- ✔ TCP/IP compliant with Winsock Version 1.1 or later (If you have an Internet connection, you most likely have this. If you don't, or if you're unsure, give your guru a call.)

If you want to use the Bonus Pack, you need additional hard disk space:

- ✔ 11MB for Microsoft Internet Explorer
- ✔ 1MB for the Microsoft Personal Web Server
- ✔ 1MB for the Web Publishing Wizard
- ✔ 2MB for the Internet Mail and News Reader
- ✔ 11MB minimum, 17MB preferred for the Microsoft Image Composer

If you intend to use the Microsoft Image Composer, you need

- ✔ 16MB of memory (32 recommended)
- ✔ A VGA, 256-color monitor (Super VGA TrueColor with 2MB video memory recommended)

Part I
Getting Friendly with FrontPage

The 5th Wave · By Rich Tennant

"What do you mean you're updating our Web home page?"

In this part . . .

*F*aced with mastering a new piece of software, the scariest moment probably occurs as you launch the new program for the first time and stare at all those unfamiliar buttons and menu items. The situation's kind of like walking into a party and not recognizing anyone.

In this part, however, you get fully acquainted with FrontPage. I make the introductions, pass around a few drinks, and pretty soon, you're going to feel right at home with the two most popular personalities: the FrontPage Explorer and the FrontPage Editor.

Chapter 1

Weaving a Web
with FrontPage Explorer

• •

In This Chapter

▶ What is Web publishing, exactly?

▶ Creating a new Web site

▶ Simplifying site creation with templates and Wizards

▶ Importing an existing Web site into FrontPage

▶ Opening a FrontPage Web site

▶ Deleting a Web site

• •

Microsoft likes the name *Explorer*. The term conjures up images of adventure and romance. So think about the term this way: The Internet Explorer browser is your all-terrain vehicle for the World Wide Web; the Windows 95 Explorer charts your hard drive; and now, you have the FrontPage Explorer to tame your passion for trail-blazing in the Web publishing frontier.

FrontPage isn't a single program, like Microsoft Word or Excel. It is actually a Web publishing team, with individual programs that work together to help you create, manage, and publish a site on the World Wide Web. When you launch FrontPage, you begin your Web publishing adventure with the FrontPage Explorer.

The Explorer is where you create, view, and manage your *Web site*. A Web site is a collection of related files that are linked together to form an information "unit" that you eventually publish on the World Wide Web. Among other things, you use the Explorer to create new Web sites and to import existing sites that you want to update and maintain with FrontPage.

What Is Web Publishing, Exactly?

Before you hang your shingle as a FrontPage Web publisher, you need to understand what you're actually doing when you create and publish a Web site.

If you've looked around the World Wide Web (I call it "the Web" from now on), you've already seen a Web site. Web sites are the places you visit while zooming along the electronic highway. Some folks refer to their own Web site as their *home page*. FrontPage has its own special name for Web sites: *FrontPage Webs*. A FrontPage Web is simply a Web site that was created in or is maintained with FrontPage. A FrontPage Web is no different from any other Web site, aside from the unique capabilities FrontPage can add.

As a book is made up of individual pages, a Web site is made up of individual files called *Web pages*. Web pages contain the text and graphics you see when you visit a Web site (I talk more about the unique qualities of Web pages in Chapter 3).

When you construct a Web site, you create individual Web pages and string them together with links so that visitors can easily jump from page to page. (Chapter 2 goes into more detail about how these links work.) The FrontPage Explorer simplifies the process with built-in Web site templates and Wizards: It cranks out a boilerplate Web site, complete with linked Web pages, to which you simply add your own text and graphics.

When you publish a Web site, you make it visible to the rest of the world on the Web. This isn't automatic; for a Web site to be live, two things must happen:

- ✔ All the site's pages and files must be stored on a computer running a special program, called a *Web server*.

- ✔ That computer must be connected to the Internet 24 hours per day. (A constantly connected computer running a Web server program is called a *dedicated Web server.*)

Usually, the only folks with dedicated Web servers are Internet service providers and big companies. FrontPage is the first Web publishing program to come with its own built-in Web server program: the FrontPage Personal Web Server. The FrontPage Personal Web Server is a big deal because it enables you to create a sophisticated Web site and then check out all its features to make sure that they work — on your own computer. Web publishers without FrontPage (poor souls) need to transfer their Web pages and files to a *remote* Web server (a different computer to which they are connected via the Internet) to test the Web site before they make it public.

When it comes time to publish your site, you still need the services of an Internet service provider or company Web server because you probably don't want to leave your computer connected to the Internet all the time. I talk about the nitty-gritty of publishing your Web site in Chapter 18.

Creating a New Web Site

Creating a new Web site is akin to sitting at your typewriter (if you still have one of those antiquated pieces of equipment) with a blank piece of paper tucked in the carriage. Sometimes, brilliant concepts, fully formed, spring from your brain right onto the page. Other times, you need a little nudge to get those creative juices flowing.

FrontPage provides a comfortable balance of direction and flexibility. If you want help getting started, use a Web site template. If you need hand-holding, call on a FrontPage Wizard to guide you through setting up a complete site. If you already have a sense of how you'd like your site to look and act, build your own Web site from scratch (you can always change it later).

After you create a new Web site in the Explorer, you add content — text, pictures, and everything else that you want to display in your Web site — by editing the individual Web pages in the FrontPage Editor. (I introduce you to the Editor in Chapter 3.)

By using a template

The Explorer contains *templates* that produce standard Web sites that you customize to suit your own needs. Although sites created with cookie-cutter templates lack the flair of custom-designed Web sites, they give you a good foundation on which to begin building your own site. Templates also enable you to see the typical structure of different types of Web sites.

FrontPage comes with templates for several purposes:

- **Customer Support Web:** The Customer Support Web is for companies that want to make product help and support information available on the Internet. Customers access the Web site to read about product news, have their questions answered, discuss the product with other users, and more. This template is geared toward the needs of software companies and includes pages from which customers can download new versions of the product and to which users can submit bug reports. You can easily customize the Customer Support Web for your own business.

- **Personal Web:** The Personal Web template sets up a no-frills site that you can use to share information about yourself, talk about your current projects, display a list of your favorite spots on the World Wide Web, and tell people how to contact you. The template also includes a feedback form that visitors can use to tell you what they think of your site (and your life).

✔ **Project Web:** The Project Web template is perfect for use on an *Intranet* — a company's internal network accessible only to employees and "insiders." This site tracks the status of a project and includes space for project team members, status reports, schedules, an archive, a search form, and a discussion forum.

To create a new Web site by using a template (using the Personal Web template as an example), follow these steps:

1. **Launch FrontPage by double-clicking the Microsoft FrontPage icon on your desktop.**

   Or select the icon from the Windows 95 Start menu.

   You're greeted by the Getting Started with Microsoft FrontPage dialog box (Figure 1-1). This dialog box enables you to choose from a menu of options to open or create a Web site.

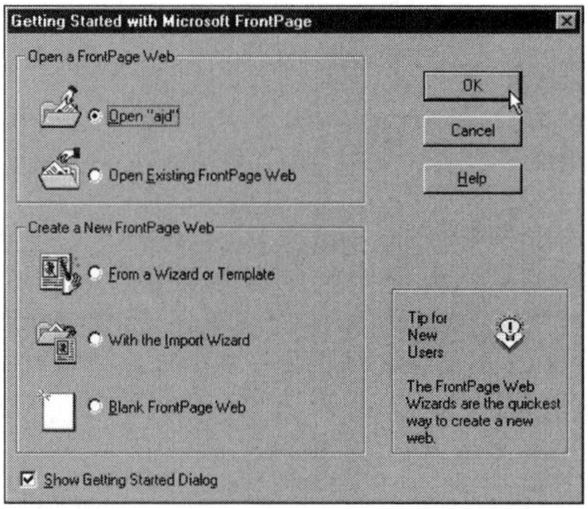

Figure 1-1:
The Getting Started with Microsoft FrontPage dialog box awaits your first wish.

2. **Select the From a Wizard or Template radio button.**

3. **Click OK.**

   The New FrontPage Web dialog box appears.

4. **In the Template or Wizard text box, select Personal Web.**

   (If you want to use the Customer Support Web or Project Web template instead, you select the appropriate template name here.)

5. **Click OK.**

   The Personal Web Template dialog box appears. Here, you specify where you want FrontPage to store the new Web site files.

FrontPage creates all new Web sites using the FrontPage Personal Web Server. (If you're not sure what a Web server is, glance at the section "What Is Web Publishing, Exactly?" earlier in this chapter.) The name visible in the Web Server or File Location text box is the name FrontPage assigned to the Personal Web Server during the installation process.

You can create new Web sites on another Web server or in another location on your computer. For details on why and how to accomplish this task, consult the FrontPage Help system by selecting Help⇨Microsoft FrontPage Help.

6. **In the Name of New FrontPage Web text box, type a one-word name.**

   The Web site name is a one-word label that describes the content or purpose of your Web site. You can use upper- and lowercase letters in the name.

7. **Click OK.**

   After a pause, the Name and Password Required dialog box appears.

8. **In the Name and Password text boxes, type the administrator name and password that you chose when you installed FrontPage.**

   Make sure that you type the name and password *exactly* as you entered it originally. If you can't remember your administrator name or password, take a moment to feel foolish. (I did the first time I forgot my password.) Then read the upcoming sidebar "Help! I forgot my password!"

9. **Click OK.**

   Your computer's hard drive clicks and hums, letting you know that FrontPage is setting up your Web site. In a moment, the Personal Web appears in the Explorer.

FrontPage stores all new Web sites in a subdirectory of the C:\FRONTPAGE WEBS\CONTENT folder on your hard drive.

You may have noticed the Learning FrontPage Web template listed with the other options in the New FrontPage Web dialog box. This template creates an example Web site which is used as part of the tutorial in the "Getting Started With FrontPage" manual.

TIP

Help! I forgot my password!

In your excitement to play with FrontPage, you paid half-hearted attention to the administrator name and password you chose during the installation process. Then, when the Explorer requested the information, you drew a blank. For one stomach-churning moment, you thought your Web publishing career was over before it had a chance to start (and you threw the money you spent on FrontPage down the drain).

Don't worry: FrontPage Personal Web Server's password list has a back door, and I know where it is. In fact, I even show you. It's called the FrontPage Server Administrator.

The Server Administrator lets you adjust the settings of the Web server installed on your computer. You can ignore most of the program's features because they are useful only to Webmasters, system administrators, and other techie folks who run Web servers. One feature is worth remembering, however, and that is how to use the Server Administrator to choose a new password. Here's how:

1. **Open the FrontPage Server Administrator by double-clicking its icon on your desktop.**

   You'll find it wherever you originally installed FrontPage on your hard drive — most likely at C:\PROGRAM FILES\MICROSOFT FRONTPAGE\BIN\FPSRVWIN.EXE.

   The FrontPage Server Administrator opens.

2. **Click Security.**

   The Administrator Name and Password dialog box appears. <Root Web> appears in the Web name text box. That's good.

3. **In the Name text box, type an administrator name.**

4. **In the Password text box, type a password.**

   (One you'll remember this time!)

5. **In the Confirm password text box, type the password again.**

6. **Click OK.**

   The Administrator Name and Password dialog box closes.

7. **Click Close to close the FrontPage Server Administrator.**

In the future, you can change password settings from within the Explorer. (I show you how in Chapter 17.) Use the Server Administrator only in times of desperation when you forget your password.

By using a Wizard

A *Wizard* takes you through a process of creating a Web site by presenting you with a series of dialog boxes and prompting you to fill in and select information. FrontPage comes with Wizards for its two most elaborate Web templates: The Corporate Presence Web and the Discussion Web. (FrontPage also contains an Import Web Wizard that helps you import an existing Web site into FrontPage. You discover how in the section "Importing an Existing Web Site into FrontPage," later in this chapter.)

✔ **Corporate Presence Web Wizard:** The Corporate Presence Web Wizard (shown in part in Figure 1-2) sets up a corporate Web site complete with graphics. Depending on the options you choose, the site can contain anything from a product catalog to a discussion forum to company contact information. The Wizard even places items on the FrontPage To Do list, reminding you to customize aspects of the finished site. (Chapter 16 shows you how to work with the FrontPage To Do List.)

Figure 1-2:
The
Corporate
Presence
Web
Wizard.

✔ **Discussion Web Wizard:** The Discussion Web Wizard creates an interactive site that enables visitors to post comments and read others' replies about a given topic. Visitors are also able to search the text of the Discussion Web replies for specific information. You can use this Wizard to create a new Discussion Web site or to add a discussion forum to an existing Web site. You find out how to use this Wizard in Chapter 15.

To create a business Web site by using the Corporate Presence Web Wizard:

1. **Launch FrontPage by double-clicking the Microsoft FrontPage icon on your desktop.**

   Or select the icon from the Windows 95 Start menu.

   The Getting Started with Microsoft FrontPage dialog box appears.

2. **Select the From a Wizard or Template radio button and then click OK.**

   You can also choose File➪New➪FrontPage Web, press Ctrl+N, or click the New FrontPage Web button in the toolbar.

   The New FrontPage Web dialog box appears.

3. **In the Template or Wizard text box, click Corporate Presence Web Wizard and then click OK.**

   The Corporate Presence Web Wizard dialog box appears. Here, you choose where you want FrontPage to store the new Web site files.

4. **If not already visible, select the name of the Personal Web Server from the Web Server or File location drop-down list.**

5. **In the Name of New FrontPage Web text box, type a Web site name and then click OK.**

   For example, an appropriate name for the Acme Incorporated Web site is **acme**.

   The Name and Password Required dialog box appears.

6. **In the Name and Password text boxes, type your administrator name and password and then click OK.**

   Make sure that you type the name and password *exactly* as you entered it originally. If you can't remember your administrator name or password, run, don't walk, to the sidebar "Help! I forgot my password!" earlier in this chapter.

   After you click OK, there is a pause as FrontPage summons the Corporate Presence Web Wizard. In a moment, the introductory Corporate Presence Web Wizard dialog box appears.

7. **Click Next.**

   The next Corporate Presence Web Wizard dialog box appears. The dialog box lists typical categories of information included in a business Web site. The Wizard creates a separate Web page for each category.

8. **Select the check boxes next to the pages that you want to include in your Web site.**

   For example, select What's New to include a page in your Web site devoted to new product and service announcements.

9. **Click Next.**

   The next Corporate Presence Web Wizard dialog box appears. Here, you choose the topics that you want to appear on the Web site's entry page (also referred to as the *home page*).

   Net-dwellers use the term *home page* to refer to three different things: a Web site ("I spent seven hours this weekend working on my home page"), the default or entry page of a Web site ("My e-mail address is listed at the bottom of my Web site's home page"), and the page that automatically appears each time you open your Web browser. ("I like to read the headlines every morning, so I set my home page to *CNN Interactive.*")

10. **Select the check boxes next to the topics that you want to include in your home page and then click Next.**

   For example, if you want the home page to display a company profile and contact information, select Company Profile and Contact Information.

The next Corporate Presence Web Wizard dialog box appears. This dialog box is the first in a series that enable you to customize the pages you selected in step 8. The options available in this dialog box differ depending on the page being customized.

11. **Customize the page by selecting options and filling in information and then click Next.**

    Customization dialog boxes appear for each page you chose in step 8.

12. **Complete each customization dialog box; click Next.**

    After you're through customizing the individual pages, a dialog box appears, prompting you to select header information (stuff that appears at the top of every page) and footer information (stuff that appears at the bottom of every page).

13. **For information that should appear at the top of each page, select the check boxes next to the items that you want to include.**

    For example, if you want links to all of your Web site's main pages to appear at the top of every page, click Links to your main Web pages.

14. **For information that should appear at the bottom of each page, select the check boxes next to the items that you want to include and then click Next.**

    The next Corporate Presence Web Wizard dialog box appears. Here, you choose the graphic style for your Web site. Each style — Plain, Conservative, Flashy, and Cool — has its own set of graphics that FrontPage uses for the page background, page banners, and clickable buttons.

15. **Select the radio button next to the style that you want and then click Next.**

    The next Corporate Presence Web Wizard dialog box appears. Here, you choose your site's color scheme.

16. **Select new options for any of the settings that you want to change; click Next.**

    For example, click the Pattern drop-down list and select a new background pattern. In Part II, "Creating Web Pages That Make You Look Like a Genius," I explain each option in detail.

    The next Corporate Presence Web Wizard dialog box appears. Here, you can choose to include an "Under Construction" graphic on pages that aren't yet finished.

17. **Click Yes to include the graphic or No to leave pages as they are and then click Next.**

    The next Corporate Presence Web Wizard dialog box appears. Here, you identify your company.

18. **Type your company name, an abbreviated company name, and the company's address in the appropriate text boxes and then click Next.**

   The next Corporate Presence Web Wizard dialog box appears. Here, you list your company's contact information.

19. **Type your company's phone number, fax number, and contact e-mail addresses in the appropriate text boxes and then click Next.**

   The next Corporate Presence Web Wizard dialog box appears. (You're nearing the end, I promise!) Here, you can tell FrontPage to open the To Do List after it creates the Web site.

20. **If you do not want FrontPage to display the To Do List, deselect the Show To Do list after web is uploaded check box.**

21. **Click Finish.**

   Based on your choices, the Wizard creates an entire Corporate Web site. This process may take a moment or two. Relax and get a snack.

   Pretty soon, the Corporate Web appears in the Explorer.

FrontPage templates and Wizards make use of *WebBots*, which are miniprograms that add special features to your Web site. (For a look at what WebBots can do, jump ahead to Chapter 12.) For these WebBots to function, the dedicated Web server on which you publish your Web site must support *FrontPage Server Extensions.* FrontPage Server Extensions are a set of files and programs that work together with the Web server program to enable certain FrontPage features to work. Although you can still publish FrontPage Webs on servers that *don't* have FrontPage Server Extensions installed, you can't take advantage of certain extra-cool FrontPage features. Throughout the book, I point out features that require the assistance of FrontPage Server Extensions. Chapter 18 explains everything you need to know about publishing your Web site.

By starting from scratch

If you're a control freak, as I am, you may want to oversee every aspect of the structure, look, and function of your site. Templates and Wizards are helpful, but if you already understand enough about Web sites to have a basic sense for how you want yours to look, you may prefer to build yours from the ground up.

The seeds of the home-grown site are the Normal Web and the Empty Web templates. To call them templates overstates what they are, because they do little more than create a blank page from which you begin to build a site.

- **Normal Web:** The Normal Web template creates a site containing one blank page.

- **Empty Web:** The Empty Web template creates, well, an empty Web — that is, a Web site with nothing in it. This option is useful if you want to import an existing Web site into FrontPage.

The easiest way to import a Web site into FrontPage is to use the Import Web Wizard, explained in the following section, "Importing an Existing Web Site into FrontPage."

To create a new Web site by using the Normal template, follow these steps:

1. **Launch FrontPage by double-clicking the Microsoft FrontPage icon on your desktop.**

   Or select the icon from the Windows 95 Start menu.

   The Getting Started with Microsoft FrontPage dialog box appears.

2. **Click Blank FrontPage Web.**

3. **Click OK.**

   FrontPage creates a new, single-page Web site.

You find out how to attach additional pages to your blank Web site in Chapter 3.

To create a blank Web site without the help of the Getting Started dialog box, choose File⇨New⇨FrontPage Web, press Ctrl+N, or click the New FrontPage Web button in the toolbar. When the New FrontPage Web dialog box appears, double-click Normal Web (or, Empty Web, if you'd rather use that template), and follow the steps listed in the section "By using a template" earlier in this chapter.

Importing an Existing Web Site into FrontPage

If you want to use FrontPage to maintain and update a Web site assembled with another program, you must import that site into the FrontPage Explorer. The easiest way to accomplish this task is to use the Import Web Wizard, a handy-dandy tool that performs most of the work for you. Figure 1-3 gives you a sneak peek at the Import Web Wizard.

To import a Web site into FrontPage, follow these steps:

1. **Launch FrontPage by double-clicking the Microsoft FrontPage icon on your desktop.**

   Or select the icon from the Windows 95 Start menu.

   The Getting Started with Microsoft FrontPage dialog box appears.

2. **Select With the Import Web Wizard and then click OK.**

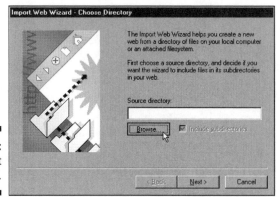

Figure 1-3:
The Import
Web Wizard.

Or choose File➪Import or click the New FrontPage Web button and double-click Import Web Wizard in the New FrontPage Web dialog box.

The Import Web Wizard dialog box appears.

3. **If not already visible, select the name of the Personal Web Server from the Web Server or File location drop-down list.**

4. **In the Name of New FrontPage Web text box, enter a one-word name.**

The name you choose should reflect the content or purpose of the Web site you're importing.

5. **Click OK.**

After a brief pause, the Import Web Wizard - Choose Directory dialog box appears. Here, you select the folder on your computer (or network, if you're connected to one) that contains the Web site files you want to import.

6. **Type the location of the Source directory.**

The Source directory should look something like C:\FOLDERNAME.

If you don't know the folder's location offhand, click Browse to select it from a hierarchical list of folders on your computer.

7. **If you want the Import Web Wizard to include the files stored in folders inside the folder you selected, select the Include Subdirectories check box and then click Next.**

The Import Web Wizard - Edit File List dialog box appears, with all the files contained in the source directory listed in a text box. This dialog box allows you to exclude files that you don't want to import along with the rest of your Web site.

8. **Select the files that you want to exclude by clicking their names in the text box.**

To select a range of files, press and hold the Shift key while clicking the filenames. To select more than one file, press and hold the Ctrl key as you click filenames. To start all over with a fresh file list, click the Refresh button.

9. **Click the Exclude button and then click Next.**

   The Import Web Wizard - Finish dialog box appears, congratulating you on a job well done. If you want to double-check your choices, click the Back button, otherwise. . . .

10. **Click Finish.**

   The Import Web Wizard performs its magic, and in a moment, your Web site — now a full-fledged FrontPage Web — appears in the Explorer.

   (I dare you to say "full-fledged FrontPage Web" five times fast.)

 If, in the Explorer's Hyperlink view, your home page isn't preceded by a little house icon, you can change the filename that FrontPage uses to recognize the site's default page. I show you how in Chapter 2. I also introduce you to the Explorer's views and icons in that chapter.

You may notice a few broken links where everything was fine before you imported the site into FrontPage. (Broken links are flagged by torn-page icons and broken lines.) Links break if FrontPage can't find the link's destination page or file. I show you how to fix broken links in Chapter 6.

Open, Sesame!

Well, actually, you don't need a special incantation to open a FrontPage Web (that is, a Web site previously created in or imported into FrontPage). Just follow these easy steps.

To open an existing FrontPage Web site, follow these steps:

1. **Launch FrontPage by double-clicking the Microsoft FrontPage icon on your desktop.**

    Or select the icon from the Windows 95 Start menu.

   The Getting Started with Microsoft FrontPage dialog box appears.

2. **Click Open Existing FrontPage Web.**

3. **Click OK.**

    Or you can choose File➪Open FrontPage Web or click the Open Web button.

   The Open FrontPage Web dialog box appears.

Opening Web sites on other Web servers

In this chapter (and throughout the book), I assume that you do your Web-building on your own computer and then publish your Web site on a dedicated Web server (a different computer most likely belonging to your company or your Internet service provider). I recommend this approach because, this way, you create Web sites in the privacy of your own hard drive and make only the finished, perfect stuff visible to the world on the Web. This approach also minimizes the time you spend connected to the Internet, which can save you a bundle if you pay for access time.

In a few instances, however, you may need to open a Web site located on another server, such as if you're working as part of a site-building team or if you want to adjust your Web site's permissions. (I discuss permissions in Chapter 17.) In the Explorer, you can open Web sites stored on other Web servers, as long as the Web server has FrontPage Server Extensions installed. (For more information about FrontPage Server Extensions, see Chapter 18.)

In step 4 of "Open, Sesame!" instead of selecting the name of the Personal Web Server, enter the name of the remote server in the Web Server or File location text box and then click List Webs. FrontPage establishes a connection with the remote server, and in a moment, the names of the Web sites stored on that server appear in the FrontPage Webs text box. Double-click the name of the Web site that you want to open. The Web site opens in the Explorer, and you can update and change the site just as if it were stored on your own computer. One word of caution: If the remote server is connected to the Internet, any changes that you make are immediately visible to the world, so do so with care.

4. **If not already visible, select the name of the Personal Web Server from the Web Server or File location drop-down list.**

5. **Click the List Webs button.**

   A list of the Web sites stored on the Personal Web Server appears in the FrontPage Webs text box.

6. **In the FrontPage Webs text box, double-click the name of the Web site that you want to open.**

   FrontPage may require you to enter a name and password. If so, the Name and Password Required dialog box appears.

7. **In the Name and Password text boxes, enter your name and password.**

8. **Click OK.**

   FrontPage opens the Web site.

You can open only one Web site at a time. If you open a Web site while another site is open, the FrontPage Explorer closes the current site.

The Explorer saves shortcuts to the last three Web sites that you opened at the bottom of the File menu.

If you find the Getting Started dialog box more annoying than helpful (as I did after using FrontPage for about a week), you can turn it off. Here's how: The next time you launch FrontPage and the dialog box appears, click the Show Getting Started Dialog check box in the lower-left corner to remove the check mark, select whatever operation you want (create a new Web site, open an existing Web site, and so on), and click OK. You can also choose Tools⇨Options. The Options dialog box appears. In the General tab, deselect the Show Getting Started Dialog check box and click OK.

Deleting a Web

Remove those dusty old Webs lurking in the corners of your computer. You know — the ones that are obsolete or that you no longer use. You're rewarded with a tidy hard drive and lots of extra disk space.

To delete a Web site currently open in the Explorer, follow these steps:

1. **In the Explorer, choose File⇨Delete FrontPage Web.**

   The Confirm Delete dialog box warns you that if you delete the Web, you can't change your mind later.

2. **Throw caution to the wind and click Yes!**

   But click Yes only if you're really sure that you want the Web gone for good. If not, click No.

   FrontPage deletes the Web.

Screaming . . . er, I mean, calling for Help

By now, I'm sure you've developed an inkling of the power and complexity of FrontPage. (No doubt, that's what motivated you to buy this book!) Never fear: Help is as close as your mouse. Choose Help⇨Microsoft FrontPage Help to access a nicely organized set of FrontPage crib notes. Refer to them whenever this book isn't handy and you need assistance.

If you find yourself wondering what a button or menu item does, click the Help button in the Explorer Toolbar. (The button looks like a pointer sitting next to a question mark.) Then click the button or select the menu item you don't understand. FrontPage automatically flips to the appropriate Help screen.

If you still can't find answers to your question, refer to the Cheat Sheet at the front of the book for more places to go for help.

What's a Root Web?

When you open a Web site stored on the FrontPage Personal Web Server (as outlined in the section "Open, Sesame!" earlier in this chapter), a mysterious name appears at the top of the FrontPage Webs list: `<Root Web>`.

The Root Web is the Personal Web Server's top-level Web site. I can best explain the concept of a Root Web by using an example: the Microsoft Web site. If you visit the Microsoft Web site at `http://www.microsoft.com`, you are looking at the Microsoft Root Web. It is the top-level Web site for the Microsoft Web server. The FrontPage Web site, located at `http://www.microsoft.com/frontpage`, is stored on the same Web server as the main Web site but in its own directory. To access it, you need to add the directory reference `/frontpage` to `http://www.microsoft.com`. In FrontPage lingo, the FrontPage Web site is known as a *Child Web* because it is stored on the same server as the Root Web but in a secondary level of directories. The accompanying figure illustrates the relationship between the Root Web and Child Webs on the same Web server.

A Web server can have an unlimited number of Child Webs but only one Root Web. The Root Web can be linked to Child Webs (creating a network of interlinked Web sites), or each Web site can stand on its own.

FrontPage comes installed with a standard Root Web that acts as a placeholder for your top-level Web site. After you create your main Web site, you can copy it to the Root Web, replacing its standard pages with your own. (I show you how in Chapter 2.)

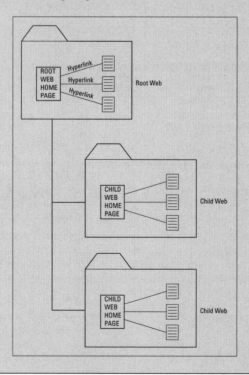

Chapter 2

Explorer Essentials

● ●

In This Chapter

▶ Getting familiar with the Explorer's views

▶ Working with the files in your Web site

▶ Creating new Web site folders

▶ Renaming your Web site

▶ Copying your Web site

● ●

Consider the FrontPage Explorer as your Web publishing Command Central. From the Explorer, you can do just about anything to change, update, or repair your Web site.

In this chapter, you delve deeper into the site-management capabilities of the Explorer. You become familiar with the Explorer's Hyperlink and Folder views. You also discover how to use the Explorer to update and change your Web site.

Taking in the Views

The Explorer's charm lies in its *views*, or ways of displaying the structure of your Web site. The Explorer contains two views — the *Hyperlink View*, which illustrates the site's network of links, and the *Folder View*, which enables you to see all the site's files and folders (similar to how the Windows 95 Explorer lets you see the files and folders on your hard drive).

Hyperlink View

The Hyperlink View displays your Web site as a network of linked files. These links, also known as *hyperlinks*, are the glue that keep the Web stuck together. Hyperlinks connect Web pages to each other and to sites on the World Wide Web. When you click a hyperlink in a Web page, you are transported to another page. (In Chapter 6, I explain hyperlinks in detail.)

The links between the pages in your Web site create a path visitors follow when they explore the site. The Hyperlink View is like a road map; it illustrates the Web site's navigational path so that you can make sure that your Web site is easy to get around.

The left pane of the Hyperlink View contains a hierarchical outline of the pages in your Web site. You expand and collapse parts of the outline by clicking the plus and minus icons to view the different "levels" of hyperlinks. When you click a page icon in the outline, a magnified view of the page appears in the right pane, with incoming and outgoing links clearly listed. Figure 2-1 shows how a typical personal home page looks in the Hyperlink View.

In the right pane see how some hyperlinks are indicated with arrows, while the link to the file PORTRAIT.GIF ends with a dot? In the Hyperlink View, lines ending with dots indicate links to files that appear inside the source page (as does the image PORTRAIT.GIF in Asha's Home Page). (When viewed with a color monitor, the arrows are blue, and the lines ending with dots are gray.)

Menu bar   Toolbar   Title bar

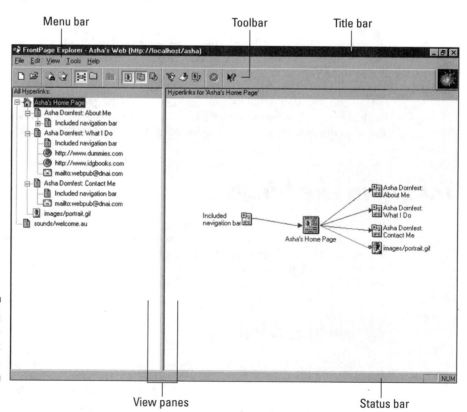

Figure 2-1:
The Hyperlink View.

View panes   Status bar

To display the Hyperlink View (if the view isn't already visible), click the Hyperlink View button in the Explorer toolbar or choose View⇨Hyperlink View.

Can't figure out what one of those icons in the Hyperlink view stands for? Refer to Table 2-1, the Hyperlink View Icon Decoder, for speedy assistance.

Table 2-1	Hyperlink View Icon Decoder
This Icon	*Means This*
🏠	The entry page, also known as the home page. If the door is red, you can expand the page by clicking its plus icon. If the door is blue, the home page is already expanded.
📄	A Web page.
⊞	Sits next to a page icon that you can expand to show its links. Click the plus icon to expand the page.
⊟	Sits next to a page icon that is expanded. Click the minus icon to collapse the page.
🖼	An image file.
🌐	A link to a page located outside the Web site.
✉	A link to an e-mail address, otherwise known as a *mailto link*.
🔗	A broken link.
⚠📄	Flags a page containing a WebBot that is set up incorrectly. (You find out about WebBots in Chapter 12.)

Tinkering with the Hyperlink View

The Hyperlink View boasts lots of handy features that help you tinker with the Web site's display.

- ✔ For more information about a particular link, in the right pane, pass your mouse pointer over a page icon. After a moment, the line indicating the link turns red, and a label, listing the type of link and the page's filename, pops up.

- ✔ If your Web site contains a broken link — that is, a link to file that has moved — the broken link appears in the Hyperlink View as a broken line. I talk about broken hyperlinks, and how to fix them, in Chapter 6.

- ✔ To move a page to the center of the right pane without having to hunt for that page in the left pane, right-click the page's icon and select Move to Center from the pop-up menu that appears.

- ✔ To expand the magnified view in the right pane, click the plus icon on the page that you want to expand. (The plus icon appears in the upper-left corner of the page icon.)

✔ To adjust the size of each view, pass your mouse pointer over the middle divider until the pointer turns into a vertical line with arrows sticking out on either side. Click the mouse button and then drag the divider to the left or right. Release the button after you're satisfied with the new size of the view.

✔ To give yourself a teensy-weensy bit more viewing space, temporarily hide the Explorer toolbar and status bar. Choose View➪Toolbar and View➪Status Bar.

Hyperlink View housekeeping

The right pane of the Hyperlink View can get a bit cluttered, especially if you are viewing a page containing lots of links. Three helpful Explorer tools let you control which links are visible in the Hyperlink View.

✔ **Hyperlinks to images:** To quickly survey your site's hyperlinks, you can temporarily hide links to images. To *toggle* (turn on and off) the display of image links, click the Hyperlinks to Images button or choose View➪Hyperlinks to Images.

✔ **Repeated hyperlinks:** If a page contains more than one hyperlink to the same destination page, the Explorer displays only one link. If you want repeated links visible, too, you must click the Repeated Hyperlinks button or choose View➪Repeated Hyperlinks.

✔ **Hyperlinks inside pages:** If a page contains hyperlinks to locations within itself (that is, links to *bookmarks*), the Explorer doesn't display these links. If you want these links inside pages visible as well, you need to click the Hyperlinks Inside Page button or choose View➪Hyperlinks Inside Page. (I explain what bookmarks are in Chapter 6.)

Folder View

Where the Hyperlink View enables you to look "inside" your Web site at its system of hyperlinks, the *Folder View* displays the Web site as a group of files and folders (see Figure 2-2). This view serves the same purpose for your Web site as the Windows 95 Explorer serves for your hard drive: It helps you manage and organize your Web site's file system.

To display the Folder View (if the view isn't already visible), click the Folder View button in the Explorer toolbar or choose View➪Folder View.

The Folder View even works like the Windows 95 Explorer.

✔ Click a folder in the left pane to display its contents in the right pane.

✔ To sort the list of files and folders in the right pane, click the header label of your choice.

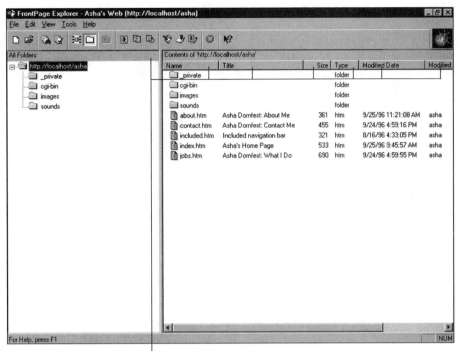

Figure 2-2:
The Folder
View.

Header labels

✔ To change the width of the list's columns, pass the mouse pointer over the
   boundary between the header labels until the pointer turns into a vertical
   line with arrows sticking out on either side. Click the mouse button and
   drag the divider to the left or right. Release the button after you're satisfied with the new column width.

✔ To move a page into a folder, click the page icon, drag it on top of the
   folder, and release the mouse button. The Explorer updates any of the page's
   associated hyperlinks to reflect the page's new location. (I show you how to
   create new folders in the section "Creating new folders," later in this chapter.)

Working with Web Site Files

The Explorer gives you easy access to the files that make up your Web site.
Use the Explorer as your starting point whenever you want to open, import,
or rearrange files in your Web site.

Home is where the filename is

When you create a Web site, FrontPage assigns the filename INDEX.HTM to the Web site's entry page (also known as the home page). If you import a Web site into FrontPage, and the home page is named something other than INDEX.HTM, the home page appears in the Hyperlink View as a regular page icon. Without a home page, the outline in the left pane has no place to "begin" and therefore inaccurately displays the hierarchy of your Web site's links.

More importantly, the Web server on which you publish your Web site may use yet *another* filename to identify the home page (examples include INDEX.HTML and HOME.HTM).

To solve this problem, you need to make a tiny adjustment to one of the FrontPage Personal Web Server configuration files. Adjusting the file is easy. To do so:

1. **Launch your favorite word processor or text editor, such as Windows 95 Notepad.**

2. **Open the file named SRM.CNF.**

   The file is located at C:\FRONTPAGE WEBS\SERVER\CONF. (If you don't see the file, select All Files (*.*) from the Files of _type_ drop-down menu in the Open dialog box.)

   Microsoft thoughtfully explains everything in the configuration file by using *comments*.

Comments are all the lines preceded by a #. Anything without a # at the beginning is an actual configuration setting used by the Personal Web Server.

3. **Look for a line that reads as follows:**

   `# DirectoryIndex filename`

4. **Change** `filename` **to the filename you want FrontPage to recognize as your home page.**

   For example, change it to `default.htm` or `index.html`. You should choose the home page filename recognized by your dedicated Web server (the Web server on which you will eventually publish your Web site). If you're not sure which filename the Web server recognizes, ask your system administrator or the staff of your Internet service provider. For more details about publishing your Web site, jump ahead to Chapter 18.

5. **Delete the # sign.**

   By deleting the # sign, you transform the line from a comment into a configuration setting.

6. **Save the file and close the text editor or word-processing program.**

The next time you create a new FrontPage Web site, your home page has the filename you specify.

Opening files

From the Explorer, you can open any file in your Web site so that you can update or change the file. FrontPage launches the editing program associated with that file type, and you're on your way. For example, if you open a Web page, the Explorer launches the FrontPage Editor, the program in charge of editing Web pages. (I introduce you to the Editor in Chapter 3.)

Weird FrontPage folders

No doubt, when you switched to Folder View, you noticed unfamiliar folders with odd names like _PRIVATE and CGI-BIN lurking in your Web site. All FrontPage Web sites contain a standard set of folders, each of which has its own role:

✔ **_PRIVATE:** documents stored in the _PRIVATE folder remain hidden from browsers and from the FrontPage Search WebBot (which you get to know in Chapter 12).

✔ **CGI-BIN:** FrontPage reserves the CGI-BIN folder for server-based programs called CGI scripts, which process information submitted from a Web form. (I talk more about CGI scripts in Chapter 10.)

✔ **IMAGES:** The IMAGES folder is where FrontPage stores images that appear inside Web pages. I recommend keeping all your images in that folder, too, just so that your Web site remains neat.

To open a file from the Explorer, do one of the following things:

✔ Right-click an icon and choose Open from the pop-up menu.

✔ Click the icon and then choose Edit⇨Open (or press Ctrl+O).

✔ Double-click an icon in the right pane of either Explorer view.

FrontPage automatically associates Web pages with the FrontPage Editor, and image files with the Microsoft Image Composer (an image editing program included in the Bonus Pack). If your Web site contains files the Explorer doesn't recognize, however, you need to tell FrontPage which program to launch when you open that type of file.

To associate a file type with an editing program, follow these steps:

1. **In the Explorer, choose Tools⇨Options.**

   The Options dialog box appears.

2. **In the Option dialog box, click the Configure Editors tab.**

   The Configure Editors tab contains a list box in which FrontPage lists the editors the Explorer already recognizes.

3. **To add a new file type and associated editing program, click the Add button.**

   The Add Editor Association dialog box appears.

4. **In the File Type text box, type the three-letter extension of the file type that you want to associate with an editor.**

   For example, type **doc** for Microsoft Word documents.

5. **In the Editor name text box, type the name of the editing program.**

6. **In the Command text box, enter the location of the editing program or click Browse to locate the editor.**

   If you click Browse, the Browse dialog box appears. Navigate your hard drive until you see the editor's program icon and double-click the icon to select the editor. When you select the editor, the Browse dialog box closes, and the editor's location appears in the Command text box.

7. **Click OK.**

   The Add Editor Association dialog box closes, and the new file type and editor appear in the list of associated editors in the Configure Editors tab. You can change or remove any entry on the list by clicking the Modify or Remove buttons.

8. **Click OK to close the Options dialog box.**

To open a file with an editing program *other* than the one with which the file type is associated, in any Explorer view, right-click the file's icon and choose Open With from the pop-up menu. The Open With Editor dialog box appears. All associated editors are listed in the Editor list box. In the list box, double-click the name of the program in which you want to open the file.

Importing files and folders

If you want to add an existing file to your FrontPage Web site — say, a Web page stored on your hard drive but created using a different program — you must import the file with the Explorer. When you import a file, the Explorer places a copy of the file in the Web site.

To import an entire Web site into the Explorer — as opposed to a single file or a folder — take the Import Web Wizard for a spin. I show you how in Chapter 1.

To import a single file or folder, use the quick-and-dirty approach: Simply drag the file or folder from your Windows 95 desktop (or the Windows 95 Explorer) into either view of the FrontPage Explorer.

If you're importing several files or folders, it's easier to create a list of all the files and folder and then import them in one go.

To create an import list:

1. **With a Web site open in the Explorer, choose File⇨Import.**

   The Import File to FrontPage Web dialog box appears.

   (If you choose File⇨Import when no Web site is currently open in the Explorer, the Import Web Wizard launches.)

2. Click the Add File button.

The Add File to Import List dialog box appears (see Figure 2-3). You use this dialog box to navigate your hard drive to select the files that you want to import.

Figure 2-3:
The Add
File to
Import List
dialog box.

3. Navigate your hard drive and select the files that you want to import.

To select multiple files, hold down the Ctrl key while clicking file icons in the Add File to Import List dialog box. To select a range of files, hold down the Shift key while clicking on file icons. If you don't see the file that you want to import, select All files (*.*) from the Files of type drop-down menu.

4. Click the Open button.

The Add File to Import List dialog box closes, and the file appears in the import list in the Import File to FrontPage Web dialog box.

5. Click OK to import the file.

A pause occurs as FrontPage imports the file(s) to your Web site. After the file is imported, the dialog box closes.

If you would rather put off importing the files, click the Close button in the Import File to FrontPage Web dialog box. FrontPage saves the import list, which you can access later by choosing File➪Import.

If you close the Web site before importing the files on the import list, FrontPage erases the list.

To import an entire folder to your Web site, in step 2, click the Add Folder button. The Browse for Folder dialog box appears, enabling you to select the folder that you want to import (see Figure 2-4). Click the folder and then click the OK button. The Browse for Folder dialog box closes, and the folder's contents appear in the import list.

Imported files appear in alphabetical order in the Hyperlink View and at the bottom of the list in the Folder View. When you are ready, you can create hyperlinks to the file from other pages in the Web site. (I show you how to create hyperlinks in Chapter 6.)

Exporting files

Exporting files from a FrontPage Web site simply means copying the files to a different location on your computer. Frankly, I can't think of an occasion to use this feature, but you might, so I show you how to export files anyway.

To export files from a Web site, follow these steps:

1. **In either Explorer view, click the icon of the file that you want to export.**

   In the Folder View, you can select several files by holding the Shift or Ctrl key while clicking the files' icons.

Figure 2-4:
The Browse
for Folder
dialog box.

2. **Choose File⇨Export.**

   The Export Selected As dialog box appears.

3. **Navigate to the folder in which you want to copy the file.**

4. **Click Save.**

   The dialog box closes, and FrontPage exports the file. When the task is finished, the FrontPage Explorer dialog box appears, letting you know that the file was copied successfully.

5. **Click OK to close the dialog box.**

Renaming files

I admit it. The power of this feature makes me weak in the knees. If, for any reason, you need to change the name of a file in your Web site, FrontPage automatically updates all the file's associated hyperlinks.

You can rename a file several ways, but the easiest way is to follow these steps:

1. **If the Folder View is not already visible, in the Explorer toolbar, click the Folder View button (or choose View⬄Folder View).**

2. **In the right pane, click the icon for the file that you want to rename and then click its filename.**

   A box appears around the filename, and the filename is selected.

3. **Type a new name.**

   Make sure that you keep the same three-letter extension so that the Explorer knows what kind of file you're renaming.

4. **Press Enter.**

   If the file contains associated links, the Rename dialog box appears, asking if you'd like to update the links to reflect the new name. (The power! Be still my beating heart!)

5. **Click Yes.**

   The dialog box closes, FrontPage updates the links, and all is well with the world.

Deleting files

If your Web site contains a file that has outlived its usefulness or is otherwise cluttering your Web site, you can boot the file out of your Web site with one swift click.

To delete a file, do the following:

1. **In either Explorer view, click the icon of the file that you want to delete.**

   To select more than one file, in the Folder View, hold down the Shift or Ctrl key while clicking the files' icons.

2. **Press the Delete key.**

   Or choose Edit⬄Delete. Or right-click the icon and choose Delete from the pop-up menu.

   The Confirm Delete dialog box appears, making sure that you want to delete the file.

   3. Click Yes to delete the file.

   If you are deleting more than one file, click Yes to All to delete them all in one step (instead of having the Confirm Delete dialog box pop up before deleting each file). If you change your mind about deleting the file, click No or Cancel to close the dialog box without deleting the file.

Be careful — if you delete a file that's the destination of a link from elsewhere in your Web site, you break the link.

Working with a Web

In addition to exerting its influence over individual files, the Explorer can make Web-wide changes as well.

Creating new folders

You can add new folders to your Web site. If you have a large site with lots of pages divided into categories, adding new folders is a good way to keep the files organized.

Say, for example, that your company's home page has four main sections — About Acme Consulting Company, Acme Services, Acme Staff, and Contact Acme — and each section contains several files. You can store each section's files in its own folder to keep your file system spic-and-span.

To create new folders, follow these steps:

   1. If the Folder View is not already visible, in the Explorer toolbar, click the Folder View button (or choose View⇨Folder View).

   2. Choose File⇨New⇨Folder.

   A new folder appears in the right pane of the Folder View. The folder name (New_Folder) is selected.

   3. Type a new folder name and press Enter.

   FrontPage renames the folder.

Renaming a Web site

When you create a Web site in FrontPage, you choose a one-word Web name. (Chapter 1 shows you how to create a new Web site.) FrontPage stores the Web site's files in a subfolder of the main Web site folder (located at C:\FRONTPAGE WEBS\CONTENT) and gives the subfolder the same name as the Web site. If, later on, you want to change the Web site's name (and, by extension, the name of the folder in which the Web site is stored), you can easily do so.

You can also give your Web site a descriptive title. When you open Web sites in the Explorer, the title is listed along with the Web name in the FrontPage Webs list box in the Open dialog box. If you've created several Web sites with similar names, titles make the list easier to sort through.

To change a Web site's name and title, follow these steps:

1. **In the Explorer, choose Tools⇨Web Settings.**

   The FrontPage Web Settings dialog box appears with the Configuration tab visible.

2. **In the Web Name text box, type a new name.**

   Jennifer is nice. Or Quincy.

3. **Enter a descriptive title in the Web Title text box.**

4. **Click OK to close the dialog box.**

Copying Web sites

The FrontPage Explorer enables you to copy your Web site to other locations. This feature comes in handy on several occasions.

- ✔ **You can easily copy one Web site *into* another, merging them into a single Web site.** This technique is helpful if you want to combine two Web sites' files and folders so that you can more easily manage the Web site's file system.

- ✔ **You can create a working copy of your Web site to use as a "scratch pad" so that you avoid making permanent changes to the original.**

- ✔ **Most important, this technique is how you transform your main Web site into the FrontPage Root Web.** (If you don't know what a Root Web is, refer to the Chapter 1 sidebar "What's a Root Web?")

FrontPage comes installed with a standard Root Web. After you create your main Web site, you copy the Web site into the Root Web, replacing its place-holder pages with your own. After you transform your main Web site into the Root Web, you can link it to the other Web sites that you create in FrontPage (by definition, all other FrontPage Web sites are Child Webs because each Web server can have only one Root Web). You can also take advantage of unique FrontPage features, such as registration systems (explained in Chapter 14), discussion groups (explained in Chapter 15), and permission settings (explained in Chapter 17).

If you merge two Web sites, FrontPage overwrites any files in the destination Web site that have the same name as those in the Web site that you're copying. This action is fine in the case of the Root Web because you want your Web site's pages to replace the standard FrontPage Root Web pages. In other cases, however, you can avoid the problem by renaming such files *before* you copy the Web site. (Refer to the section "Renaming files," earlier in this chapter).

To copy a Web site, follow these steps:

1. **In the Explorer, choose File➪Publish FrontPage Web.**

   The Publish FrontPage Web dialog box appears. (Incidentally, this feature is the same one that you eventually use to publish your completed Web site on a dedicated Web server, which I explain in Chapter 18.)

2. **If not already visible, select the name of the Personal Web Server from the Web Server or File location drop-down list.**

3. **In the Name of the Destination FrontPage Web text box, enter the name of the Web site into which you want to copy the current Web site.**

   If you are copying your main Web site to the Root Web, leave the text box empty. To make a duplicate copy of the Web site, enter a new Web name here (for example, if you are making a backup copy of your current Web site, enter the name **backup**).

4. **To copy only those pages that have changed since the last time you copied the Web site to this location, select the Copy changed pages only check box.**

   If this is the first time you are copying the Web site to this location, uncheck the check box.

5. **If you are copying the current Web site into another Web site, select the Add to an existing FrontPage Web check box.**

   If you are creating a duplicate copy of the current Web site, uncheck the check box.

6. **Click OK.**

   FrontPage copies the Web site to the new location and tells you when the process is complete.

Chapter 3

Playing with Pages in the FrontPage Editor

. . . .

In This Chapter

▶ What is a Web page?

▶ Creating a new Web page

▶ Opening a Web page

▶ Converting another type of document into a Web page

▶ Using a Web browser to preview a page

▶ Printing a page

▶ Saving a page

. . . .

*M*y artistic period took place between the ages of 6 and 10, when my teachers set aside part of each school day for "creative time." I drew pictures of unicorns, wrote poems, and perfected the subtle art of finger painting.

As I got older, my artistic ability dwindled to stick figures and scribbling on restaurant napkins. Then, one day, I discovered Web publishing and entered my renaissance. I no longer work with construction paper, tempera paints, or Elmer's glue; I now use the FrontPage Editor to create stacks of colorful Web pages.

The FrontPage Editor contains all the tools you need to embellish the basic pages created by the Explorer's Web site templates and Wizards. You also use the Editor to create new pages to add to your Web site. This chapter introduces you to the basic workings of the Editor, including creating, opening, saving, and printing Web pages, converting other documents into Web pages, and previewing pages in a Web browser. If you want to jump into page-building right away, turn to the chapters in Part II, "Creating Web Pages That Make You Look Like a Genius."

What Does the FrontPage Editor Do?

Where you use the Explorer to create Web sites, you use the Editor to make changes to the individual pages that make up the Web site or to add new pages to the Web site. The Editor is one of many *HTML editors,* programs that specialize in building Web pages. The FrontPage Editor is one of the most powerful HTML editors around, packing in more features than a ten-screen multiplex cinema.

HTML stands for *Hypertext Markup Language,* a set of codes that defines the layout and structure of a Web page. These codes (called *tags*) control how the page looks and acts. (Figure 3-1 illustrates a bare, naked Web page with its HTML tags showing — oh, my!) As you surf the World Wide Web, your Web browser translates HTML tags into the beautiful Web page you see on-screen (Figure 3-2 shows how the page in Figure 3-1 looks as seen through the flattering lens of a Web browser).

Not so long ago, you needed to learn all of HTML's tags to create a Web page. Although not difficult, memorizing tags does take time. Because most of us would rather frolic on the beach than spend sunny weekends in front of the computer, learning HTML (along with programming your VCR) stayed tucked away in the techie zone.

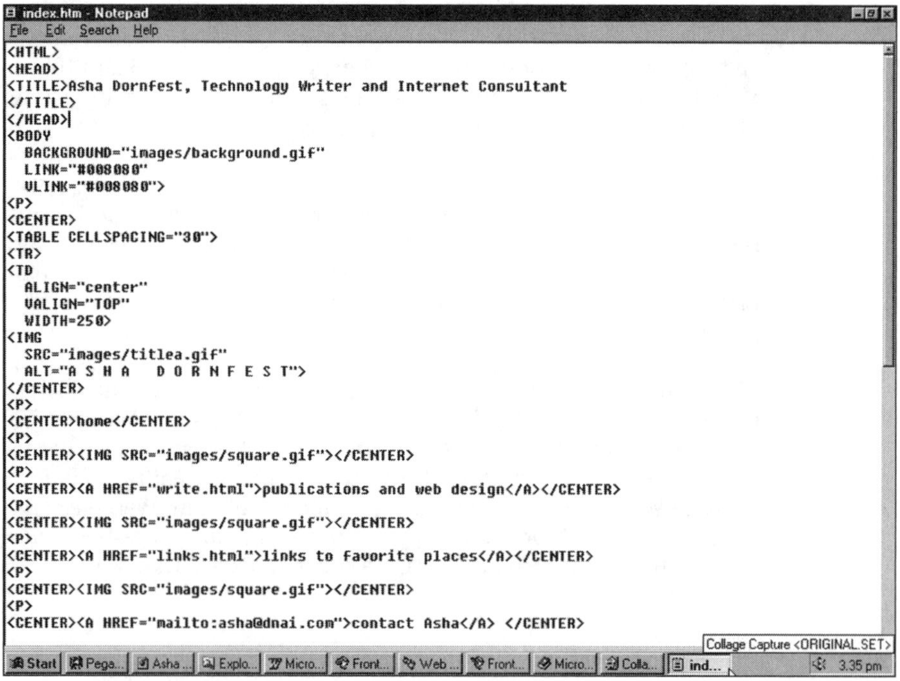

Figure 3-1: Kindly avert your eyes: This page's HTML tags are showing.

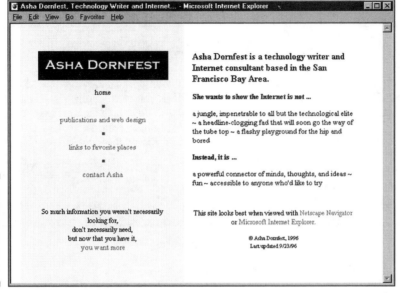

ASHA DORNFEST

home

publications and web design

links to favorite places

contact Asha

So much information you weren't necessarily
looking for,
don't necessarily need,
but now that you have it,
you want more

Asha Dornfest is a technology writer and
Internet consultant based in the San
Francisco Bay Area.

She wants to show the Internet is not ...

a jungle, impenetrable to all but the technological elite
~ a headline-clogging fad that will soon go the way of
the tube top ~ a flashy playground for the hip and
bored

Instead, it is ...

a powerful connector of minds, thoughts, and ideas ~
fun ~ accessible to anyone who'd like to try

This site looks best when viewed with Netscape Navigator
or Microsoft Internet Explorer.

© Asha Dornfest, 1996
Last updated 9/23/96

Figure 3-2:
The same
page, as
seen with
a Web
browser.

That is, until programs like the FrontPage Editor came along. The Editor does
the HTML grunt work for you, freeing your brain cells for such creative things
as deciding what to put in your page. You get to click menus and push buttons,
and the Editor generates all the HTML behind the scenes — which means that
you can create sophisticated Web pages without sacrificing precious beach time.

Creating a New Web Page

Back in my artistic heyday, I could sit in the corner with a piece of scratch
paper and some crayons, and, an hour later, emerge with a masterpiece. Today,
I sometimes need a little help getting started.

If you want to add a new page to your Web site, but don't know how to begin
building a page, rely on the Editor's page templates and Wizards for a helpful
nudge in the right direction. *Templates* are boilerplate versions of common page
formats you can customize for your own purposes. *Wizards* ask you questions
about the information that you'd like to include and then generate a page based
on your answers.

If your creative juices are flowing freely, you can, of course, build your own page
from scratch. Please do not draw on the screen with crayons, however.

HTML isn't just for geeks anymore

Although you don't *need* to learn HTML anymore, a bit of HTML knowledge certainly doesn't hurt. In fact, learning HTML is well worth your while. HTML is constantly evolving, with new tags and design effects making impressive debuts. Later versions of FrontPage are sure to support these features, but you don't really want to wait for (or, heaven forbid, *pay* for) an upgrade so that you can use hot, new effects in your Web, do you? So consider learning at least a bit of HTML. You gain a greater appreciation of Web publishing, and you can take advantage of HTML's latest features. At the very least, you can impress your colleagues at the next staff mixer.

In Chapter 4, I introduce you to some elementary HTML, just to prove how easy the stuff is.

By using a template

Templates are to a page what a jump-start is to an engine. If your Web publishing inspiration is tapped out, templates jolt you back into action.

Templates are skeleton pages, to which you add your own information and design effects. The Editor contains templates for pages that commonly appear in commercial and educational Web sites, such as lists of FAQs (pronounced *eff-ay-cues,* which is Web-lingo for *frequently asked questions*), product descriptions, and job listings, to name a few.

To create a new page with the help of a template, follow these steps:

1. **Launch FrontPage and, in the Explorer, open the Web site to which you want to add a new page.**

   If you don't know how to launch FrontPage or open a Web site in the Explorer, refer to Chapter 1.

2. **In the Explorer toolbar, press the Show FrontPage Editor button.**

   Or choose Tools⇨Show FrontPage Editor.

   The Editor launches.

3. **In the Editor, choose File⇨New (or press Ctrl+N).**

   The New Page dialog box appears, displaying a smorgasbord of templates and Wizards from which to choose.

4. **In the Template or Wizard list box, select a template name for a description of what that template does.**

5. **After you find the template you want, click OK.**

If you know exactly what template you want and don't need any description of what it does, you can simply double-click the name in the list to create a new page based on that template.

If the built-in FrontPage templates don't meet your specific needs, you can always create your own template. I explain how in the section "Saving a page as a template," later in this chapter. I also include my own custom-designed page templates on the CD that comes with this book. Refer to Appendix C for a list of the templates, as well as instructions for using them.

A new page, based on that template, appears (see Figure 3-3).

The purple text at the top of the new page is a *comment*. (In Figure 3-3, the comment appears black.) Comments are visible as you edit the page in the Editor, but not as you view the page with a browser. FrontPage uses comments to give you hints about how to customize the template. You can leave the comments for reference, or you can delete them after you understand how the template works. To delete a comment, click anywhere on the purple text and press either the Backspace or Delete key. (I show you how to add your own comments to a page in Chapter 5.)

Title bar   Menu bar   Comment   Editing window   Toolbars

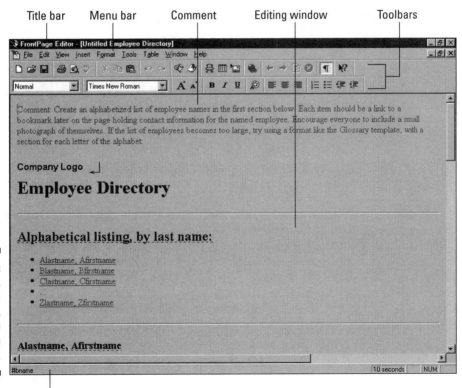

Figure 3-3:
A new page, based on a template, opens in the FrontPage Editor.

Status bar

By using a Wizard

The Editor contains page Wizards for four particularly complex pages:

- ✔ **Form Page Wizard:** This Wizard takes you through the steps necessary to create an interactive form. Chapter 10 explains what forms are, how they work, and how you can use forms to keep in touch with your visitors.

- ✔ **Frames Wizard:** This Wizard helps you create a page divided into sections called *frames,* each of which can display another page. You discover how to use the Frames Wizard in Chapter 11.

- ✔ **Personal Home Page Wizard:** This Wizard recites the Personal Home Page incantation, asking you a bunch of questions about yourself and then generating a page based on your responses. Incidentally, the finished page is almost identical to the one you can create by using the Explorer's Personal Web template.

- ✔ **Database Connector Wizard:** This Wizard creates a *database connector file* that specifies how your Web interacts with a database connected to the Internet. I discuss databases in Chapter 10.

To create a page with the help of a Wizard, follow these steps:

1. **In the Editor, choose File⇨New (or press Ctrl+N).**

   The New Page dialog box appears.

2. **In the Templates and Wizards dialog box, double-click the name of the Wizard that you want to use.**

   The Wizard launches, and you're presented with a series of dialog boxes prompting you for more information. Fill in the info requested for each dialog box and then click the Next button to advance to the following dialog box or click the Back button to return to the preceding dialog box to review or change what you entered there.

3. **After you're done filling in information in the Wizard dialog boxes, click the Finish button.**

   Alakazam! The Wizard creates a new page based on your selections.

Creating pages from scratch

If you already have a good idea about what you want to include in the new page, create a blank page. To do so, choose one of the following options:

✔ Click the New Page button. (This button bypasses the New Page dialog box and automatically creates a new, blank page.)

✔ Choose File⇨New to open the New Page dialog box and double-click Normal Page in the Templates and Wizards list box. (Or press Enter because Normal Page is automatically selected as the default option.)

A new, blank page appears in the Editor, patiently awaiting your additions.

Opening a Page

If you want to make changes to the pages in your Web site, open them in the Editor. The FrontPage Editor can open any Web page, even those created with other programs. The page may live inside your Web site, elsewhere on your computer, or in the wilds of the World Wide Web.

In the current Web site

If you're already working in the Editor and want to open one of your Web site's pages, you don't need to switch to the Explorer to do so. You can open a page directly in the Editor.

To open a page that's part of a FrontPage Web site, the Web site must be open in the Explorer.

To open one of your Web site's pages, follow these steps:

1. From the Editor, click the Open button.

Or choose File⇨Open.

The Open File dialog box appears (see Figure 3-4). The dialog box contains two tabs that describe the location of the page that you want to open: the Current FrontPage Web tab and the Other Location tab. When a Web site is open in the Explorer, the Current FrontPage Web tab is visible, with all the Web site's files and folder listed in the tab's list box.

2. In the list box, select the page that you want to open and click OK.

If the page is stored inside a folder, double-click the folder to open it, select the page, and then click OK.

The Editor opens the page. Be patient — the page may take a few moments, especially if it contains lots of graphics.

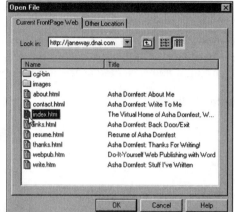

Figure 3-4:
The Open
File dialog
box.

From a file

In FrontPage parlance, *opening a page from a file* means opening a page that exists outside of a FrontPage Web site. Use this option if you want to open a Web page that lives elsewhere on your computer.

To open a page from a file, follow these steps:

1. **Click the Open button.**

   Or choose File➪Open or press Ctrl+O.

   The Open File dialog box appears (refer to Figure 3-4).

2. **If not already visible, click the Other Location tab.**

   The Other Location tab becomes visible.

3. **Select the location of the file that you want to open in the From File text box and click OK.**

   Or click the Browse button to select the file by browsing the contents of your hard drive. If you click Browse, another Open File dialog box appears. Navigate your hard drive until you see the file's icon and double-click the icon to open the file.

   The Editor opens the file.

FrontPage does not check HTML tags created in other programs for errors; the Editor just opens the Web page as-is. If FrontPage encounters an HTML tag it doesn't recognize, it displays an Unknown HTML icon (a yellow box containing a question mark) inside the Web page. In Chapter 5, I show you how to correct invalid HTML tags.

From another Web server

The FrontPage Editor enables you to open a Web page stored on another Web server (as opposed to your own computer). This ability is extremely useful if you want to open a Web page directly from the World Wide Web or from your company *intranet* (an internal company network based on Internet technology, but only accessible to company insiders).

 If you open a page stored on another Web server, FrontPage opens the *copy* of the page for you to edit. When you save the page, FrontPage saves the page (plus any embedded graphics) on your computer. Any changes you make aren't visible on the Internet until you transfer the edited document back to the Web server on which the original document is stored. For more details on how to publish Web pages, see Chapter 18.

To open a page stored on another Web server, follow these steps:

1. **Click the Open button.**

   Or choose File⇨Open or press Ctrl+O.

   The Open File dialog box appears.

2. **If it's not already visible, click the Other Location tab.**

   The Other Location tab becomes visible.

3. **Select the From Location radio button.**

   The From Location text box turns from gray to white, indicating that you can type something into it.

4. **In the From Location text box, type the URL of the page that you want to open.**

   The *URL* is the page's address on the Web server. A URL should look something like the following address: `www.dnai.com/~asha/write.html`. (You don't need to type **http://** first because FrontPage already knows that you're looking for a page on a Web server, and all Web URLs begin with `http://`.)

5. **Click OK.**

   FrontPage retrieves the page from the server and displays a copy on your screen.

Converting Other Documents into Web Pages

FrontPage has its evangelical tendencies. The Editor can convert the following popular document formats into Web pages, just by opening the files:

✔ Microsoft Word documents (for Windows, Versions 2.x, 6, and Word 97; and for Macintosh, Versions 4.0 to 5.1 and 6) (*.DOC, *.MCW)

✔ Microsoft Works 3.0 and 4.0 documents (*.WPS)

✔ WordPerfect 5.x and 6.x documents (*.DOC, *.WPD)

✔ Microsoft Excel worksheets (*.XLS)

✔ RTF documents (*.RTF)

✔ Text documents (*.TXT)

This feature is one of the Editor's most lovable because a lot of your Web site's content may already exist in other formats.

Make sure to create backup copies of the original files *before* you convert the files into Web pages with the Editor. Otherwise, when you save the newly HTML-ified page, it writes over the original file. The other option is to change the filename at the time that you save the page. See the section "Saving a Page," later in this chapter, for details on how to save pages in the Editor.

Word-processing documents

The FrontPage Editor can convert Microsoft Word, Microsoft Works, and WordPerfect documents to Web pages in the blink of an eye. Even more thrilling, the Editor maintains much of the document's text and paragraph formatting by converting the formats to the closest HTML style.

To convert a word-processing document into a Web page, you simply need to open the file in the Editor. To do so, follow the steps listed in the "Opening a page from a file" section, earlier in the chapter. In step 3, if you click the Browse button to locate the file, a second Open File dialog box appears. Select the appropriate document format from the Files of type drop-down list to make those files visible in the Open File dialog box's file list.

Microsoft Excel worksheets

If you've never worked with a *spreadsheet,* it's a type of program that simplifies numerical calculations. Microsoft Excel, the undisputed spreadsheet boss, is loved by engineers, accountants, and other number-crunchers worldwide.

Excel *worksheets* (what a spreadsheet program calls its documents) are arranged in rows and columns of information. In the past, converting spreadsheets into Web pages meant transferring the data into a Web page *table,* a painstaking and time-consuming process. (If you're not sure what a table is, check out Chapter 9.). Today, the FrontPage Editor can convert Excel worksheets into tables with nary a thought.

To convert an Excel worksheet into a Web page, follow the steps listed in the "Opening a page from a file" section, earlier in the chapter. In step 3, if you click the Browse button to locate the file, a second Open File dialog box appears. Select Microsoft Excel Worksheet (*.XLS, *.XLW) from the Files of type drop-down list to make Excel worksheets files visible in the Open File dialog box's file list.

RTF documents

RTF stands for *Rich Text Format.* This format saves certain types of text styles and layout in a format readable by all kinds of word-processing programs. RTF is often used by folks who want to share formatted documents with others who are using different types of computer systems.

The Editor makes short work of converting RTF documents into Web pages. In fact, if you blink, you don't even realize that the conversion took place.

To convert an RTF document into a Web page, follow the steps listed in the "Opening a page from a file" section, earlier in the chapter. In step 3, if you click the Browse button to locate the file, a second Open File dialog box appears. Select Rich Text Format (*.RTF) from the Files of type drop-down list to make RTF files visible in the Open File dialog box's file list.

Text documents

Text documents contain no formatting whatsoever. No bold or italics, no tables or curly quotes ("") — just regular old characters and spaces. The Editor can convert a text document to a Web page in one of the following four different ways:

- **One formatted paragraph:** The Editor stuffs all the document's paragraphs into a single paragraph, to which the program applies the *Formatted* style. In a Web page, the Formatted style appears as a monospaced font (usually Courier) with line breaks and multiple spaces between characters preserved. (The upcoming sidebar, "Font fun," explains what a monospaced font is.) If your text document contains rows and columns of information separated by spaces or tabs, this style is a good choice.

- **Formatted paragraphs:** FrontPage retains individual paragraphs and applies the Formatted style to each one. Use this style if you want the individual paragraphs in your document to remain distinct.

- **Normal paragraphs:** FrontPage applies the *Normal* style to each of the document's paragraphs. The Normal style is the default style for Web page text. The Normal style appears as a *proportional* font (usually Times) and ignores multiple spaces and tabs. (The "Font fun" sidebar also explains what a proportional font is.) This style is a good choice if you just need to convert the document's text into a Web page without regard for spaces or line breaks.

✔ **Normal paragraphs with Line Breaks:** FrontPage applies the Normal style to the document's paragraphs and retains line breaks. Use this style if you want your document's line breaks to remain intact.

Now that you know your options, here's how to convert a text document into a Web page:

1. **Follow the steps listed in "Opening a page from a file," earlier in the chapter.**

   Before the file opens in the Editor, the Convert Text dialog box appears.

2. **Select the radio button next to the conversion method that you want to use.**

   Your choices are One formatted paragraph, Formatted paragraphs, Normal paragraphs, and Normal paragraphs with line breaks.

3. **Click OK.**

   The Editor opens the document and converts the file according to your preference.

If you don't like the way FrontPage converts your document, close the file without saving it. Then reopen the file and choose another conversion method.

Font fun: Monospaced versus proportional

Quite a few printing and typography buzzwords have made their way into the Web publishing lexicon. Two you should remember are *monospaced* and *proportional font*.

A monospaced font is one in which each character and space is exactly the same width.

```
This paragraph appears in Courier, the
most common monospaced font on the Web.
This font often appears in pages on
which the author wants to control the
placement of each character.
```

A proportional font is more elegant and readable than a monospaced font. The width of each character and the amount of space between characters differs, making the text more visually appealing.

This paragraph appears in Times, the most common proportional font on the Web. The majority of Web page text appears in this font, because its text is compact and easy to read.

Previewing a Page in a Web Browser

As you create pages in the Editor, the pages look very similar to how they appear as viewed with a Web browser. In techno-speak, this similarity is called *WYSIWYG* (pronounced *wizzy-wig*), which stands for What-You-See-Is-What-You-Get.

Even so, previewing your pages in an honest-to-goodness browser is a good idea. That way, you get an accurate representation of how your pages appear to your visitors. The FrontPage Editor, handily enough, enables you to quickly preview your pages by opening the pages in a Web browser with the click of a button.

Even better, if you have more than one Web browser installed on your computer, you can choose which browser you'd like FrontPage to launch to preview your pages. You can also select different window sizes so that you can see how your page looks to visitors who have monitors smaller or larger than yours.

Because FrontPage makes previewing your pages in several browsers so easy, consider downloading and installing more than one browser program (preferably ones that can display different features). If you have the room on your hard drive, the understanding you can pick up about how different pages may look in different programs is worth the extra bit of effort required in installing the extra browsers.

Visit Browserwatch at `http://browserwatch.iworld.com` for an up-to-date account of Web browser happenings and links to download sites.

In the Editor toolbar, click the Preview in Browser button to open the current page in your default Web browser.

To choose the browser in which you want to open the page or to control the window size, follow these steps:

1. **Choose File⇨Preview in Browser.**

   The Preview in Browser dialog box appears (see Figure 3-5).

2. **In the Browser list box, select the name of the browser you want to use.**

3. **Select the radio button for the Window Size that you want to view.**

   The numbers listed next to each radio button represent standard *resolution values* in pixels. A monitor's resolution refers to the number of pixels that monitor displays on-screen. The larger the that number, the higher is the resolution of the picture and the more information a monitor can display. The majority of Web surfers have 800 x 600 resolution monitors.

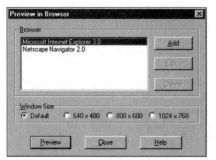

Figure 3-5:
The Preview
in Browser
dialog box.

4. Click the Preview button.

FrontPage opens your page in the browser of your choice.

To edit the page, return to the Editor by clicking the Editor's button in the Windows 95 taskbar (or pressing Alt+Tab). Make any changes to the page you want. To view changes, save the page (see the section "Saving a Page," later in this chapter for details), switch back to the browser window, and choose the browser's Refresh or Reload command.

You can easily add browsers to the FrontPage Preview in Browser dialog box's Browser list. Click the Add button, type the name of the browser in the Name field, and click Browse to locate the browser's icon on your hard drive.

Printing a Page

Web pages don't make the best transition to print because the concept of a "page" on the Web is tied to a discreet bit of information rather than to a physical piece of paper. Still, you may, from time to time, need to print your Web pages if, say, your Net-challenged boss wants to check on your work.

If you use FrontPage print settings, you affect how FrontPage prints your pages, not how your pages print after you post them on the Web. If your visitors want to print out your Web site, their Web browsers' print settings determine how the finished product looks.

To print a page, do the following:

1. In the Editor, click the Print button.

Or choose File⇨Print or press Ctrl+P.

The Print dialog box appears.

2. **If not already visible in the Name drop-down list, select the name of the printer that you want to use.**

3. **In the Print Range section, select the All radio button to print all pages or select the Pages radio button to specify a range of pages.**

   "Pages" refers to the number of pieces of paper it takes to print all the information in your Web page. If you click Pages, type the number of the first page in the range in the from text box and the number of the last page in the range in the to text box.

4. **In the Number of copies text box, type the number of copies that you want to print.**

5. **If you are printing more than one page and want to collate the pages, select the Collate check box.**

6. **Click OK to spur your printer into action.**

Here are a few printing tips:

- ✔ Choose File⇨Print Preview to display a preview of the Web page as it will appear on the printed page.

- ✔ FrontPage automatically sets 0.5" page margins. To change the margins, choose File⇨Page Setup. The Print Page Setup dialog box appears. Enter new values in the Margins text boxes and click OK.

- ✔ Each page prints with the page title at the top of the page (the *header*) and the page number at the bottom (the *footer*). You can change the header and footer by choosing File⇨Page Setup. The Print Page Setup dialog box appears. Enter a new header and footer in the Header and Footer text boxes and click OK.

Saving a Page

Your Web publishing masterpiece is only as grand as the last time you saved your pages. So save your work often. My fingers instinctively press Ctrl+S every time I write a particularly brilliant sentence.

You can save a page as part of a FrontPage Web site, as a file, or as a page template. Pay close attention to the steps because how you save a page depends on how you originally opened the page.

 If you've made lots of changes to your page but haven't yet saved the changes, you can erase all the changes and revert to the previously saved version of the page. To do so, press the Refresh button (or choose View⇨Refresh) and then click No after FrontPage asks whether you want to save the changes.

As a page in your Web site

If you create a new Web page or open a page from elsewhere, you can easily add the page to your Web site simply by saving the page.

To save a page as part of a FrontPage Web site, the Web must be open in the FrontPage Explorer.

To save a page to your Web site, follow these steps:

1. **If you're saving a new page or a page you originally opened from another Web server, choose File➪Save.**

    Or click the Save button or press Ctrl+S.

   If you're saving a page you originally opened from a file, choose File➪Save As.

   The Save As dialog box appears.

   (If you're saving a page you opened from within your Web site, choosing File➪Save doesn't cause any dialog boxes to appear — the command just saves your changes.)

2. **Type a descriptive title in the Page Title text box.**

   FrontPage automatically generates a filename based on the title you choose.

3. **If you want to change the page's filename, type a new name in the File path within your FrontPage web text box.**

4. **Click OK.**

   If you're saving a page originally opened from another location, FrontPage asks whether you want to import the page's graphics (if the page contains any). Click Yes to import each image one-by-one or click Yes to All to import everything in one go.

   FrontPage saves the page and adds that page to the Web site.

As a file

If you want to save the page to another location on your hard drive (that is, outside of your Web site), you can do that, too.

1. **If you're saving a new page or a page originally opened from another Web server, choose File➪Save.**

   Or click the Save button or press Ctrl+S.

If you're saving a page that you originally opened from within your Web site, choose File⇨Save As.

The Save As dialog box appears.

(If you're saving a page you originally opened from a file, choosing File⇨Save doesn't cause any dialog boxes to appear — the command just saves your changes.)

2. **Enter a descriptive title in the Page Title text box.**

3. **If you want to change the filename, type a new name in the File path within your FrontPage web text box.**

4. **Click As File.**

   The Save As File dialog box appears.

5. **Navigate your hard drive and open the folder in which you want to save the file.**

6. **Click Save.**

   If the page contains graphics, FrontPage asks whether you also want to save the page's graphics as files. Click Yes.

   FrontPage saves the page to the selected folder.

If you save a page originally opened from within your Web site to a file, FrontPage saves a *copy* of the edited page to the file. The original, unchanged page remains in your Web site.

As a template

You can save any page as a page template. This feature saves countless hours if you create lots of pages with standard layouts.

1. **If you're saving a new page or a page originally opened from another Web server, choose File⇨Save.**

   Or click the Save button or press Ctrl+S.

   If you're saving a page you originally opened from within the Web site or from a file, choose File⇨Save As.

   The Save As dialog box appears.

2. **Click the As Template button.**

   The Save As Template dialog box appears.

3. **Enter a descriptive title in the Title text box.**

4. **In the Name text box, type a filename.**

Just type a short word — the Editor automatically applies the correct three-letter extension (TEM, in case you're curious).

5. **In the Description text box, type a short description of what the template does.**

6. **Click OK.**

FrontPage saves the page as a template.

If the page you're saving contains graphics, FrontPage asks whether you want to save the page's graphics as separate files. Click Yes to save the graphics this way.

The next time you create a new file, your template appears with all its friends in the Templates and Wizards list box inside the New Page dialog box.

Part II
Creating Web Pages That Make You Look Like a Genius

The 5th Wave   By Rich Tennant

"No, Thomas Jefferson never did 'the Grind,' however, this does show how animation can be used to illustrate American history on the Web."

In this part . . .

Mastering FrontPage is one thing. . . . Understanding how to construct a great-looking, easy-to-navigate Web site is another. Part II helps you do both.

In this part, you discover how to build Web pages from the ground up. You delve into the inner workings of the FrontPage Editor, your tool for everything from creating hyperlinks to adding dazzling sound and video to your Web site.

Chapter 4

Web Design Fundamentals

*T*he desktop-publishing revolution of the '80s taught wannabe designers a lesson: Buying a big, fat desktop publishing program doesn't guarantee clear, professional-looking newsletters and reports. The crucial ingredient — *design sense*, or an "*eye*" — isn't built into the software.

In the same way, creating standout Web sites using FrontPage requires a thorough understanding of the program's publishing capabilities *and* an eye for what makes a Web site work. This chapter pumps up your design muscles so that you can build a site that's easy to navigate, loads quickly, and looks fantastic.

Clients and Servers 101

To understand Web design, you first need to understand the basic relationship between *clients* and *servers* on the Web. The client-server relationship is the yin and yang that keeps the Internet running.

A *server* is any computer that contains and distributes information. A *client* is the program on your computer that requests and processes or displays that information. On the Web, Web servers store and serve Web pages, and Web clients (more often referred to as Web browsers) display the pages on your screen. Clients and servers are useless without each other, much like separate halves of a piece of Velcro.

If you're unclear about the client-server relationship, think of your television. After you turn on your TV, the device hunts for signals from a broadcast station, assembles them into *Melrose Place,* and displays the show on your TV screen. In this example, the broadcast station is the server, and your TV set is the client. Without the signals sent by the broadcast station, your TV is an empty box. By the same token, without TVs to pick up and display these signals, broadcast stations have no purpose. Figure 4-1 illustrates the client-server relationship.

When you publish a site on the World Wide Web, you place all the site's linked files on a Web server. The server waits patiently, listening for client requests from the Internet or company intranet. As soon as the server receives a request (a visitor types the file's URL into his or her Web browser), the server springs into action and delivers the requested file. *How* the file looks after appearing on your visitor's screen depends in large part on the particular features of the visitor's computer and Internet setup, such as the choice of Web browser, operating system, and size of monitor.

Return to the TV analogy for a moment. The broadcast station (the server) spits signals into the ether, which your TV (the client) picks up and translates into *Melrose Place* (the file). You're watching the same show as everyone else. What you see on your color, 17-inch screen, however, looks different from what your neighbor sees on the old black-and-white set in her kitchen (see Figure 4-2).

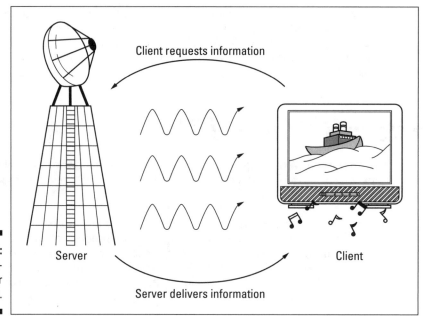

Figure 4-1:
The client-
server
relationship.

Client requests information

Server

Client

Server delivers information

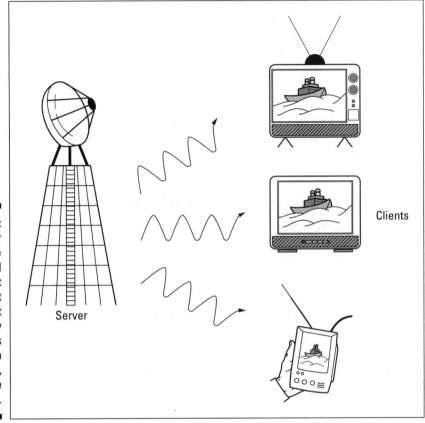

Figure 4-2:
The server
serves the
original
content, but
how that
content
ultimately
looks
depends, in
large part,
on the
client.

In a fit of sick pleasure, you adjust the contrast so that Heather Locklear appears green. She doesn't turn green all over America — just on your set — and there's not a thing the broadcast station can do about it.

The moral of this story is that you have only so much control over how your Web site looks after it ends up on your visitors' screens. Read on if you want to discover more about the specific differences between clients and how to accommodate those differences in your site's design.

Cross-Platform Mania

Designing for the World Wide Web is often compared to taming a large, hairy beast. Where conventional design enables you to control how the finished product looks down to the finest detail, Web design is, at best, a crap-shoot.

Why? Because the Web is a *cross-platform* medium, which means that people browse the Web using any number of hardware devices, software programs, and operating systems. Each piece of the platform affects how Web sites ultimately look after the sites show up on the visitor's screen.

The challenge (or, as those less tactful may say, pain-in-the-butt) for Web publishers is to design sites that account for platform variations and still manage to look great. Doing so is not difficult after you accept a few truisms about the Web as a publishing medium. You soon realize that the Web design beast, although still big and hairy, is really just a teddy bear after you come to know it.

Web truism #1: Your visitors use different computers

Just as people drive to work in buses, Bugs, and BMWs, folks cruise the Net with all sorts of computers. Some drive old clunkers with tiny black-and-white monitors. Others speed along with turbo-charged processors and a big, full-color display. The beauty of the Web is that the vehicle of choice doesn't matter — whether you use a Mac, a PC, or a UNIX workstation, all you need is a Web browser, and you're ready to roll. The problem, however, is that Web sites look different depending on the visitor's computer setup.

A particular Web site viewed on different computers doesn't necessarily look *so* different that you wouldn't recognize the site, but slight differences such as color, text alignment, and font size are all affected (in varying degrees) by your visitor's monitor size and choice of operating system. I created my personal home page on a PC running Windows 95, for example, and I gave my page a lovely lemon-yellow background color. To my chagrin, however, my designer friend — a die-hard Mac user — looked at my page with his Web browser and told me that my page was a sickly green. (Fortunately, this problem was easy to fix — I share the secret in Chapter 7.)

Web truism #2: Your visitors use different browsers

Not only do your visitors use different computers, but they also use different programs to browse the Web. As with platform differences, Web pages appear slightly different in each Web browser — and even in older versions of the same browser.

Ninety percent of the Web surfing population uses Netscape Navigator or Microsoft Internet Explorer, the David and Goliath of the battle to dominate the browser field. The other ten percent use other browsers, such as Spyglass

Mosaic, Lynx (a text-only browser), and proprietary browsers belonging to online services. "Feh," you say, "why worry about a measly ten percent?" Because ten percent of an estimated tens of millions of Net cruisers ain't no handful. To see what I'm talking about, take a peek at Figures 4-3 and 4-4.

Figure 4-3:
The
Microsoft
home page,
as seen
using
Microsoft
Internet
Explorer.

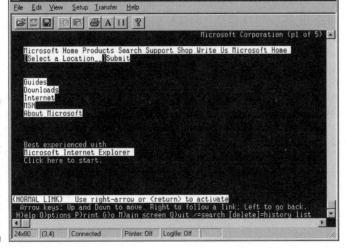

Figure 4-4:
The
Microsoft
home page,
as seen
using Lynx,
a text-based
browser.

The situation is further convoluted by *browser-specific extensions to HTML.* In an effort to encourage folks to use their products, Netscape and Microsoft each invented HTML tags that produce fantastic design effects — but only if viewed by the companies' own browsers and, often, only by the most recent version. If you're one of the unfortunate ten percent using another browser, too bad.

Web truism #3: Your visitors connect to the Internet at different speeds

Speed is an obsession on the Internet. Suddenly, a few seconds spent waiting for a Web site to appear feels like an eternity. Those seconds can stretch into agonizing minutes for those of your visitors using slow Internet connections.

What causes a Web site to load at tortoise speed? Graphics are the worst culprit. Big graphics with lots of colors take a long time to load and are not always worth the time spent waiting.

The length of a Web page also affects its speed. Pages containing several screenfuls of text load more slowly than shorter pages.

Other notorious sloths include multimedia goodies, such as sounds, videos, and embedded miniprograms, called *Java applets* or *ActiveX components.* These Web publishing extras, so loved by designers with lightening-fast Internet connections, are the bane of normal folks surfing with a 28.8 modem.

Web truism #4: Your visitors come from diverse cultures

Consider your visitors' cultural backgrounds as central to your design as platform differences because cultural differences in outlook affect how your visitors experience your Web site just as much as do their choices of computer or browser. Beyond its appearance, your site must speak to people of different cultures, nationalities, and value systems. No, you don't need to learn a new language to publish on the Web. You do, however, need to keep a diverse audience in mind as you build your site. By making sure that each page is easy to navigate and is clearly written, you make your site accessible to the largest audience possible.

Five Steps to a Brilliant Web Site

The Boy Scout motto "Be Prepared" applies to Web publishing. Now that you're aware of the Web truisms, you can account for these factors as you design your site. The following sections describe how to do so in five easy steps.

Give your site a purpose

As I write this book, my purpose isn't to document the Internet or even to explain every nook and cranny of Web publishing. My purpose is to show you how to use FrontPage to create a beautiful Web site — and have fun at the same time.

Your site needs a similar clarity of purpose to be effective. Focus on what you want your site to accomplish: Do you want to educate your visitors? Do you want to sell them a product? Do you just want to share your warped vision of the world? After you decide what you want your site to do, make the purpose clear to your visitors right away so that they know what to expect if they decide to stay for a while.

You can state your site's purpose directly. ("Welcome to the Hurricane-A-Day home page, your source for the latest information on tropical storms.") Or you can use a more subtle approach by listing your site's different parts, thereby enabling your visitors to know, at a glance, what kind of information they can find there.

Remember your visitors

Establishing a purpose can be daunting unless you concentrate on your most important visitors: your *target audience.* Just as *Seventeen* targets teenyboppers and *Wired* targets technology addicts, your site must target a specific group of people.

Visualize your target audience. No, don't try to divine your visitors' hair color or astrological signs. Ask yourself the following questions: "Are they technically savvy? How old are they? What kind of information do they want?" The more answers you come up with, the better you can communicate your message to visitors of your site.

(In Chapter 14, I show you how to add a registration system to your Web site — this system is an excellent way to gather more information about your target audience after your Web site is live.)

Cultivate an image

Elvis, Nike, and Ross Perot all have something your Web site needs: an image. Your site's image is everything it says without words — in advertising and design lingo, its "look and feel." So think about how you'd want your target audience to describe your site — "friendly," "cutting edge," "useful," "bizarre" — and choose your site's graphics and layout accordingly.

Make your site easy to navigate

If you've ever driven a car in San Francisco, you know it's not what one would call a user-friendly city. One-way streets, nosebleed hills, and elusive parking make driving in San Francisco a frightening experience for the first-time visitor. (Of course, you can always double-park while you hop out for a cappuccino, which more than makes up for the hassles.)

Your Web site should be just the opposite. Your site must be easy to navigate the very first time around. Guide your visitors with clearly categorized information and thoughtfully placed links. Break information into manageable bits, keeping pages short and easy to read. (As a bonus, short pages load faster, too.) If your visitors get lost, give them a map containing links to all the pages in your site or, better, set the site up so that visitors can search your site for key words. (The FrontPage Search WebBot, which you discover in Chapter 12, enables you to perform this task.)

For an excellent discussion of the merits of mapping out your site's navigational flow, read *Site Blueprints: The Key to Web Hygiene* by Lou Rosenfeld. You can find this useful guide on the Web at `http://webreview.com/design/arch/sept15/index.html`.

Plan for the future

Web sites, like little babies and national deficits, grow. As time goes on, you're bound to add new pages, even new sections to your site. Build some growing room into your site's organization. Minimize repetitive tasks by creating page templates. Use the FrontPage Include WebBot to automate the inclusion of standard elements in your pages. (I show you how in Chapter 12.) Most important, keep the growth of your Web site in perspective by refining your site's purpose and remaining focused on your target audience.

The Web loves to talk about itself — hence, the enormous number of Web sites devoted to the topic of Web design. Here are a few of the best:

✔ David Siegel's Web Wonk at `http://www.dsiegel.com/tips`

✔ The Top Ten Ways to Improve Your Home Page at `http://www.glover.com/improve.html`

✔ Webmastery's Style Resources at `http://union.ncsa.uiuc.edu/HyperNews/get/www/style.html`

Irrefutable Evidence That HTML Is Easy

And you thought you'd sneak out of here without any mention of HTML, the language used to create Web pages (for a more in-depth definition of HTML, refer to the beginning of Chapter 3).

You don't *need* to know HTML to publish fully functional, great-looking Web sites with FrontPage. If you want to get serious about Web publishing, however, there is no substitute for HTML fluency. HTML evolves faster than Microsoft can crank out new versions of FrontPage, so knowing HTML enables you to integrate the latest, hottest Web design effects into your site *today.*

You don't need programming experience to learn HTML because HTML isn't a programming language. HTML is a *markup language,* which means that it's just a series of codes that signal your Web browser to display certain formatting and layout effects. These codes, called *tags,* are easy to pick up on. Don't believe me? Keep reading: I prove my point in the following paragraphs.

Figure 4-5 shows a line of text as the words look viewed by Microsoft Internet Explorer.

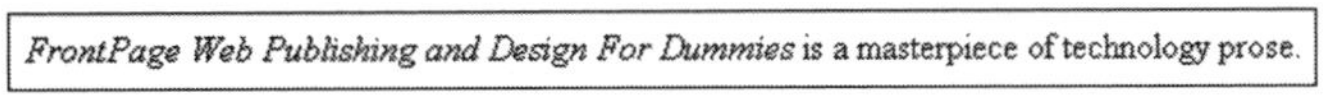

Figure 4-5:
Regular and
italic text,
as seen on
a Web
browser.

> *FrontPage Web Publishing and Design For Dummies* is a masterpiece of technology prose.

Figure 4-6 shows the HTML tags behind that same line of text.

The HTML tags that define italic text (`<I>` and `</I>`) surround the words `FrontPage Web Publishing and Design For Dummies`. The opening code, `<I>`, tells the Web browser where the italic text begins, and the closing code, `</I>`, indicates where the italics end.

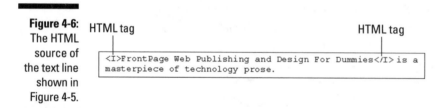

Figure 4-6:
The HTML source of the text line shown in Figure 4-5.

```
<I>FrontPage Web Publishing and Design For Dummies</I> is a
masterpiece of technology prose.
```

That's the basic premise behind HTML. Not as difficult as you thought, eh?

No doubt my HTML teaser has captivated your imagination. Find out more by visiting one or several of the wonderful HTML tutorials on the Web. Visit `http://www.yahoo.com/Computers_and_Internet/Software/ Data_Formats/HTML/Guides_and_Tutorials`, for example, for an overview. Or add *HTML For Dummies* (IDG Books Worldwide, Inc.), by Ed Tittel and Steve James, to your computer book library.

Chapter 5
Tweaking Your Text

. . . .

In This Chapter

▶ Adding text

▶ Creating stylish fonts and paragraphs

▶ Adding headings

▶ Creating lists

▶ Inserting symbols

▶ Creating a marquee

▶ Working with horizontal lines

. . . .

*Y*ou didn't buy this book just to find out how to use FrontPage. Figuring out FrontPage is simply a means to an end; your ultimate goal is to create a spectacular Web site. So in this and the following chapters, I show you how to build beautiful pages with the FrontPage Editor at your side.

The Editor contains a gazillion tools and commands that control various aspects of a page. In this chapter, I concentrate on the tools that affect the main ingredient of a page: its text.

Getting Started

Words, letters, numbers, characters. Text. Seems rather humble compared to the Web's flashy graphics and interactive effects. Yet text is the most important part of each page that you create, because the text makes up the *content*. You may dazzle your visitors with cutting-edge visuals and multimedia tricks, but the content — fresh, interesting, useful information — is what keeps people coming back for more.

(If you haven't already done so, you may want to take the time now to read Chapter 4. In that chapter, I do my best to persuade you to resist the temptation to play with FrontPage without first giving some thought to your readers.)

Adding text

Enough with the lecture. I promised to get you started on your page, didn't I? Okay, so launch the Editor and create a new, blank page (refer to Chapter 3 if you're not sure how), and as soon as you see the blinking cursor, start typing. Type whatever you want. Better yet, type something close to what you'd like a page in your Web to contain. Your screen should look something like the one shown in Figure 5-1. If you don't see similar toolbars, choose View➪Standard Toolbar and View➪Format Toolbar. (A check mark by a toolbar name means that the feature is already visible.)

Sanity-saving Editor shortcuts

FrontPage shares many attractive features (its ease of use, its good looks) with its Microsoft Office siblings — most notably, Microsoft Word. As you add and work with text in your Web page, you notice a resemblance between the Editor and a word processor. As does Word, the FrontPage Editor contains the following time-saving Office editing features that may tempt you to give your computer a big, affectionate squeeze:

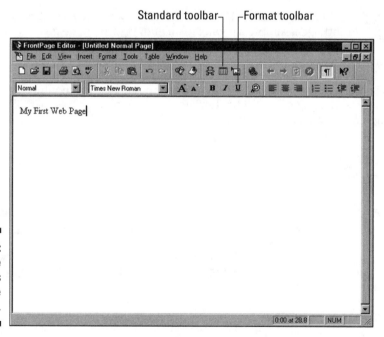

Figure 5-1:
Every page has its humble beginnings.

✔ **Undo:** If you type (or, worse, delete) something you didn't want typed (or deleted), the Undo button enables you to take back what you've done, up to the last 30 actions. You can also choose Edit⇨Undo or press Ctrl+Z.

✔ **Redo:** You can Redo anything you've undone just by clicking the Redo button, choosing Edit⇨Redo, or pressing Ctrl+Y.

 ✔ **Cut, Copy, and Paste:** You can cut, copy, and paste stuff (text, images — just about anything that you can select with your cursor) between open pages in the Editor and between documents in different applications. Just click the appropriate button or choose Edit⇨Cut (or press Ctrl+X), Edit⇨Copy (or press Ctrl+C), or Edit⇨Paste (or press Ctrl+V).

✔ **Drag and Drop:** You can drag and drop text, graphics, and other elements to different locations in your page.

✔ **Find and Replace:** The Edit⇨Find command enables you to jump directly to the location of a character, word, or phrase. You can even replace all instances of that character/word/phrase with another character/word/ phrase by using the Edit⇨Replace command. (The FrontPage Explorer also contains a Find and Replace function so that you can find and replace words throughout your Web site. To use it, click the Cross File Find button in the Explorer toolbar or choose Tools⇨Find or Tools⇨Replace.)

✔ **Thesaurus:** The built-in Thesaurus (accessible by choosing Tools⇨Thesaurus or pressing Shift+F7) instantly boosts your vocabulary by thousands of words.

 ✔ **Spell checking:** The spell checker takes care of any last-minute typo cleanups. Just click the Check Spelling button, choose Tools⇨Spelling, or press F7. (The FrontPage Explorer also contains a spell checker so that you can check your entire Web site's spelling in one go. To use it, click the Cross File Spelling button in the Explorer toolbar, choose Tools⇨Spelling, or press F7.)

✔ **Right-click pop-up menus:** The Editor contains shortcuts to commonly used commands in pop-up menus that appear after you pass the mouse pointer over an element (a piece of text, a hyperlink, a graphic, anything) and click the right mouse button. The pop-up menu that appears contains commands pertaining to the selected element.

Foolin' with Fonts

In FrontPage lingo, *font* refers to how text looks in your Web page. Characteristics such as boldface or italics, size, color, and typeface all make up a character's font. *Characters* — the thingies that appear on-screen after you press keyboard buttons — can be an unruly bunch. FrontPage Editor includes a pile of font-formatting tools with which to rein in those rowdy . . . er, characters.

Using font tools

All font tools are in the Font dialog box and the Format toolbar. (I introduce you to each of them in a moment.) You can use font-formatting tools in either of the following two ways:

✔ Type a bunch of text, select the stuff you want to format, and activate the appropriate tool, either by selecting an option in the Font dialog box or clicking a button in the Format toolbar. (Throughout this chapter, I specifically explain how to use each tool.)

✔ Activate the tool first, type the formatted text, and then deactivate the tool after you're done.

You can apply more than one font format to a piece of text. (You can, for example, make a word both bold and italic at the same time.)

To turn off all font formatting as you type, press Ctrl+spacebar. To remove all font formatting from a selected chunk of text, choose Format⇨Remove Formatting.

The Font dialog box

The Font dialog box (shown in Figure 5-2) contains every tool you need to control your characters. The options in this dialog box enable you to change the font, style, color, and size of text in your page.

To access the Font dialog box, choose Format⇨Font or right-click a piece of text (selected or not) and choose Font Properties from the pop-up menu.

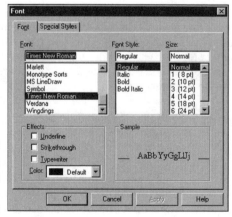

Figure 5-2:
The Font
dialog box.

The Format toolbar

The Format toolbar contains buttons for all the text tools you use most often, including a selection of font tools shown in Figure 5-3. The toolbar contains buttons for the following font tools: Bold, Italic, Underline, Increase and Decrease Text Size, and Text Color.

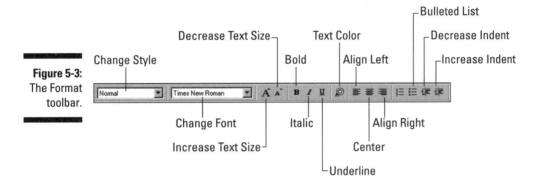

Figure 5-3:
The Format
toolbar.

Changing text font

Usually, when folks talk about a document's *font,* they're referring to its *typeface,* or the style and shape of the characters. (See Figure 5-4 for an example of different fonts.) The right choice of font sets the tone for your document and makes the text easy to read. (For an example of how font choices can enhance a page, check out the Resume template included in the CD that comes with the book; Appendix C shows you how to access CD contents.)

Until recently, Web publishers had no control over their pages' fonts and had to content themselves with the default fonts of most Web-browsing programs: Times and Courier. Now, because of advances in HTML and Web browser technology, you can apply any font to your Web pages — with certain restrictions, of course.

If you use special fonts in your Web pages, your visitors' computers must also have these fonts installed for your text to appear correctly on their screens. If your visitors don't have a particular font on their machines, any text you format in that font appears to them in their browsers' default font.

If, for example, you use the Garamond font in your pages and a visitor who doesn't have Garamond installed on her machine browses your page, she sees your page's text in Times (which is most browsers' default font).

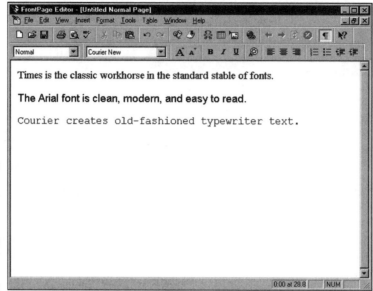

Figure 5-4:
The font or typeface you choose helps set the tone for your page.

Additionally, not all browsers can display font changes. Font variation is visible only in recent versions of advanced browsers such as Microsoft Internet Explorer and Netscape Navigator. (For more information about browser-specific effects, refer to Chapter 4.)

Bottom line: If you vary the font in your Web pages, keep in mind that a number of your visitors can't see the variations.

To change text font, perform one of the following actions:

✔ Select a new font from the Change Font drop-down list in the Format toolbar (see Figure 5-5).

Figure 5-5:
The Change Font drop-down list.

✔ Choose Format➪Font (or right-click text and choose Font Properties from the pop-up menu) to open the Font dialog box, select a font from the Font list, and click OK.

Be bold (or italic or underlined)!

Bold and *italic* attributes are the foundation of the font-formatting team. You pull these formats out like a trusty hammer every time you build a page. Apply these attributes for emphasis or to add variety to your text.

You have a few more font effects at your disposal: *underline, strikethrough,* and *typewriter.* The underline and strikethrough effects speak for themselves (see Figure 5-6). The typewriter effect, however, deserves a bit of attention. The typewriter effect applies a monospaced font to the selected text, which means that each character is of exactly the same width, creating a look similar to typewritten pages. Most Web browsers display the typewriter effect as Courier.

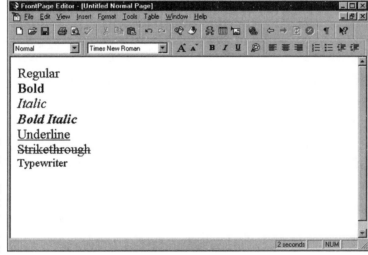

Figure 5-6:
You have several font styles at your disposal.

Why would you ever use the typewriter effect? I use the effect to set off blocks of text such as quotes or pieces of code. Some folks like the look of Courier better than that of Times (the default font for most Web browsers), so those people use the typewriter effect for all the text in their pages.

To apply a font style, perform one of the following actions:

✔ Click the style's button in the Format toolbar. (Buttons are available for Bold, Italic, and Underlined text.)

✔ Press Ctrl+B for bold, Ctrl+I for italics, or Ctrl+U for underlined text.

✔ Choose Format⇨Font (or right-click text and choose Font Properties from the pop-up menu) to open the Font dialog box, choose a style from the Font Style list, select the check box next to the effect you want (if any), and click OK.

Changing text size

Text size in print documents is measured in absolute units called *points* or *picas*. Because of the way HTML works, text size in Web pages is based on a relative system of *increments*.

HTML text sizes range in increments from 1 (the smallest size) to 7 (the biggest). In the Editor, the point-size equivalents range from 8 points (for size 1) to 36 points (for size 7). How many points each increment value turns out to be when viewed by a *Web browser,* however, depends on the reader's individual browser settings. Here's where you run into some cross-platform prickles, because you can't control the absolute point size of text as it appears on your reader's screen — only its size in relation to the other text in the page.

In FrontPage, for example, the default or Normal text size is 3, which the Editor displays as 12-point type. A visitor's Web browser, on the other hand, may display size 3 text as 14-point type. As you change the text size in the Editor, you simply increase or decrease the text size by one increment.

To change text size, perform one of the following actions:

- ✔ Click the Increase Text Size or Decrease Text Size buttons.
- ✔ Choose Format⇨Font (or right-click text and choose Font Properties from the pop-up menu) to open the Font dialog box and choose a size from the Size list. The Size list displays the range of size increments, along with their point sizes, as displayed in the Editor.

The point sizes apply *only* to how text appears in FrontPage, not necessarily to how the text appears in your reader's browser, because browser settings determine each increment's point size.

Changing text color

You can dress up your text in any color of the rainbow (plus a few fluorescent shades that don't appear in nature). Color gives your text panache, highlights important words, and, if coordinated with the colors of the page's graphics, unifies design.

The steps in this section show you how to change the color of individual characters and words you select. To set the color of an entire page full of text, read the section "Setting body text color," in this chapter.

To change text color, perform one of the following actions:

  ✔ Click the Text Color button to display the Color dialog box, click the color swatch you like in the Basic Colors area, and click OK.

  ✔ Choose Format⇨Font (or right-click text and choose Font Properties from the pop-up menu) to open the Font dialog box, choose a color from the Color drop-down list, and click OK.

Defining custom colors

You're not limited to the range of basic colors displayed or listed in the Color or Font dialog boxes. You can define up to 16 customized colors of your very own. To do so, just follow these steps:

1. Click the Text Color button to open the Color dialog box and then click the Define Custom Colors button.

Figure 5-7 shows the Color dialog box.

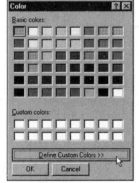

Figure 5-7:
The Color
dialog box.

The Color dialog box expands and displays a pretty rainbow palette and several technical-sounding text boxes containing different numbers (see Figure 5-8).

2. Choose the color you like.

The easiest way to choose a color is to drag the little crosshatch around the rainbow palette and drag the arrow up and down the side of the Luminance box (the thin vertical band on the right side of the dialog box) until the color you want appears in the Color I Solid box. If you prefer precise measurements, you can enter Hue, Sat (saturation), and Lum (luminance) values into the appropriate text boxes, or you can specify Red, Green, and Blue values.

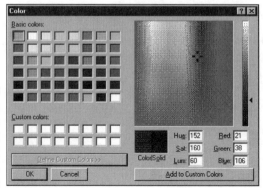

Figure 5-8:
The
expanded
Color dialog
box.

3. Click the Add to Custom Colors button.

The color appears in one of the blank Custom colors swatches.

4. Click OK.

The Color dialog box closes.

The next time you display the Color dialog box, the custom color is visible in one of the Custom colors swatches, and you can use it just as you would a basic color.

The Editor doesn't always display custom colors correctly as you apply them to text. For a more accurate picture of how the color appears on the Web, use the Preview in Browser button. (Refer to Chapter 3 for details.)

Setting body text color

To set the body text color for the entire page (as opposed to selected text), follow these steps:

1. With the cursor anywhere inside the page, choose Format⇨Background.

The Page Properties dialog box appears, with the Background tab visible.

2. Select a color from the Text drop-down list.

3. Click OK.

All the page's text changes color (except for the stuff you previously colored by using the steps outlined in the section "Changing text color," earlier in this chapter).

You can also base your page's text color on that of another page. You discover how in Chapter 6.

What's so special about special styles?

The Font dialog box contains a second tab, mysteriously labeled *Special Styles* (see Figure 5-9). (A more accurate label could be *Random HTML Styles You Rarely Have Occasion To Use,* but I guess the programmers at Microsoft couldn't fit all those words onto the tab.) The Special Styles are a hodgepodge of HTML styles that you rarely use or that duplicate more commonly used styles (those available in the main panel of the Font dialog box).

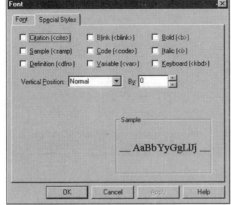

Figure 5-9:
The Special Styles tab of the Font dialog box.

One style deserves special mention: the *Blink* style. The Blink style, a Netscape-created extension to HTML, causes text to flash on and off, like a faulty neon sign outside a cheap motel. Trust me — the instances are *very few* where the Blink style is anything but tacky. Luckily, only those visitors using the Netscape Navigator browser can even see this style.

To apply a special style, follow these steps:

1. **Choose Format⇨Font (or right-click the text and choose Font Properties from the pop-up menu).**

   The Font dialog box appears.

2. **Click the Special Styles tab.**

   The Special Styles tab becomes visible.

3. **Click the check box next to any style (or styles) that you want to use.**

   The Sample box enables you to preview how the stylized text looks.

4. **Click OK to close the dialog box.**

Physical versus logical text styles

HTML contains styles that have less to do with what the text looks like through a Web browser and more to do with what the text *means*. In techno-speak, this difference is called *physical* versus *logical* styles. Physical styles control the physical look of the text. Logical styles convey meaning or context or display certain types of standard text.

Logical styles were in vogue back when academics and technicians used the Web mainly to post their communications and reports. Today, the Web is populated by a more design-oriented crowd, and logical styles, for the most part, have fallen out of use because these styles merely

create some of the same visual effects as more commonly used styles such as bold, italic, and typewriter do. The Citation style, for example, simply creates italic text. FrontPage supports logical styles (Citation, Sample, Definition, Code, Variable, and Keyboard being choices in the Font dialog box) mainly to accommodate older pages that you may eventually open and update by using the FrontPage Editor.

What does all this techno-speak mean? Well, 99 percent of the time, it means that you can banish the preceding history lesson from your brain and ignore logical styles altogether.

Making text superscript or subscript

Superscript and *subscript* text styles show up in scientific notations and footnotes, where you need to place a letter or number a hair above or below its normal alignment, as shown in Figure 5-10.

To make selected text superscript or subscript, follow these steps:

1. **Choose Format⇨Font.**

   The Font dialog box appears.

2. **Click the Special Styles tab.**

3. **In the Vertical Position drop-down list, select Superscript or Subscript.**

4. **To change the offset, type a new number in the By text box (or use the increment arrows).**

   The *offset* is the number of pixels the selected text sits above or below the line of the normal text.

5. **Click OK.**

   The dialog box closes, and the selected text nudges up or down, depending on your selection.

Superscript   Subscript

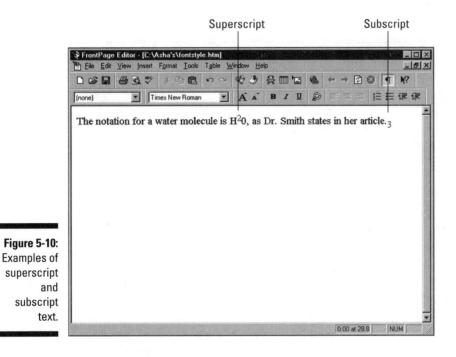

The notation for a water molecule is H^2O, as Dr. Smith states in her article.$_3$

Figure 5-10:
Examples of
superscript
and
subscript
text.

Creating Stylish Paragraphs

Unlike font styles, which you can apply to individual letters and words, *paragraph styles* operate on entire paragraphs. Use paragraph styles if you want to make widespread changes throughout your page.

A FrontPage paragraph is different from a paragraph as defined by your composition teacher. To the FrontPage Editor, every time you press the Enter key, you create a new paragraph. Even if you type only one word and then hit Enter, FrontPage considers that word a paragraph. Did you hear that, Mrs. Bagley of English 101? (To find out how to create a new line without creating a new paragraph, read the sidebar "New paragraphs versus line breaks," in the following section.)

The FrontPage Editor contains three paragraph styles: *Normal, Formatted,* and *Address.* (Headings and lists also are paragraph styles, but these styles require explanation, so I place them in their own sections, which follow this section.)

Practicing safe styles

I remember the first time that I used a word processor. I was seduced by the millions of fonts and type styles at my disposal and proceeded to use every one in my first document. (I think it was a letter to a pen pal.) The finished product looked like the cut-and-paste ransom notes you see in old private eye movies. The text was readable, but it was a gaudy mess.

I'm not implying, however, that *you* lack restraint. I use the example only to illustrate how moderate use of text and paragraph styles enhances a page's readability and visual appeal, while overuse sends your readers screaming to a new Web destination.

> ✔ **Normal** is the default style for paragraphs. Nothing fancy — just regular old left-aligned paragraphs with a proportional font. (Times appears in most Web browsers.)
>
> ✔ **Formatted** creates paragraphs with a monospaced font — just like the typewriter font effect. The big difference, however, is that the Formatted paragraph style preserves white space (such as tabs and multiple bangs on the spacebar), while the typewriter font (along with every other HTML text style) reduces tabs and multiple spaces into one space. (For more information about white space, see the sidebar "White space — when nothing is something important," later in this chapter.) So if you want to create columns of text by hitting your spacebar several times, you need to use the Formatted style. (A more elegant way to create columns is to use a table, which I discuss in Chapter 9.)
>
> ✔ **Address** is a holdover from the olden days, back when logical font styles were still in use. (Refer to the sidebar "Physical versus logical text styles," earlier in this chapter, for more information about logical text styles.) The Address style was used to designate the page creator's e-mail address so that visitors could get in touch. Today, folks like to format their contact information any number of ways, so the Address style has, for the most part, become obsolete. Besides, the style merely creates italic text, just as the italic font style does, so why use the old clunker anyway?

To change the style of a paragraph, follow these steps:

1. **Place the cursor anywhere within the paragraph you want to format.**

2. **In the Format toolbar, select the style you want from the Change Style drop-down list shown in Figure 5-11.**

Normal ▾
Address
Bulleted List
Defined Term
Definition
Directory List
Formatted
Heading 1
Heading 2
Heading 3
Heading 4
Heading 5
Heading 6
Menu List
Normal
Numbered List

Figure 5-11:
The Change
Style drop-
down list.

Alternatively, you can choose Format➪Paragraph (or right-click the paragraph and choose Paragraph Properties from the pop-up list) to open the Paragraph Properties dialog box. In the Paragraph Format list box, click the name of the style you want and then click OK.

Adding Headings

Each chunk of text in this book is identified by *headings*. You can tell that you're about to begin a new chapter, because the Chapter Title heading appears at the top of the page. Lower-level headings separate the categories of information within each chapter so that you can keep track of where you are inside the chapter.

Headings serve a similar purpose in Web pages. Large headings, usually located at the top of the page, identify what the page is all about, and smaller headings, sprinkled throughout, divide the page's information into manageable bits.

Headings in Web pages come in six sizes, or *levels.* Strangely enough, Heading 1 is the largest size, and Heading 6 is the smallest. (Figure 5-12 illustrates heading sizes.)

New paragraphs versus line breaks

Whenever you press the Enter key, FrontPage thinks that you want to create a new paragraph and puts a little bit of space between the two paragraphs. If you simply want to create a new line without any space between the new line and the line above it, use a *line break* instead. To create a line break, press Shift+Enter or choose Insert➪Break. The Break Properties dialog box appears, with the Normal Line Break radio button selected. This radio button is the one you want, so click OK to close the dialog box and insert the line break. (The other break options apply to positioning text next to graphics, which I explain in Chapter 7.)

To distinguish between line breaks and new paragraphs in the Editor, click the Show/Hide ¶ button in the standard toolbar or choose View➪Format Marks. Line breaks are indicated by left-pointing arrows.

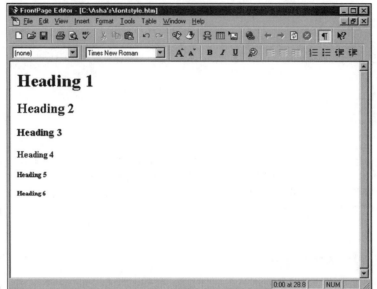

Figure 5-12:
The Heading gang's all here!

To apply a heading style to selected text, perform one of the following actions:

- ✔ Select a heading from the Change Style drop-down list in the Format toolbar.

- ✔ Choose Format➪Paragraph (or right-click the paragraph and choose Paragraph Properties from the pop-up menu) to open the Paragraph Properties dialog box. In the Paragraph Format list box, select the level of heading you want and then click OK.

The List of Lists

Lists. I love 'em and hate 'em. I love 'em because lists promote the illusion that I'm in control. I hate 'em because lists show me just how much work I still need to do.

Lists in Web pages, on the other hand, do nothing but make life easier. As do headings, these lists help organize your page's information so that your text is easy to read and understand.

Bulleted lists

Bulleted lists are not lists that were attacked with an assault weapon. Instead, such lists are groups of items, each of which is preceded by a solid dot, called a *bullet*.

White space — when nothing is something important

White space — the blank space that surrounds your page's content — is just as important to your site's design as the content itself. Generous amounts of white space "open up" the page, making the entire page easier to read and more pleasing to the eye.

You'd think that adding white space is as easy as pressing Enter or the spacebar a few times, right? Wrong. Different browsers treat multiple spaces and blank paragraphs differently, with most ignoring them.

What's a Web publisher to do? Resort to HTML loopholes that achieve the desired effect, that's what. You can use many tricks to add white space to your document. The easiest, however, is to switch to the Formatted paragraph style, press Enter however many times you need vertical lines of white space, and then switch back to the Normal style whenever you're ready to add more text. Because HTML leaves Formatted paragraph text as is, your page retains the extra space.

For horizontal space and precise control over vertical space (down to the pixel), you can insert an invisible spacer graphic. I reveal this trick in Chapter 7.

To create a bulleted list, follow these steps:

1. **Place the cursor in the location where you want the list to begin.**

2. **Click the Bulleted List button or select Bulleted List from the Change Style drop-down list.**

   A bullet appears at the beginning of the first line.

3. **Type your first list item after the bullet and press Enter.**

   A bullet appears on the next line.

4. **Type your second list item (and so on and so on).**

5. **After you're done adding items to your list, press Enter twice to end the list (and the creation of bullets).**

   You also may end lists by pressing Ctrl+End.

You can also convert existing paragraphs into a bulleted list by selecting all the paragraphs you want included in the list and clicking the Bulleted List button.

You can change the bullet's shape by choosing Format⇨Bullets and Numbering, but I don't recommend doing so because, as of this writing, bullet shape changes are visible only to those among your visitors who use the Netscape Navigator browser.

Numbered lists

A *numbered list* is just like a bulleted list, except that FrontPage substitutes numbers for bullets. Numbered lists are great if you need to list a series of chronological steps (such as those that follow — what a coincidence!).

To create a numbered list, follow these steps:

1. **Place the cursor in the location where you want the list to begin.**

2. **Click the Numbered List button or select Numbered List from the Change Style drop-down list.**

   A number 1 appears at the beginning of the first line.

3. **Type your first list item after the number and press Enter.**

   A number 2 appears on the next line.

4. **Type your second list item (and so on and so on).**

5. **After you're done adding items to the list, press Enter twice (or Ctrl+End) to end the list.**

You can also convert existing paragraphs into a numbered list by highlighting the paragraphs you want to include in the list and clicking the Numbered List button.

To split a long numbered list into two separate lists, click at the end of a list item and press Enter twice. The list splits into two lists and renumbers itself automatically.

Changing the list's starting number

You can easily change the starting number of a numbered list. To do so:

1. **Click anywhere inside the list and choose Format⇨Bullets and Numbering.**

   Or right-click inside the list and choose List Properties from the pop-up menu.

   The List Properties dialog box appears with the Numbered tab visible.

2. **In the Start At text box, enter the number with which you want the list to begin and click OK.**

   The dialog box closes, and the list's numbering changes.

Changing numeral style

Should the whim overtake you, you can tell FrontPage to display your Numbered list with roman numerals or letters instead of regular numbers. To do so, follow these steps:

1. **Click anywhere inside the list and choose Format⇨Bullets and Numbering.**

   Or right-click inside the list and choose List Properties from the pop-up menu.

   The List Properties dialog box appears with the Numbered tab visible.

2. **In the Numbered tab, click the box that shows the numeral style you want and click OK.**

   The dialog box closes, and the numbering style changes.

Definition list

A *definition list* enables you to present information in dictionary format — with the term you want to define listed first and its definition listed on the following line, slightly indented. Definition lists turn up infrequently on the Web but can come in handy every now and then.

Although you can create definition lists several ways (as you can the other types of lists), the easiest way is to follow these steps:

1. **Place the cursor in the location where you want the list to begin.**

2. **Select Defined Term from the Change Style drop-down list.**

3. **Type your first term and press Enter.**

   FrontPage creates a new line, slightly indented.

4. **Type the term's definition and press Enter.**

   FrontPage creates a new line, flush left.

5. **Type your second term — and so on.**

   Follow steps 2 through 4 for each new term and its definition.

6. **To end the definition list, press Enter twice.**

List-in-a-list

Sometimes a simple list doesn't cut it. Say that you need something more sophisticated, such as a multilevel bulleted list or a numbered list with bullets following certain items (similar to the one shown in Figure 5-13). No problem! With the Editor, you simply create the main list (the numbered items in Figure 5-13) and then insert a separate list containing the secondary items (the bulleted items in Figure 5-13).

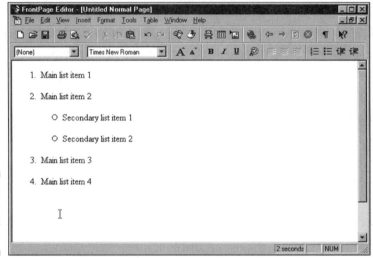

Figure 5-13:
A number-bullet combo list.

To create such a fancy-shmancy combo list, follow these steps:

1. **Create a list of any type.**

   The list should contain only the main, or *top-level,* items.

2. **Click at the end of the line *above* where you want to insert the second level of list items and then press Enter.**

   A new line appears in the list.

 3. **Click the Increase Indent button.**

   The list item turns into a blank line.

 4. **Click the Bulleted List or Numbered List button (depending on the type of list you want to insert).**

 Or select Bulleted List or Numbered List from the Change Style drop-down list.

   Depending on the style you choose, the blank line turns into a bulleted or numbered line. (If bulleted, the bullets appear white instead of solid black.)

5. **Type the list, pressing Enter each time to create new items.**

6. **After you finish, click the cursor anywhere on the page outside the list.**

    Pressing Enter twice to end the list doesn't work in this case; it simply adds extra space to the list.

Aligning Paragraphs

Normal paragraphs are left-aligned. (This sentence is *not* a political statement.) You may center and right-align paragraphs as well.

To change a paragraph's alignment, click inside the paragraph (or select multiple paragraphs) and perform one of the following actions:

- ✔ Click the Align Left, Center, or Align Right button.

- ✔ Choose Format⇨Paragraph (or right-click a paragraph and choose Paragraph Properties from the pop-up menu) to open the Paragraph Properties dialog box. Select an alignment setting from the Paragraph Alignment drop-down list and click OK.

Indenting Paragraphs

You can indent entire paragraphs so that the paragraphs appear set in from the left margin. This effect is especially useful for quoting large pieces of text or to add white space to large blocks of text on the page.

To indent a paragraph, click inside the paragraph (or select multiple paragraphs) and click the Indent Paragraph button. You may click the button as many times as you want to achieve the desired effect.

To decrease the level of an indented paragraph, click the Decrease Indent button.

Increasing and decreasing indents works only on *left-aligned* paragraphs (unless you are using the Increase Indent command to create a multilevel list, as described in the section "List-in-a-List," earlier in this chapter). Although the Editor's display changes as you attempt to change the indentation of a centered or right-aligned paragraph, the change doesn't appear in most Web browsers.

Inserting Symbols

Symbols are the odd little numerals and symbols that occasionally pepper documents. Some of these symbols turn up in scientific writing (Latin characters, for example), while others are more commonplace (such as the copyright and trademark symbols).

To include a special character in your page, follow these steps:

1. **Place the cursor where you want the symbol to appear.**

2. **Choose Insert⇨Symbol.**

   The Symbol dialog box appears, containing all sorts of tiny characters. If you squint, you can actually make out the characters.

3. **Select the character you want to insert.**

   The character appears (magnified, thank goodness!) at the bottom of the dialog box (see Figure 5-14).

Figure 5-14:
The Symbol
dialog box.

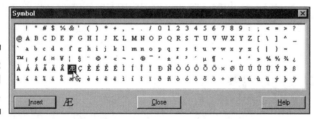

4. **If this character is the one you want, click Insert; if not, keep hunting around until you find the right character and then click Insert.**

   The symbol appears in your page at the location of the cursor.

5. **Click Close to close the Symbol dialog box after you finish inserting symbols.**

Inserting Comments

You can insert explanatory text and reminders to yourself (or to other Web authors) in the form of *comments*. Comments are notes that appear only in the Editor, not as a visitor views the page through a Web browser.

To insert a comment, place the cursor where you want the comment to appear and choose Insert⇨Comment. The Comment dialog box appears. In the Comment text box, type your comment and click OK. The comment appears in your page as purple text. To edit a comment, double-click the comment. To delete a comment, click the comment and press the Backspace key.

Viewing and editing HTML tags

"But I bought FrontPage precisely to *avoid* dealing with HTML," you say. That's okay — you can create incredible Web sites in FrontPage without one spot of HTML knowledge. In fact, you may just want to ignore this feature altogether.

If you know any HTML, however — even a little bit — you already know how useful directly viewing and editing your page's HTML tags can be. You can add to your page HTML tags for which FrontPage doesn't yet have built-in support. If your page contains a glitch that you can't figure out, you can hunt down the problem inside the HTML code.

To view a page's HTML, choose View⇨HTML.

The View or Edit HTML dialog box appears, displaying your page's underlying HTML tags. Inside the dialog box, FrontPage color-codes the HTML so that you can easily distinguish between tags and page text.

To edit the HTML, just click anywhere inside the document and make your desired changes. After you're done, click OK, and you return to the regular Editor display.

If you enter HTML tags the Editor doesn't recognize, an Unknown HTML icon (a little yellow rectangle with a question mark inside) appears inside your page. To correct the HTML tags, double-click the icon. The Show HTML Markup dialog box appears, containing the invalid (or otherwise unrecognizable) tags. Edit the tags in the dialog box and click OK to close the dialog box. (The Unknown HTML icon remains in your page even after you correct the offending HTML tag but disappears as soon as you refresh your page's display by clicking the Refresh button in the Editor's standard toolbar.)

You can also work with HTML without leaving the coziness of the Editor's WYSIWYG display. To insert a line or two of HTML, place the cursor where you want to insert the HTML and click the Insert HTML button in the Advanced toolbar (or choose Insert⇨HTML Markup). The HTML Markup dialog box appears. In the HTML Markup to insert text box, enter the HTML tags and then click OK. Because FrontPage does not check HTML tags that you enter by using this method, the Unknown HTML icon appears, even if the HTML tag is valid. If you preview the page in a Web browser, the inserted HTML effect is visible. (For details on how to preview your page in a Web browser, refer to Chapter 3.)

Creating a Marquee

A *marquee* is a rectangular banner that contains scrolling text. Marquees are a fun and popular way to highlight announcements or other important information on your Web pages.

The big bummer is that, as of this writing, marquees are visible only in Microsoft Internet Explorer. If you view a marquee in another browser, the thing just appears as regular text.

Other ways to include scrolling banners in your page are possible: For example, you can add a banner by inserting into your page a *Java applet,* which is a special miniprogram written in the Java programming language. (You find out all about Java applets, plus all sorts of other components you can add to your pages, in Chapter 13.) Unfortunately, Java applets also are visible in only a limited number of Web browsers.

So if you decide to use a marquee in your page, realize that many of your visitors can see the marquee only as regular text.

To insert a marquee, follow these steps:

1. **Place the cursor where you want the marquee to appear.**

2. **Choose Insert⇨Marquee.**

   The Marquee Properties dialog box appears.

3. **In the Text box, type the message that you want to appear inside the marquee.**

4. **In the Direction area, click the radio button next to the direction you want the text to scroll.**

   The Left option creates text that begins at the right side of the marquee and scrolls left, while the Right option creates text that does the opposite. Left is generally the better choice, because this direction enables visitors to read the marquee text from beginning to end as the banner scrolls by.

5. **In the Delay text box, type the number of milliseconds to pause between each successive movement of the marquee text.**

   The smaller the number is, the faster the marquee text scrolls by.

6. **In the Amount text box, type the amount of distance (in pixels) that you want the marquee text to move each time.**

   The smaller the number is, the slower and smoother the marquee text scrolls.

7. **Select a radio button next to an option in the Behavior area of the dialog box.**

   The Scroll option creates continually scrolling text (that is, text that scrolls to one side until it disappears). The Slide option creates text that originates at one side of the marquee, scrolls to the other side, and stops. The Alternate option creates text that scrolls from one side of the marquee and, after the text reaches the opposite margin, bounces back the other direction.

8. **Select a radio button next to an option in the Align with Text area.**

   The Align with Text area controls where the text sits inside the marquee boundaries. Your choices are Top, Middle, or Bottom.

9. **If you want to specify the marquee size, select the Specify Width and Specify Height check boxes and type a percentage or pixel value in each field.**

   The easier course is to leave this section alone and resize the marquee by hand. (I explain how to do so at the end of this section.)

10. **If you want the marquee text to repeat a limited number of times, remove the check from the Repeat Continually check box and then specify the number of repetitions you want in the text box beneath the check box.**

11. **Select a color from the Background Color drop-down list.**

    The Default option makes the marquee background color the same as the page's background color. If you choose a different color, the marquee stands in contrast to the background color of the page. (You find out how to set your page's background color in Chapter 7.)

12. **Click OK.**

    The dialog box closes, and the marquee appears in your page, surrounded by a dashed line.

To see the marquee in action, preview the page in Internet Explorer. (For information on how to preview a page in a Web browser, refer to Chapter 3.) To edit the marquee, double-click it (or right-click the marquee and choose Marquee Properties from the pop-up list) to open the Marquee Properties dialog box.

To resize your marquee by hand, click one of its *size handles* (the square dots sitting along the dashed marquee boundary) and, while holding down the mouse button, drag the handle in the appropriate direction to change the marquee's height and/or width.

Working with Horizontal Lines

Horizontal lines are thin gray stripes that run the width of your Web page. How do they fit into a chapter about tweaking text, you ask? Because, as is true of font and paragraph formatting, horizontal lines group together bunches of related information. You can use a horizontal line if you need a quick-and-dirty way to divide your Web page into different sections. You can even change the line's width and height for a little variety. (Figure 5-15 displays several examples of horizontal lines that you can create in FrontPage.)

Keep in mind, however, that overusing horizontal lines can wreak design havoc on your page. A line or two can provide a much-needed visual break. Too many lines make your page look as though it's trapped behind bars.

To insert a horizontal line, place the cursor where you want the line to appear and choose (surprise!) Insert⇨Horizontal Line.

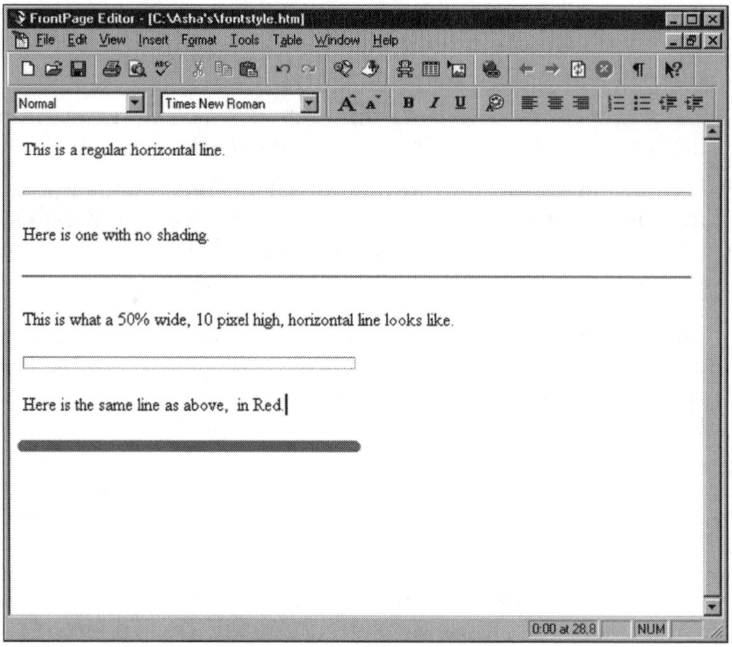

Figure 5-15:
A bevy of
horizontal
lines.

To customize how the line looks, follow these steps:

1. **Double-click the horizontal line (or right-click the line and choose Horizontal Line Properties from the pop-up menu).**

   The Horizontal Line Properties dialog box appears.

2. **In the Width area, specify the width of the line by typing a value into the text box and selecting the Percent of window or Pixels radio button.**

   You can indicate the width as a percentage of the width of the browser window, or you can specify an absolute number of pixels. See my Tip at the end of these steps if you're not sure which measurement to use.

3. **In the Height text box, type the line's height (its thickness) in pixels.**

4. **In the Align area, select the Left, Center, or Right radio button.**

5. **Select a color from the Color drop-down list.**

   Variations in horizontal line color are visible only in Microsoft Internet Explorer.

6. **If you want the line to appear solid instead of engraved, select the Solid line (no shading) check box.**

7. **Click OK to close the dialog box.**

Chapter 6

Hyperlinks: Your Web's Ticket to Ride

. . . .

In This Chapter

▶ Creating text and image hyperlinks

▶ Using bookmarks to jump to a specific spot in a page

▶ Editing hyperlinks

▶ Changing hyperlink color

▶ Fixing broken hyperlinks

▶ Unlinking hyperlinks

. . . .

*H*yperlinks (also known as *hotlinks* or just *links*) are the gems that make the Web so addictively surfable. Click a link, and you find yourself somewhere else — maybe on another page in your Web or, just as easily, on a page stored on a server in Sri Lanka or Cheyenne. Too bad Web surfing doesn't earn Frequent Flyer miles.

The heady nature of Web travel may lead you to believe that hyperlinks are difficult to create. Relax and discover how easily you can hitch your Web to the global conga line that's the Internet.

The Hyperlink Two-Step

Hyperlinks are bits of text or images that connect to another location. Hyperlinks between pages and files in a Web site transform the site from a jumble of documents into a cohesive unit. Hyperlinks to locations outside the Web site connect the site to the rest of the Internet.

Hyperlink creation is a two-step process. Here are the basic steps (the rest of this chapter fills in the details):

1. **Select the thing that you want to transform into a hyperlink.**

   I call this "thing" the *hyperlink source*. A hyperlink source can be a character, a word, a phrase, or an image. (If you don't know how to insert an image into your page, read Chapter 7.)

2. **Connect the hyperlink source to the place visitors end up after they click the hyperlink.**

   This location can be inside the same page, in another page in the Web site, or in a site on the Internet. From now on, I call this location the *hyperlink destination*. If the hyperlink destination is inside the same page as the hyperlink source, the destination is identified with a *bookmark*. (I show you how to create bookmarks in the section "Using Bookmarks," later in this chapter.) If the hyperlink leads to another page inside the Web site or on the Internet, the destination is identified with its Internet address, or *URL* (short for *Universal Resource Locator*).

Source-destination, source-destination. . . . Keep reciting this mantra, and you can soon do the hyperlink two-step with the best of 'em.

Linking to an open page

If you have several of your Web site's pages open in the Editor, you can easily create hyperlinks between the pages.

Use the steps in this section *only* if linking together pages opened from within a FrontPage Web site. (Refer to Chapter 3 for detail on opening pages in the Editor.) Although FrontPage enables you to create hyperlinks between pages opened from files (that is, pages on your computer that exist outside the Web site), I strongly advise against doing so. If you create a hyperlink to a file, FrontPage uses the file's location on your hard drive as the destination. If you publish your finished Web site on a dedicated Web server, the link no longer works because the location is specific to your computer's file system (not the Web server's). Read the sidebar "Dissecting hyperlinks," later in this chapter, for more information.

To create hyperlinks between pages open in the Editor, follow these steps:

1. **In a page open in the Editor, select the element you want to turn into a hyperlink (the hyperlink source).**

   Highlight a bit of text, click a picture, double-click a word — whatever.

2. **Click the Create or Edit Hyperlink button in the standard toolbar.**

   Or you can choose Edit⇔Hyperlink or press Ctrl+K.

   The Create Hyperlink dialog box appears with the Open Pages tab visible (see Figure 6-1). The titles of all the pages currently open in the Editor are visible in the Open pages text box.

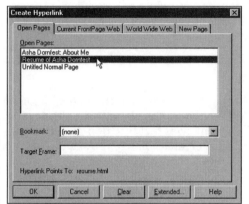

Figure 6-1:
The Create
Hyperlink
dialog box.

3. **Click the title of the page to which you want to link the element selected in step 1.**

   The page you select is the hyperlink destination. The filename of the hyperlink destination appears in the lower-left corner of the dialog box (next to the words `Hyperlink Points To`).

4. **Click OK.**

   The dialog box closes, and a hyperlink is born.

If the hyperlink source is text, that text now displays the proud markings of a link: underlining and color. (You can still apply the same font formatting styles — bold, italic, and so on — to text hyperlinks as you can to regular text.)

If the hyperlink source is an image, the image itself looks no different than before its transformation. Trust me, however — that image is still a link. If you want proof, pass your mouse pointer over any text or image link, and its destination appears in the lower-left corner of the Editor window. To differentiate linked images from regular images, give linked images a border. The borders of image links are the same color as text links, giving visitors a visual cue to click the image to jump elsewhere. (I show you how to add borders to images in Chapter 7.)

Choosing hyperlink words wisely

Hyperlinks' colorful and charming nature immediately attracts attention, especially if your visitors are quickly scanning the page for information. Choose the clearest, most meaningful text for promotion to linkhood. Avoid the temptation to create links that say things such as "Click here to see a picture of Harold, my pet ferret."

(The underlined word here is the hyperlink in the previous sentence, by the way.) Instead, choose a word that clues the visitor in on what's sitting at the other end of the hyperlink. If you insist on immortalizing Harold in your home page, you're doing better to use the following link text: "See a picture of Harold, my pet ferret."

Instant hyperlink shortcut: Without first selecting a bit of text or an image (the hyperlink source), click the Create or Edit Link button to display the Create Hyperlink dialog box. In the Open Pages text box, double-click a page title. The dialog box closes, and the Editor creates a link to the selected destination page, using the destination page's title as the hyperlink text.

Linking to a page in the same Web site

A page doesn't need to be open in the Editor to become the target of a link. You can create a link to any page in your Web site (as long as the Web site is currently open in the Explorer). Just follow these steps:

1. **In an open page in the Editor, select the hyperlink source.**

2. **Click the Create or Edit Hyperlink button to open the Create Hyperlink dialog box.**

3. **Click the Current FrontPage Web tab to make the tab visible.**

4. **In the Page text box, type the filename of the page to which you want to create a link.**

   If you can't remember the filename, click the Browse button. The Current Web dialog box appears, displaying a list of all the pages and folders in your Web site. Double-click the page to which you want to link. If the page is stored inside a folder, double-click the folder to open it and then double-click the page. The Current Web dialog box closes, and the filename appears in the Page text box.

5. **Click OK to close the Create Hyperlink dialog box.**

   Poof! — another link is born.

Linking to a page in another FrontPage Web site

If you're creating a large-scale Web site and have sectioned the site into a core Root Web and auxiliary Child Webs, creating links *between* these FrontPage Web sites (that is, the Web sites stored on the FrontPage Personal Web Server) involves some fancy footwork using both the FrontPage Editor and the Explorer.

(If you're not sure what a Root Web is, refer to the Chapter 1 sidebar "What's a Root Web?" For details on how to transform your main Web site into the FrontPage Root Web — as well as the benefits of doing so — refer to Chapter 2.

Strangely enough, the Editor's Create Hyperlink dialog box contains no tab that helps you create hyperlinks between two FrontPage Web sites. To create a link from a page inside one FrontPage Web site (say, the Root Web) to a page inside another FrontPage Web site (say, a Child Web), you need to engage in some creative maneuvering, as outlined in the following steps:

1. **In the Editor, open the page in your Web site in which you want to create the link.**

   For instructions on how to open a page in the Editor, refer to Chapter 3.

2. **Click the Show Microsoft Explorer button in the Editor's standard toolbar.**

   Or choose Tools⇨Show FrontPage Explorer.

   The Explorer, with the current Web site open, becomes visible.

3. **In the Explorer, open the Web site containing the destination page to which you want to link.**

   For instructions on how to open a Web site, refer to Chapter 1. The current Web site closes, and the destination Web site opens in the Explorer.

4. **In the Explorer toolbar, click the Show FrontPage Editor button to switch back to the open page in the Editor.**

   Or choose Tools⇨Show FrontPage Editor.

   The Editor appears.

5. **In the page open in the Editor, select the hyperlink source.**

6. **Click the Create or Edit Hyperlink button to open the Create Hyperlink dialog box.**

7. **Click the Current FrontPage Web tab to make the tab visible.**

8. **In the Page text box, type the filename of the page in the destination Web site to which you want to link.**

   If you can't remember the filename of the destination page, click the Browse button. The Current Web dialog box appears, displaying a list of all the pages and folders in the destination Web site. Double-click the page to which you want to link. If you stored the page inside a folder, double-click the folder to open it and then double-click the page. The Current Web dialog box closes, and the path to the destination page appears in the Page text box.

9. **Click OK to close the Create Hyperlink dialog box.**

   FrontPage creates a hyperlink to the destination Web site.

When you're ready to save the page containing the link, you must return to the Explorer and open the original Web site (the one in which the page containing the link belongs). Otherwise, the Editor saves the page to whichever Web site is currently open in the Explorer. (The Editor warns you before it saves the page to a different Web site.)

Drag-and-drop hyperlinks

If drag and drop is your style, you can create hyperlinks by dragging Explorer page icons into an open page in the Editor. The process is more cumbersome than is creating hyperlinks by using the Editor alone, but if you're a right-brain, visual sort of person, you may prefer this method.

Just follow these steps:

1. **In the Editor, open the page that is to eventually contain the hyperlink.**

2. **If the Explorer isn't already showing, click the Show FrontPage Explorer button or choose Tools⇨Show FrontPage Explorer in the Editor.**

3. **Resize and arrange the Explorer and Editor windows so that they are both fully visible.**

   This task is the cumbersome part of the process. Your mission is to arrange the screen so that you can see both the spot in the page open in the Editor where you want the hyperlink to appear and the icon of the destination page (in the Explorer).

4. **Drag the destination page icon from the Explorer and drop it in the spot in the open page in the Editor where you want the hyperlink to appear.**

   The Editor inserts a hyperlink leading to the destination page, using the destination page's title as the hyperlink text.

Linking to a page on the World Wide Web

Linking to a site on the World Wide Web is just as easy as linking to a page inside your Web site. Just follow these steps:

1. **In a page open in the Editor, select the hyperlink source.**
2. **Click the Create or Edit Hyperlink button to open the Create Hyperlink dialog box.**
3. **Click the World Wide Web tab to make the tab visible.**
4. **In the URL text box, type the URL of the link destination.**

Internet URLs look different depending on their *protocols*. A URL's protocol notation tells the visitor's Web browser the type of file to which the browser's linking. The sidebar, "Becoming a Protocol Pro," in the following section, gives you a crash course in Internet URLs if you don't know how yours should look.

If you can't remember the URL, click the Browse button to launch your Web browser. Surf to your destination, switch back to the FrontPage Editor (by clicking the Editor's button in the Windows 95 taskbar or pressing Alt+Tab) and — huzzah! — the URL appears in the URL text box!

5. **Click OK to close the dialog box and create the hyperlink.**

If you goof while typing a URL for a site on the Web, FrontPage doesn't know that you made a mistake and creates the link anyway. You can double-check all the links in your Web site by using the Explorer's Tools➪Verify Hyperlinks command, or you can check individual hyperlinks by using the Editor's Tools➪Follow Hyperlink command. I explain both procedures in the section "Do-It-Yourself Hyperlink Repair," later in this chapter.

If, while adding text to your Web page, you type an Internet URL (such as `http://www.microsoft.com`), the Editor automatically turns the text into a hyperlink to that URL.

Linking to a new page

If, as you're building your Web site, inspiration for a new page suddenly hits you, you can use a hyperlink as the starting point for an entirely new page. Just follow these steps:

1. **In a page open in the Editor, select the hyperlink source.**
2. **Click the Create or Edit Hyperlink button to open the Create Hyperlink dialog box.**

Becoming a protocol pro

Protocols are flags that tell your visitor's Web browser what type of information it's accessing and what to do after finding it. A URL that begins with `http://` (short for Hypertext Transfer Protocol), for example, tells the browser that its connection is to a Web site and to display the requested page. If the URL begins with `mailto:`, this protocol indicates that the browser is activating a connection to an e-mail address and to fire up its e-mail component (if the browser has one). The following table gives you the rundown on the different protocols you're likely to see, what each protocol means, and how a typical URL for each protocol looks.

If you don't recognize the different server types listed here and you want to know what they do, take a look at *The Internet For Dummies* (IDG Books Worldwide, Inc.), by John R. Levine, Carol Baroudi, and Margaret Levine Young. By the way, that's my e-mail address (`webpub@dnai.com`) in the "`mailto:`" entry — make me feel popular by sending me a flattering note.

Protocol	Connects To	A Typical URL Looks Like
`file:`	A file on the local disk	`file:///c:\folder\file name.txt`
`ftp:`	An FTP server	`ftp://ftp.microsoft.com`
`gopher:`	A Gopher server	`gopher://server.microsoft.com`
`http:`	A Web server	`http://www.microsoft.com`
`https:`	A secure Web server	`https://www.microsoft.com`
`mailto:`	An e-mail address	`mailto:webpub@dnai.com`
`news:`	An Internet newsgroup	`news:alt.bunnies`
`telnet:`	A Telnet server	`telnet://server.microsoft.com`
`wais:`	A WAIS server	`wais://server.microsoft.com`

3. **Click the New Page tab to make the tab visible.**

4. **In the Page Title text box, type a title for the new page you're about to create.**

   Choose a meaningful, descriptive title. The Editor generates a filename based on the title words you choose.

5. **If you don't like the filename FrontPage assigns, type a different filename in the Page URL text box.**

6. **Decide whether you want to edit the page right away or save page editing for later and then take the appropriate actions.**

If you want to edit the page right away, click the Edit New Page Immediately radio button and then click OK. The New Page dialog box appears, prompting you to choose a template or Wizard. Select a template or Wizard from the Templates and Wizards list and click OK. The new page opens in the Editor and awaits your additions.

If you want to save page editing for later, click the Add New Page to To Do List radio button and then click OK. The New Page dialog box appears, prompting you to choose a template or Wizard. Select a template or Wizard from the Templates and Wizards list and click OK. In a moment, the Save As dialog box appears. In the Page Title text box, enter a page title (and, if you want, enter a new URL in the Page URL text box) and click OK to save the page. The Editor saves the new page, dutifully adds a task to your To Do List, reminding you to complete the page another time, and returns you to your original source page. (I show you how to use the To Do List in Chapter 16.)

Using Bookmarks

A *bookmark* is a clump of text inside a Web page that is defined as the target of a link. Later, after you link to that page, you can jump straight to the bookmark instead of to the top of the page (as a link without the benefit of a bookmark would).

To link to a bookmark in your page, you must first create the bookmark and then create the hyperlink that leads to the bookmark.

Creating bookmarks

A bookmark can be any bit of text: a word, a phrase — even a letter. Text defined as a bookmark looks (and acts) no different from regular text — the text is simply flagged with a marker that you can target with a hyperlink.

After you create a bookmark in the Editor, a dotted line appears underneath the bookmark text. In real life, bookmarks are invisible. Surfers viewing your finished page on the Web can't distinguish bookmarks from regular text.

To create a bookmark, follow these steps:

1. **In a page open in the Editor, select the clump of text you want to turn into a bookmark (eventually becoming the hyperlink destination).**

Dissecting hyperlinks

Hyperlinks come in two types: *relative* and *absolute*. On the surface, these hyperlink varieties look and act the same. Underneath, however, the two types are very different.

The hyperlinks that connect your Web site's pages and files to each other are relative hyperlinks. These links are called relative because each link expresses the location of the destination page *in relation to* the location of the source page. If you create a link to another page in your Web site, for example, its underlying HTML simply contains the filename (and folder name, if any) of the destination page. After a Web browser encounters this hyperlink, the browser looks for the destination page in the same folder as the file that contains the hyperlink (or, if a folder notation is present, inside that particular folder). If the file isn't found in that location, the link doesn't work.

The hyperlinks in your Web site that point to locations on the Internet are absolute hyperlinks. An absolute hyperlink contains the full URL of its destination, including the protocol (`http://`, for example) and the server name (`www.microsoft.com`, for example). After a Web browser encounters an absolute hyperlink, the browser goes straight to the destination URL, no matter where the hyperlink source page is located.

2. Choose Edit⇨Bookmarks.

The Bookmark dialog box appears, with the selected text visible in the Bookmark Name text box. (The Editor wisely assumes that you want to give the bookmark the same name as the text it's made of. If you want to choose a different name, type that name in the Bookmark Name text box.)

3. Click OK.

The dialog box closes, and a dotted line appears underneath the selected text. (If you don't see a dotted line, click the Show/Hide ¶ button or choose View⇨Format Marks.)

Linking to a bookmark

Bookmarks are like ballroom dancers: They need a partner to do their thing. Without a hyperlink, a bookmark is as lonely as a wallflower.

You can create a link to a bookmark in the same page, in a different page in your Web site, or in a page on the World Wide Web.

Linking to a bookmark in the same page

Linking to bookmarks inside a page helps visitors find their way around long pages that otherwise require lots of troublesome scrolling and searching to navigate. You can create a link at the top of the page to bookmarks in the interior of the page so that visitors can jump around with swift clicks of the mouse. Likewise, you can create a link at the bottom of the page to a bookmark at the top of the page so that visitors don't need to scroll to return to the beginning of the page.

Several FrontPage templates use bookmarks to make getting around in a long page easy. (The Glossary of Terms and the Frequently Asked Questions templates come to mind.) Even if you don't use those templates as foundations for your own pages, you may want to take a look at the templates to see how bookmarks and links work together.

To link to a bookmark in the same page, follow these steps:

1. **In a page open in the Editor, select the hyperlink source.**

   This step is the same as that for creating a regular link: Select the word, phrase, or image you want to turn into a hyperlink.

2. **Click the Create or Edit Hyperlink button to open the Create Hyperlink dialog box.**

   Ditto.

3. **Click the Bookmark drop-down list box.**

   A drop-down list appears, containing all the page's bookmarks.

4. **Select from the list the bookmark to which you want to link your source text.**

   After you select the bookmark, notice how the URL notation in the lower-left corner of the dialog box reads #bookmark name. I talk more about this designation at the end of these steps.

5. **Click OK.**

   The dialog box closes, and the bookmark and hyperlink live happily ever after. Trumpets sound.

The # sign is Web shorthand for "bookmark." If you see a URL that looks something like cookies.htm/#oatmeal, the # simply means that the hyperlink jumps to the oatmeal bookmark in the page named cookies.htm. This bit of trivia is *not* obscure, geek-only information — you put this info to use whenever you link to a bookmark in a page on the World Wide Web (as described in the section "Linking to a Bookmark in a Page on the World Wide Web," a little later in this chapter).

Linking to a bookmark in an open page

Create a link to a bookmark in another page if you want the hyperlink to lead to a specific location inside the destination page, not just to the top of the page.

If several of your Web site's pages are open in the Editor, creating a link to a bookmark in one of those pages is just as easy as linking to a bookmark in the same page. No kidding.

Just follow these steps:

1. **In a page open in the Editor, select the hyperlink source.**

2. **Click the Create or Edit Hyperlink button to open the Create Hyperlink dialog box.**

3. **In the Open Pages list box, click the title of the page to which you want to link (the hyperlink destination).**

4. **Select the bookmark to which you want to link from the Bookmark drop-down list box.**

5. **Click OK.**

   The dialog box closes, and the Editor creates the hyperlink.

Linking to a bookmark in another page in your Web site

Any bookmark on any page in your Web site is an eligible candidate for a link. To forge this link, follow these steps:

1. **In a page open in the Editor, select the hyperlink source.**

2. **Click the Create or Edit Hyperlink button to open the Create Hyperlink dialog box.**

3. **Click the Current FrontPage Web tab to make the tab visible.**

4. **In the Page text box, type the filename of the destination page.**

   The Browse button is here for you if you need to search for the page.

5. **In the Bookmark text box, type the name of the bookmark to which you want to link your source text.**

   Unfortunately, you don't have the benefit of a drop-down list here, so you need to remember the bookmark name on your own.

6. **Click OK.**

   The dialog box closes, and the Editor creates the hyperlink.

To link to a bookmark located inside a page in another FrontPage Web site, create the hyperlink following the steps outlined in the section "Linking to a Page in another FrontPage Web Site," earlier in this chapter. In step 8, in addition to specifying the page to which you want to link, type the bookmark name in the Bookmark text box, and then click OK to create the hyperlink.

Linking to a bookmark in a page on the World Wide Web

The attraction between bookmarks and links is strong enough to transcend the FrontPage Web site barrier. You can create links to bookmarks in any page on the World Wide Web.

Pop quiz: Bookmarks are invisible while you're browsing the Web, so how do you know to link to one from your page? (I'm a softy, so I give you the answer here, too.)

Answer: If you're linking to a bookmark in a page you created, presumably you know where you placed and what you named the bookmarks. If you didn't create the page (or if you can't, for the life of you, remember all those bookmarks), you can use your browser's View HTML command to expose the page's HTML tags. Don't be afraid. Even if you don't know HTML, you can easily spot bookmarks. Take a deep breath and look through the jungle of tags for things that look similar to the following example:

```
<A NAME=oatmeal>
```

The word or phrase that follows `<A NAME=` is the bookmark name (in this case, it's `oatmeal`). Now that you know the name of the bookmark, close your browser's HTML view as quickly as possible, return to the FrontPage Editor, and proceed to create a link to that bookmark — in other words, follow these steps:

1. **In a page open in the Editor, select the hyperlink source.**

2. **Click the Create or Edit Hyperlink button to open the Create Hyperlink dialog box.**

3. **Click the World Wide Web tab to make the tab visible.**

4. **In the URL text box, type the URL of the destination page followed by a # sign and the name of the bookmark.**

   No spaces go between the URL, the # sign, and the bookmark name.

5. **Click OK.**

   The dialog box closes, and the Editor creates the hyperlink.

Visiting bookmarks

After you create bookmarks, you may become attached to those bookmarks and want to visit your creations from time to time. To jump straight to the location of a bookmark without needing to scroll around your page, follow these steps:

1. **In the Editor, choose Edit⇨Bookmark.**

2. **In the Other Bookmarks on this Page box, click the name of the bookmark you want to visit.**

   The lucky little devil.

3. **Click the Goto button.**

   The dialog box closes, and FrontPage instantly whisks you to the location of your bookmark. Make sure that you visit the others, too, so that none get jealous.

Dismantling bookmarks

You can dismantle and return to regular text status any bookmarks that outlive their usefulness. The procedure is quick and painless (for both you and the bookmark). Just follow these steps:

1. **Click anywhere inside the bookmark you want to dismantle.**

2. **Choose Edit⇨Unlink.**

   The bookmark returns to plain text status.

Editing Hyperlinks

Just as you can change hair color, you can easily change hyperlinks. You can change the text that makes up the link, the hyperlink's color, and even the destination to which it leads.

Changing hyperlink text

Say that you turn the sentence Go To My Home Page into a link, but you later decide that you want only the words Home Page to form the link, with the rest of the sentence just hanging on as regular text. (The resulting sentence is to look as follows: Go To My Home Page.) FrontPage enables you to make this type of change; to do so, follow these steps:

1. **Select the hyperlink text that you want to convert to regular text.**

2. **Choose Edit⇨Unlink.**

   The text relinquishes its color and underline and returns to regular text status.

Changing hyperlink color

Hyperlinks stand out from regular text because hyperlinks appear in a different color from their ordinary text siblings. (The default hyperlink color is blue.) You can, however, change the link's color so that the hyperlink coordinates nicely with the color scheme of your page.

Hyperlinks actually have three distinct colors: the *default color,* the *active color,* and the *visited color.* These colors appear if a visitor views the page in a Web browser, as described in the following list:

✔ **The *default color* is the link's color before anyone follows the hyperlink trail.** As visitors arrive at your page for the first time, all the page's links appear in the default color, because the visitor hasn't yet followed a link.

✔ **The *active color* is the color the link becomes after someone clicks the hyperlink text.** The active color tells visitors that they are indeed activating that particular link.

✔ **The *visited color* is the color the link changes to after visitors follow a link and then return to your page.** That way, visitors know which links they've already followed and which ones they haven't yet explored.

You can select unique hyperlink colors for each page you create. Or, if the page is part of a FrontPage Web site, you can base hyperlink color on the background settings of another page in your site.

The link colors you choose should balance the page's design with its navigational flow. Some designers use "hot" or bright colors for new links and "cool" or muted colors for visited links. Others make the default and visited link colors the same, because these designers want the page to appear uniform, no matter what. Whatever course you choose, you need to carefully consider how you can use color to make your Web easier and more pleasant for your visitors to explore.

Selecting unique hyperlink colors

To select unique link colors for a page, follow these steps:

1. **In the Editor, choose Format⇨Background.**

The Page Properties dialog box appears, with the Background tab visible. The current link colors appear in the drop-down list boxes labeled Hyperlink, Visited Hyperlink, and Active Hyperlink, as shown in Figure 6-2.

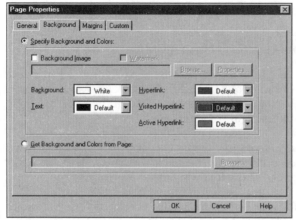

Figure 6-2:
The Background tab of the Page Properties dialog box.

2. **Select a new color from one or all the drop-down lists corresponding to each hyperlink "state."**

   If, in one of the drop-down lists, you select Custom, the Color dialog box appears. How to use the Color dialog box is fully explained in Chapter 5.

3. **Click OK.**

   The dialog box closes, and the page's links change color.

Basing hyperlink colors on another page

To base hyperlink color (as well as the two other background attributes, the body text color and the page background color or image) on that of another page in your Web site, follow these steps:

1. **In the Editor, choose Format➪Background.**

   The Page Properties dialog box appears, with the Background tab visible.

2. **Click the Get Background and Colors From Another Page radio button.**

   The text box beneath the radio button turns from gray to white, indicating that you can enter text there.

3. **In the text box, type the filename of the background color page.**

Or click B<u>r</u>owse to display the Current Web dialog box. In the dialog box, select the page and click OK. If you stored the page inside a folder, double-click the folder to open it, select the page, and click OK. The dialog box closes, and the filename appears in the text box.

4. Click OK to close the Page Properties dialog box.

The page's background and hyperlink colors change accordingly.

Changing the destination of a hyperlink

If the location of a hyperlink's destination page changes, you can edit the link so that it points to the new location. (I show you how to make sure that your Web site's hyperlinks are correct in the following section, "Do-It-Yourself Hyperlink Repair.")

To change a hyperlink destination, follow these steps:

1. Click anywhere inside the link that you want to change.

2. Click the Create or Edit Hyperlink button to open the Edit Hyperlink dialog box.

The tab that's visible depends on the destination of the hyperlink. If the hyperlink leads to a page on the World Wide Web, for example, the World Wide Web tab is visible.

3. Make the necessary change.

Type a new URL, for example, or select a different bookmark.

4. Click OK to close the dialog box.

FrontPage edits the hyperlink destination.

Do-It-Yourself Hyperlink Repair

Broken hyperlinks are like ants at a picnic. By themselves, ants are mildly annoying, but if enough ants show up, they ruin the entire afternoon.

A hyperlink breaks if the destination page the link points to moves or otherwise becomes unavailable. (The Web server on which you stored the page goes down, for example, or the page's author renamed the page.) After a visitor clicks a broken hyperlink, instead of delivering the requested page, the destination Web server delivers an error message stating that it can't find the page. Major Web-surfing bummer.

The most common cause of broken hyperlinks — renaming a page in your Web site and forgetting to update the hyperlinks elsewhere in the Web site that leads to the page — is a nonissue in FrontPage, because the FrontPage Explorer automatically updates hyperlinks if you rename or move a page. (I describe this feat of wonder in Chapter 2.)

Certain situations beyond FrontPage's control, however, still cause hyperlinks in your Web site to break, as described in the following list:

- ✔ You delete a file that has a link from elsewhere in the Web site.

- ✔ You import an existing Web site into FrontPage, and you leave out some files.

- ✔ You mistype a URL while creating a hyperlink to a site on the Internet.

- ✔ You create a link to a site on the Internet that changes location or otherwise becomes unreachable.

The FrontPage Explorer contains the Tools⇨Verify Hyperlinks command to help you find and repair broken hyperlinks throughout your Web site. If you just want to check a few hyperlinks inside a Web page, you can do so by using the Tools⇨Follow Hyperlink command in the Editor.

Verifying and fixing hyperlinks in the Explorer

The Explorer's Tools⇨Verify Hyperlinks command performs the following miracles:

- ✔ It finds all the broken links in your Web site and lists those links in the Verify Hyperlinks dialog box (as shown in Figure 6-3).

- ✔ It enables you to fix individual broken links by editing the link itself, by editing the page that contains the link, or by adding a task to the To Do List to remind you to fix the link later. (I show you how to use the To Do List in Chapter 16.)

- ✔ It updates the links in selected pages or throughout the entire Web site.

Verifying hyperlinks

You need to find broken hyperlinks before you can fix them. The Explorer is extremely helpful in this regard: It can root out pesky broken hyperlinks for you.

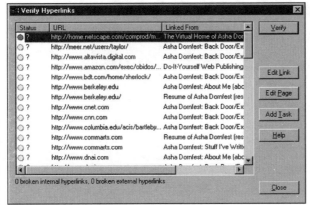

Figure 6-3:
The Verify
Hyperlinks
dialog box.

To verify the hyperlinks in your Web site, follow these steps:

1. **In the Explorer, choose Tools⇨Verify Hyperlinks.**

   The Verify Hyperlinks dialog box appears. The dialog box displays a list of all the broken internal hyperlinks (hyperlinks between pages and files in your Web site) and *all* external hyperlinks (links to locations outside the Web site). Broken internal hyperlinks are preceded by a red circle and a `Broken` label, and as-yet-unverified external hyperlinks are preceded by a yellow circle and a ? .

   (The Explorer waits for your signal to verify external hyperlinks, as this process can take a long time. You can choose to verify external hyperlinks now, or you can fix any broken internal hyperlinks and verify external hyperlinks later. If you want to skip verifying external hyperlinks for now, skip the rest of this section and jump to the following section, "Fixing Broken Hyperlinks.")

   To verify links to destinations on the Internet, you must have your Internet connection active.

2. **To verify your Web site's external hyperlinks, click the Verify button.**

   The Explorer verifies each external link by contacting the destination Web server and making sure that it can reach the page. As the verification process is going on, a progress bar appears at the bottom of the dialog box, indicating the percentage of the site's links that have been verified so far (see Figure 6-4). As each link is checked, its Status label changes from a yellow circle and a ? to either a green circle followed by OK (indicating valid links) or a red circle followed by Broken (indicating broken links).

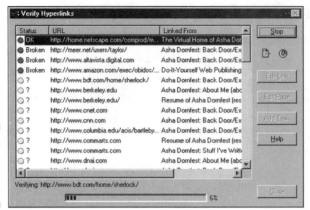

Figure 6-4:
Verifying
external
hyperlinks.

To stop the verification process, click the Stop button. (The Verify button turns into the Stop button while the verification process is going on.) To resume verifying hyperlinks, click the Resume button. (The Stop button, after you click it, turns into the Resume button.) After the verification process is complete, the Stop button turns back into the Verify button.

After the Explorer finishes verifying the external hyperlinks in your Web site, you can easily fix all the broken links from within the Verify Hyperlinks dialog box. I show you how in the following section, "Fixing Broken Hyperlinks."

Fixing broken hyperlinks

After the Explorer has unearthed the broken links, you need to fix them. Fixing broken hyperlinks is easy to accomplish by using tools available in the Verify Hyperlinks dialog box. To do so, follow these steps:

1. **If you haven't already, follow the steps in the preceding section, "Verifying Hyperlinks."**

2. **From the list in the Verify Hyperlinks dialog box, click the broken hyperlink that you want to edit.**

3. **Decide whether you want to edit the hyperlink itself, edit the page containing the hyperlink, or add a reminder to the To Do List to repair the hyperlink later and then take the appropriate action.**

   To edit the link, click the Edit Link button. The Edit Link dialog box appears, with the original link destination visible in the Replace text box (see Figure 6-5). In the With text box, type the new URL to which you want the link to point. To change the link in selected pages (as opposed to throughout the entire Web site), click the Select pages to change radio button and then click the names of the pages you want to update in the list box underneath. Click <u>O</u>K to fix the hyperlink. The Explorer repairs the link, and the link's status changes from Broken to Edited.

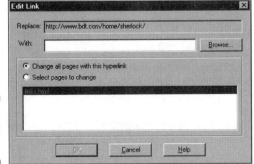

Figure 6-5:
The Edit Link
dialog box.

To edit the page containing the link, click the Edit <u>P</u>age button. The page opens in the FrontPage Editor, with the ailing link highlighted. Edit the link. (If you're not sure how, read the section "Changing the Destination of a Hyperlink," earlier in this chapter.) After you finish, click the Show Explorer button in the Editor's standard toolbar (or choose <u>T</u>ools➪Show Fro<u>n</u>tPage Explorer) to return to the Explorer. In the Verify Hyperlinks dialog box, the link's status changes from Broken to Edited.

To add a task to the To Do List, click the Add <u>T</u>ask button. FrontPage adds a task to the FrontPage To Do List. (Chapter 16 describes how to access the To Do List to complete tasks.) The link's status in the Verify Hyperlinks dialog box also changes from Broken to To Do List.

4. Continue repairing broken hyperlinks by repeating steps 1-3.

5. After you finish, click OK to close the dialog box.

I recommend verifying your site's hyperlinks every couple of weeks. Web pages on the Internet move and change all the time, breaking hyperlinks in your Web site. The Explorer makes checking your links so easy — why not make it a regular habit?

Checking individual hyperlinks in the Editor

If you simply want to check one or a few links inside a page, you can easily do so by using the Editor's <u>T</u>ools➪Follow <u>H</u>yperlink command. You don't need to be a private eye to follow hyperlinks. No one is going to think you're snooping.

Following hyperlinks enables you to check to see that the links go where you want them to go. Although the FrontPage Editor isn't a Web browser, the feature approximates browsing by enabling you to visit the destinations of the links in your pages.

As you follow a link to a bookmark in the same page, FrontPage scrolls to the location of the bookmark. If the link leads to another page or bookmark in your Web site, FrontPage opens that page. FrontPage even follows links to pages on the World Wide Web.

To follow links to destinations on the Internet, you must have your Internet connection active.

Make sure that you wear dark clothing and soft-soled shoes — and then follow these steps:

1. **Click anywhere inside the link you want to follow.**

2. **Choose Tools➪Follow Hyperlink.**

   FrontPage opens the destination page and displays it in a new window in the Editor. If it can't access the page (because the hyperlink is incorrect or the page unreachable), a FrontPage Editor dialog box appears telling you that it couldn't open the page. Click OK to close the dialog box and edit the hyperlink. (Refer to the section "Changing the Destination of a Hyperlink," earlier in the chapter.)

You can keep following links as long as you want. To reverse course, click the Back button (or choose Tools➪Back). To go forward again, click the Forward button (or choose Tools➪Forward).

This trick works only for links to pages in your Web site or to pages on the World Wide Web. FrontPage can't follow links to other protocols such as `ftp:` or `mailto:`.

Unlinking Hyperlinks

Suppose that you became so intoxicated with the power of hyperlink creation that, looking at your page now, you see more link than text. Perhaps you overindulged. Perhaps removing a few links so that the others may shine is the wise thing to do. To obtain forgiveness for your excesses, follow these steps:

1. **Click anywhere inside the hyperlink you want to unlink.**

2. **Choose Edit➪Unlink.**

Your link returns to regular text (or, if the link's an image, returns to its original state).

Chapter 7

You Oughta Be in Pictures

. . . .

. . . .

Sure, text is important. Text is, in fact, the foundation of your Web site — the basic building block of a page — and blah, blah, blah. Although that statement's essentially true, you may as well face the facts — the Web hasn't achieved worldwide fame because of a bunch of words. The pairing of information and *pictures* is what transforms the Web from a heap of data into a colorful adventure.

Web graphics, if used well, create a mood and help visitors navigate the site. High-quality, well-chosen images lend style and legitimacy. But, as with all Web design effects, too much of a good thing can be toxic. Cheesy clip art detracts from the site's message and, worse, slows its load time.

In this chapter, I unlock the secrets of Web graphics. I introduce you to the two Web graphic formats, GIF and JPEG. I let you in on tricks to keep your graphics looking good and loading quickly. And, of course, I show you how to use all the graphics capabilities of FrontPage.

Understanding the Quirks of Web Graphics

Web graphics can sometimes bewilder the novice Web publisher. No need to worry. As long as you follow the simple-but-ironclad rules in this chapter, you should have a graphic-filled, stress-free Web publishing career.

Getting to know GIF and JPEG

The alphabet soup of graphic file formats — TIF, PCT, GIF, EPS, PSD, JPEG, BMP — is enough to send anyone into fits of intimidation. Good news: You have only two format choices for Web graphics: *GIF* (some pronounce the term with a hard "g," as in *graphic;* others say "*jif* ") or *JPEG* (pronounced *jay-peg*). GIF is the oldest and most commonly used format on the Web. The JPEG format has come into use more recently and can stuff a wide range of color into a small file size. (Recent versions of Microsoft Internet Explorer can display BMP — the Windows bitmap format — graphics, but until other browsers display BMP as well, I recommend sticking with GIF and JPEG.)

Which format do you choose? The definitive answer is that . . . it depends. GIF displays a maximum of 256 colors and is therefore best suited to high-contrast, flat color images such as logos and cartoons. The JPEG format can display thousands of colors, so that format is your best choice for images displaying subtle color changes or a wide range of color, such as photographs and complex digital art.

The folks at Adobe, creators of state-of-the-art graphics software, help you choose which format is best by comparing sample images saved in each format. Check out the somewhat-technical-but-highly-informative article "GIF? JPEG? Which Should You Use?" at http://www.adobe.com/studio/ tipstechniques/GIFJPGchart/main.html.

The FrontPage Editor enables you to insert just about any type of image into a Web page. (I list specific file formats in the section "Adding an Image to Your Page," later in this chapter.) The Editor converts imported images of 256 colors or fewer to GIF and those of more than 256 colors to JPEG. If you want greater control over the conversion process, you can open your graphic file in an image-editing program such as Microsoft Image Composer (which ships with FrontPage as part of the Bonus Pack; see Appendix A for more information) or Paint Shop Pro (which comes on the CD included with this book; see Appendix C for more information and installation instructions). Then you can tweak all you like and save the file as GIF or JPEG by hand. (In the section "Editing the image itself," later in this chapter, I show you how to launch your associated image-editing program from within FrontPage.)

Is it pronounced *GIF* or *JIF*?

A dispute rages in the Web publishing community over the pronunciation of the term *GIF*. Is GIF pronounced with a hard *G*, as in *graphic*, or is the term pronounced *JIF*, like the peanut butter? For what it's worth, I say GIF with a hard G, but know-it-alls exist in both camps, so no matter how you say it, prepare to be corrected.

The GIF format has a few extra cards up its sleeve: transparency and interlacing (both of which I discuss in the section "Customizing GIFs," later in the chapter) and — its most nifty trick — simple animation (described in the accompanying sidebar, "Movin' and shakin' with GIF animation").

Picky palettes

In Chapter 4, I relate a harrowing episode from my Web publishing career: I gave my home page a background of what I thought was soothing lemon yellow — but when my friend looked at my page on his computer, the same color appeared more like pallid green. I made the mistake of ignoring an important Web graphic rule: *Stick to the browser-safe palette of colors.* Okay — an explanation.

As I said in the preceding section, GIFs display a range, or *palette,* of 256 colors. The tricky thing about color palettes, however, is that the colors are operating-system-specific. In other words, colors appear slightly different if viewed on a PC running Windows than do the same colors viewed on a Mac. Bright colors look about the same, but unusual or pastel colors may appear shockingly different on the two platforms. If your graphic contains a color that isn't present in your visitor's palette, your visitor's Web browser attempts to display the color by *dithering* — that is, by mixing other colors together to approximate the color in the graphic. Dithered graphics, although better than nothing, lack clarity and definition.

Movin' and shakin' with GIF animation

Remember those tiny "flip books" that were popular back when you were a kid? Each page contained a cartoon in a suspended state of movement, and as you quickly flipped the book's pages, the cartoon looked as though it was moving — just as though you were watching a movie.

The GIF format enables you to do something similar with individual graphics. You create individual frames of animation, save the frames as GIF files, and string them together into one file. Advanced Web browsers automatically "play" the animation, displaying the graphics in quick succession and creating the illusion of a moving picture.

The FrontPage clip-art collection contains a bunch of animated GIFs you can add to your pages. (I show you how in the section "Adding an Image to your Page," later in this chapter.) How do you create your own animation? With the help of a GIF animation tool. I include what I consider the best animation tool on the CD: Alchemy Mindworks' GIF Construction Set for Windows 95 (See Appendix C for installation instructions.)

For instructions and tips on how to create animated GIFs, visit `http://members.aol.com/royalef/gifanim.htm`.

You can eliminate dithering by using a special palette with your Web graphics: the *nondithering,* or *browser-safe, palette.* This palette gives you a range of 216 colors available in both the Windows and Macintosh system palettes. If you create graphics by using these colors or apply this palette to the graphics you convert to GIF, the issue of dithering becomes moot. And you don't have your friends calling and asking why you used such a gross color for the background of your page.

The image NETCOLPC.GIF, included on the CD that comes with this book, contains the browser-safe palette of colors. Refer to your image-editing program's documentation for instructions on how to apply the palette to your graphics.

Keeping graphics zippy

Web truism #3 states that "Your visitors connect to the Internet at different speeds." (I discuss the four Web truisms in detail in Chapter 4.) If your visitors must wait more than a few seconds for the page to appear in their browsers, your site risks falling victim to "clickitus," the chronic condition that causes surfers to click elsewhere whenever they must wait a moment for something to download to their machines. Clickitus is 100 percent preventable by keeping load times brief.

Graphics are notorious load-time hogs. Here are some ways to ensure that your graphics don't drag:

- ✔ **Wherever possible, keep picture dimensions small.**

- ✔ **Limit the number of colors in your pictures.** You can shave precious seconds off the download time while maintaining your picture's quality if you use an image-editing program to reduce the number of colors.

- ✔ **Save your graphics at a resolution of 72 dpi (dots per inch), the highest resolution possible on a computer monitor.** Anything higher, and you're adding unnecessary bulk to your graphic's file size.

- ✔ **As much as possible, use the same images throughout your site.** Web browsers *cache* images, which means that the browser saves a copy of the image on the visitor's hard drive. The first time someone visits your site, the browser downloads the images from the server; after the initial download, the browser displays the cached images instead — which load almost instantly.

The Editor displays the page's estimated download time (in seconds) in a box on the right side of the status bar (the gray stripe at the bottom of the window). Keep an eye on the download time as you add graphics to your page.

Practicing graphic restraint

The "more is better" trap is easy to fall into whenever images come into play. After all, graphics are so colorful and pretty. I urge you, however, to practice restraint. Each picture you add increases the overall load time of the page and should, therefore, be worth the wait. Use only those graphics that communicate your site's purpose and make getting around in the site easier or more pleasant for your target audience.

Finally, make sure that visitors can understand your page without the pictures. Some surfers turn off their browser's image-loading option to speed up browsing sessions.

Adding an Image to Your Page

If you add an image to a Web page, the Editor places a link between the page and the graphic file and displays the graphic at the location of the link, creating what's known as an *inline image*.

The term *inline* means that the image appears within the body of the page if viewed with a Web browser. Back in the Web publishing Stone Age, graphical Web browsers couldn't display JPEG images and had to launch a separate program called a *helper application* that opened the images in another window. Today, although all advanced browsers display both GIF and JPEG graphics inline, the name stuck.

If you insert an image into a Web page, the mechanics are the same as creating a hyperlink, because you simply link two different files: the Web page and the graphic file. So, similar to a hyperlink, an inline image link can point to a graphic file inside your Web site, to a file on your computer, or to a file stored on a remote Web server.

I recommend reading Chapter 6 (if you haven't done so already) to familiarize yourself with how links work.

The Editor converts BMP (Windows and OS/2), TIFF, MAC, MSP, PCD, RAS, WPG, EPS, PCX, and WMF graphic file formats to GIF and JPEG, saving you the extra step of converting the graphics files yourself.

FrontPage automatically converts images with 256 or fewer colors to GIF and converts those with more than 256 colors to JPEG. If, later, you want to convert JPEG images to GIF (so that you can make the images transparent or interlaced, for example), FrontPage makes doing so easy. I show you how to make these conversions in the section "Converting a JPEG to a GIF (and Vice Versa)," later in this chapter.

From the current Web site

You can insert an image that already resides in the Web site currently open in the Explorer. Just follow these steps:

1. In the Editor, place the cursor where you want the image to appear.

2. Click the Insert Image button (or choose Insert⇨Image).

The Image dialog box appears, with the Current FrontPage Web tab visible (see Figure 7-1).

Figure 7-1:
The Image
dialog box.

The tab displays your Web site's image files and folders. If you don't see any images, double-click the IMAGES folder; that's where the Explorer stores imported images (and where I recommend you store all images, just to keep them in one place).

3. Double-click the graphic you want to insert.

The dialog box disappears, and the image appears in the document.

When the time comes to save your page, FrontPage is smart. If the page you're working with was originally opened from a file (one located outside the Web site), the Editor asks, on saving the page, whether you want to export the inserted graphic to a file (because, right now, the graphic still exists inside the Web site). To avoid breaking the link between the graphic file and the page, you must store the graphic file in the same location as the page. If you click Yes, FrontPage exports a copy of the file to the same location as the page.

From a file

You also can insert an image elsewhere on your computer.

Inserting an image from a file works only if the Web page you're working with is originally opened from within the Web site. If the page was originally opened from a file, FrontPage uses the image file's location on your hard drive to create the link between the image and the Web page. If you publish your finished Web site on a dedicated Web server, the image link breaks because the image file's location is specific to your computer's file system (not the Web server's). Read the Chapter 6 sidebar "Dissecting hyperlinks" for more information on why this happens.

To insert an image from a file, follow these steps:

1. **In the Editor, place the cursor where you want the image to appear.**

2. **Click the Insert Image button (or choose Insert➪Image).**

   The Image dialog box appears.

3. **Click the Other Location Tab to make the tab visible.**

4. **Type the location of the image in the From File text box and click OK.**

   Or click the Browse button to display the Image dialog box. The dialog box lists the folders and files on your computer. Navigate your computer to the location of the graphic file. (If you don't see the file you want, make sure that you select All files (*.*) in the Files of type drop-down list box.) After you find the file, click the file, and click OK.

   The dialog box disappears, and the image appears in the document.

FrontPage asks on saving the page whether you want to import the inserted graphic into the Web site. If you click Yes, FrontPage converts the file to GIF or JPEG (if necessary) and places a copy of the image file in your Web site.

You also can copy an image from another application and paste the image into your page directly from the Clipboard. FrontPage converts the image to GIF or JPEG (if necessary) and saves the image to your Web site as you save the page.

From the World Wide Web

You can even insert graphics that dwell on a Web server on the other side of the world.

If the Web server hosting the image goes down or the location of the graphic file changes, the problem breaks the link to the image in your page. A better choice is to copy the image from its original location to your computer *first* (with permission of the host site's author, of course) and then insert the image into your page. Most Web browsers enable you to right-click any image on the Web and save a copy of the file to your computer, which you can then import into your Web.

To insert an image from the Web, follow these steps:

1. **In the Editor, place the cursor where you want the image to appear.**

2. **Click the Insert Image button (or choose Insert➪Image).**

   The Image dialog box appears.

3. **Click the Other Location Tab to make the tab visible.**

4. **Select the From Location radio button.**

   The text box underneath the radio button turns from gray to white, indicating you can type something there.

5. **In the text box, type the complete URL of the image you want to reference.**

   The URL of the image should look something like the following example: `http://www.dnai.com/~asha/title.gif`.

6. **Click OK.**

   The dialog box disappears. In a moment, the image appears on the page.

The Broken Image icon appears whenever the link between a graphic file and the Web page is broken. If this icon appears after you click OK in step 6 in the preceding steps, it means that the URL you typed in step 5 is unreachable. (Either the URL was typed incorrectly or the Web server hosting the image is down.) To correct the URL, double-click the icon to display the Image Properties dialog box, type the correct URL in the Image Source text box (on the General tab), and click OK. After you click OK, the image should appear in your page. If the Broken Image icon is still visible, it means the host Web server is down — which is beyond your control.

Gobs of graphics

Where do you find ready-made pictures to plop into your Web pages? In addition to the FrontPage Clip Art collection, plenty of excellent galleries on the Web encourage you to grab their pictures for your own personal use. Try Barry's Clip Art Server at `http://www.barrysclipart.com` (where you find both regular and animated GIFs), Pixelsight at `http://www.pixelsight.com`, and Yahoo!'s extensive index at `http://www.yahoo.com/Computers_and_Internet/Internet/World_Wide_Web/Page_Design_and_Layout/Icons`.

From the FrontPage clip-art collection

At the time you installed FrontPage, the program quietly slipped a bunch of clip art images onto your hard drive. The Editor gives you access to a bevy of buttons, bullets, banners, backgrounds, lines, and miscellaneous images that you can use to decorate your FrontPage Web.

 Inserting FrontPage clip art works only if the Web page you're working with was originally opened from within the Web site. Refer to the Warning at the beginning of the section "From a file," earlier in the chapter, for details.

To insert FrontPage clip art into a Web page, follow these steps:

1. **In the Editor, place the cursor where you want the image to appear.**

 2. **Click the Insert Image button (or choose Insert⇨Image).**

    The image dialog box appears.

3. **Click the Clip Art tab to make the tab visible.**

    FrontPage takes a moment to read the images and then displays them in the Contents box of the Clip Art tab.

4. **Select an item from the Category drop-down list to see different groups of clip art.**

    You have your choice of Animations, Backgrounds, Bullets, Buttons, Icons, Lines, and Logos. After you select a category, that clip-art group appears in the Contents box.

5. **If you see an image you like in the Contents box, double-click that image.**

    The Image dialog box closes, and in a moment, the image appears on the page.

On saving the page, FrontPage offers to import the clip-art image file to your Web site. Click Yes to import the file.

Customizing GIFs

GIF offers two features missing in JPEG: *transparency* and *interlacing*. Web publishers the world over use these two effects to make their graphics more attractive but, in the past, needed to resort to separate editing programs. Not any more. The FrontPage Editor makes applying transparency and interlacing effects to any GIF image easy.

Creating a transparent GIF

The concept of a *transparent GIF* is more easily demonstrated than explained, so I'm going to show you one first and then tell you about the concept in a moment. Figure 7-2 shows the difference between a regular and a transparent GIF. The graphic on the left is a regular GIF; see how the background color of the graphic wrestles with the background color of the page? This problem disappears if you make the GIF's background color *transparent,* as in the graphic on the right. The transparent GIF blends nicely with the rest of the page — with no unsightly clashing.

Figure 7-2:
A regular GIF on the left, and a transparent GIF on the right.

A transparent GIF has one of its colors erased (usually the background color) so that the color of the page shows through. The FrontPage Editor contains a built-in "magic eraser" so that you can make regular GIFs transparent with a couple clicks. The eraser resides in the Image toolbar, as shown in Figure 7-3. You can make this toolbar visible by choosing View⇨Image Toolbar.

Figure 7-3:
The Image toolbar.

A GIF can have only *one* transparent color. Whichever color you slate for erasure disappears throughout the graphic. Unless the color you choose is unique, your GIF resembles Swiss cheese, because see-through spots appear throughout the image. To avoid this problem, make sure that the GIF's background color does not appear anywhere else in the graphic. If you're working with ready-made graphics, you may need to alter the images in an image-editing program.

To transform a regular GIF into a transparent GIF, follow these steps:

1. Insert the GIF of your choice into your page.

Refer to the section "Adding an Image to Your Page," earlier in this chapter, for details.

2. **Click the image.**

3. **In the Image toolbar, click the Make Transparent button.**

   As you move the mouse pointer over the image, the pointer turns into a little pencil eraser with an arrow sticking out of the top.

4. **Position the pointer over the color you want to erase and click.**

   The color disappears!

   To change an image's transparent color, click the Make Transparent button and then click a different color. The original color reappears, and the newly chosen color becomes transparent. To turn a transparent GIF back into a regular GIF, click the Make Transparent button and click the transparent area. The old color comes back.

If you try this trick on a JPEG graphic, FrontPage prompts you to convert the image to GIF format. (You can make only GIFs transparent.) Proceed with care, however, because the GIF format can't accommodate as many colors as JPEG can, and your image's quality may suffer as a result.

Creating an interlaced GIF

Web surfers' greed for speed is so well-documented that many Web publishers resort to a nifty slight-of-hand called an *interlaced GIF.* Viewed in a Web browser, an interlaced GIF appears on-screen gradually, starting as a fuzzy haze and clearing up as the image loads. Interlacing creates the illusion that the image loads faster than does a regular GIF (which must download fully before the image appears, complete, on a visitor's screen). This effect is actually a tiny act of psychological subterfuge, because interlaced GIFs take just as long to load as regular GIFs. The trickery is okay, however, because your visitors usually don't mind waiting quite so much if they have something to look at in the meantime.

To turn a regular GIF into an interlaced GIF, follow these steps:

1. **Right-click the image and choose Image Properties from the pop-up menu.**

   Or click the image and choose Edit➪Image Properties or press Alt+Enter.

   The Image Properties dialog box appears with the General tab visible (see Figure 7-4).

2. **In the Type area of the General tab, select the Interlaced check box.**

3. **Click OK to close the dialog box.**

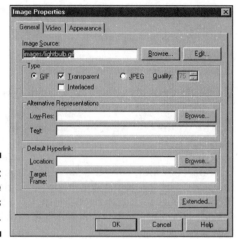

Figure 7-4:
The Image
Properties
dialog box.

 The image doesn't appear to have changed; however, it is now an interlaced GIF. To see the interlacing effect in action, preview the page by clicking the Preview In Browser button. (For more information about previewing pages in a Web browser, refer to Chapter 3.)

Converting a JPEG to a GIF (and Vice Versa)

Times may arise when you need to override the FrontPage graphic conversion feature and turn a JPEG into a GIF or a GIF into a JPEG. You may, for example, want to apply transparency or interlacing to a JPEG graphic and must, therefore, convert the JPEG to a GIF.

 Because the GIF format displays 256 colors and the JPEG format displays thousands of colors, converting a JPEG to a GIF may reduce its quality. Changing formats (both ways) also may increase the size of the file, slowing its download time. I'm not suggesting that you *never* convert graphic formats; simply remain aware of the possible consequences and balance them against your reasons for changing the format.

To convert a JPEG to a GIF, follow these steps:

1. **Right-click the image and choose Image Properties from the pop-up menu.**

   Or click the image and choose Edit⇨Image Properties or press Alt+Enter.

The Image Properties dialog box appears with the General tab visible. In the Type area of the General tab, the JPEG radio button is selected.

2. **Select the GIF radio button.**

3. **Click OK to close the dialog box.**

As you save the document, FrontPage prompts you to save a copy of the newly converted graphic file. The program uses the same filename but changes the three-letter extension from JPEG to GIF.

To convert a GIF to a JPEG, follow these steps:

1. **Right-click the image and choose Image Properties.**

   Or click the image and choose Edit⇨Image Properties or press Alt+Enter.

   The Image Properties dialog box appears. In the Type area of the General tab, the GIF radio button is selected.

2. **Select the JPEG radio button.**

   The Quality text box comes into full view. The number in this box (anything from 1 to 99) controls the amount of *file compression.* File compression removes minute details from the image, shrinking the size of the file. The higher the number is, the lower is the amount of compression and the higher is the quality of the image. The default value is 75, which, in most cases, is fine.

3. **If you want, type a new number in the Quality field.**

   In choosing a quality value for a JPEG image, you need to balance file size with image fidelity. You want the smallest possible image (*read:* the lowest quality value) that still looks good.

4. **Click OK to close the dialog box.**

As you save the document, FrontPage prompts you to save a copy of the newly converted graphic file. The program uses the same filename, but changes the three-letter extension from GIF to JPEG.

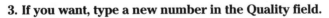

Altering an Image's Appearance

After an image is perched comfortably in your page, you can use FrontPage to control its alignment with surrounding text, the size of its surrounding white space, and the dimensions of the image as it appears when viewed in a Web browser. You can also give the image a border, or you can launch your associated image-editing program to edit the image itself.

Aligning an image with surrounding text

If you insert an image in the same line as text, you can control how the image aligns with that text.

To align an image with surrounding text, follow these steps:

1. **Right-click the image and choose Image Properties.**

   Or click the image and choose Edit⇨Image Properties or press Alt+Enter.

   The Image Properties dialog box appears.

2. **Click the Appearance tab to make the tab visible.**

3. **In the Layout area, select an alignment option from the Alignment drop-down list.**

   Here are your choices:

   - *Bottom* aligns the bottom of the image with the text.

   - *Middle* aligns the middle of the image with the text.

   - *Top* aligns the top of the image with the text.

   - *Left* places the image in the left margin and wraps surrounding text around the right side of the image (see Figure 7-5). For details on how text wraps around images, read the following section, "Controlling how text wraps around the image."

   - *Right* places the image in the right margin and wraps surrounding text around the left side of the image (see Figure 7-5).

     You can right-align an image by clicking the Align Right button in the Format toolbar, but text doesn't wrap around the image as it does if you use the Right image alignment option.

   - *Texttop* aligns the top of the image with the top of the tallest text in the line.

   - *Baseline* aligns the image with the text baseline. (The *baseline* is the invisible line that runs beneath your text to keep it straight, something like the lines on a piece of binder paper.)

   - *Absbottom* aligns the image with the bottom of the text in the line.

4. **Click OK to close the dialog box.**

   The image's alignment changes accordingly.

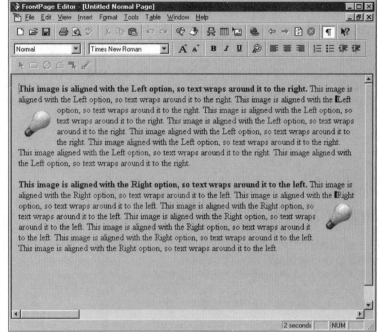

Figure 7-5:
The results
of the Left
and Right
image
alignment
options.

Many resourceful Web publishers control the precise placement of text and images by using an *invisible table* to structure page layout. I shed light on this Web design trick in Chapter 9.

Controlling how text wraps around the image

If you use the Left or Right option to align an image (as outlined in the preceding section), surrounding text flows, or *wraps,* around the image (refer to Figure 7-5).

You can control the amount of text that wraps around the image. You do so by inserting a *line break* where you want the wrapping to stop. A line break creates a new, blank line and moves all the text following the line break beneath the image, as opposed to a new paragraph — produced by pressing the Enter key — which has no effect on where the text wrapping ends.

To insert a line break, follow these steps:

1. **Place the cursor in the location you want the line break to appear.**

2. **Choose Insert⇨Break.**

   The Break Properties dialog box appears.

3. **Select the radio button next to the type of line break you want to insert.**

The type of line break you select depends on how the image is aligned.

If the image is left-aligned, select Clear Left Margin to cause text after the line break to shift to the first empty space in the left margin below the image. If the image is right-aligned, select Clear Right Margin to cause text after the line break to shift to the first empty space in the right margin below the image. If the image is left- and right-aligned, select Clear Both Margins to cause text to shift to the first empty space where both margins are clear.

4. **Click OK to close the dialog box and insert the line break.**

Controlling the amount of space surrounding the image

You can control the amount of breathing room surrounding each image. By adjusting horizontal and vertical spacing, you set the amount of space that separates an image from surrounding text.

To adjust image spacing, follow these steps:

1. **Right-click the image and choose Image Properties.**

   Or click the image and choose Edit⇨Image Properties or press Alt+Enter.

   The Image Properties dialog box appears.

2. **Click the Appearance tab to make the tab visible.**

3. **In the Horizontal Spacing text box, type the number of pixels of blank space you want between the image and the text next to the image.**

4. **In the Vertical Spacing text box, type the number of pixels of blank space you want between the image and the text above or below the image.**

5. **Click OK to close the dialog box and adjust the spacing.**

Border patrol

Image borders are useful only if the image in question is the basis of a hyperlink. Although you can place a black border around a regular image by using this feature, the border shows up only if viewed with Netscape Navigator — and in my humble opinion, it looks darn ugly.

Borders around graphic hyperlinks, on the other hand, can make your site easier to navigate. Graphic hyperlink borders are the same color as the page's text link colors, cueing neophyte Web surfers to click the image to activate the link. On the other hand, borders cause visual clutter and, worse, can clash with the colors in the image. The solution to this design dilemma is to choose your hyperlink images carefully — use graphics that implicitly whisper "click me." That way, even the greenest of visitors know to click the image to go elsewhere.

To give your image a border, follow these steps:

1. **Right-click the image and choose Image Properties.**

   Or click the image and choose Edit⇨Image Properties or press Alt+Enter.

   The Image Properties dialog box appears.

2. **Click the Appearance tab to make the tab visible.**

3. **In the Border Thickness text box, type the thickness (in pixels) of the image border.**

   I recommend nothing thicker than 1 pixel. I think anything thicker looks gaudy.

4. **Click OK to close the dialog box and apply the border.**

 The best way to apply a border to your regular (nonlinked) images is to open the image files in an image-editing program and add a border to the image itself. Read the section "Editing the image itself," later in this chapter, for details on how to launch your image-editing program from within FrontPage.

Setting image dimensions

The FrontPage Editor enables you to specify the width and height of an image as the image appears viewed with a Web browser. By doing so, you don't affect the graphic file itself; you affect only the size the image appears in a Web page.

You can use the Editor to adjust the dimensions of your Web graphics, either in pixels or as a percentage of the original graphic size. Proceed with caution, however; if you fool with the dimensions too much, your graphic may fall prey to the "jaggies" (see Figure 7-6).

To set image dimensions, follow these steps:

1. **Right-click the image and choose Image Properties.**

   Or click the image and choose Edit⇨Image Properties or press Alt+Enter.

   The Image Properties dialog box appears.

2. **Select the Appearance tab to make the tab visible.**

3. **Click the Specify Size check box.**

   The Width and Height text boxes come into full view.

Figure 7-6:
The "jaggies" occur if you overinflate the size of a Web graphic.

4. **Type new numbers in the <u>W</u>idth and <u>H</u>eight text boxes.**

You can specify a number of pixels, or you can choose a percentage of the original image size.

5. **Click OK to close the dialog box and adjust the image's dimensions.**

To quickly resize a graphic, click the graphic in the open page in the Editor and drag the size handles that appear around the graphic.

The invisible spacer GIF

This little goodie is, quite possibly, the most popular design trick on the Web. To gain precise control over the white space in your Web pages, use an "invisible spacer GIF."

Apply transparency to a tiny GIF image (as small as a single pixel) and use the image dimension controls to make the image whatever size you want. Voilà! — you now have an invisible graphic the sole purpose of which is to create white space. Place the invisible graphic anywhere you want horizontal and vertical space and simply adjust the image dimensions to adjust the amount of space in your document.

Editing the image itself

Want to add some finishing touches to your graphic? You can launch your associated image editor right from the FrontPage Editor by double-clicking any graphic in your page. Microsoft Image Composer (part of the FrontPage Bonus Pack) is the default image editor for FrontPage, although you're more than welcome to use another program if you prefer. (Paint Shop Pro is a good choice, and it comes on the CD included with this book; see Appendix C for installation instructions.) To find out how to associate editors with file types, refer to Chapter 2.

To launch your image editor independent of a graphic, choose Tools⇨Show Image Editor.

 You can also launch your associated image-editing program from the FrontPage Explorer; click the Show Image Editor in the Explorer toolbar or, from the Explorer menu bar, choose Tools⇨Show Image Editor.

Giving Your Images Multiple Identities

Images are the road-hogs of the Information Superhighway, but images are also what make the Web such a pleasant drive. A conscientious Web publisher balances these opposing forces by using graphics judiciously, keeping images small in file size, and firing the bulk of the creative power into the site's content. Because I know you're conscientious, you've already taken these steps. The following sections offer a couple more ways that you can make images easier to handle.

Including a low-resolution version of the image

Sometimes, you can't avoid using a big, slothlike image in your page. Online versions of some popular magazines, for example, use the magazine cover as the central image for the home page. Visitors click the different cover headlines to move to a related article. (By the way, an image that contains multiple clickable spots is called a *clickable image,* or an *imagemap.* In Chapter 8, you discover how to create one.) To minimize the frustration level of visitors who must wait several agonizing seconds for the picture to load, many of these sites include a *low-resolution* version of the image. (Web veterans call it a *low-res image.*) While the main image is loading, the low-res image pops up relatively quickly and is gradually replaced by the fancy version. Unlike GIF interlacing, a low-res image enables visitors to see exactly what they are waiting for, because the image appears on-screen in full clarity.

Not all your visitors benefit from this feature, because many browsers can't display low-res images. I recommend designing your site to avoid the use of big, fat central graphics that call for a low-res version in the first place.

A low-res image is a pared-down (usually black-and-white) version of the main image. Because the image contains no color, the graphic loads much faster than its full-color sibling. To create a low-res image, you must open the main image in an image-editing program, convert the image to a black-and-white version (also known as a *grayscale*), and save a copy of the new graphic.

To specify a low-res version of an image, follow these steps:

1. **Create the low-res image in an image-editing program and import the graphic into your Web site.**

   If you're not sure how to import a file into a Web site, refer to Chapter 2.

2. **Open the page containing the main image in the Editor.**

3. **Right-click the image and choose Image Properties.**

   Or click the image and choose Edit⇨Image Properties or press Alt+Enter.

   The Image Properties dialog box appears, with the General tab visible.

4. **In the Lo̲w-Res text box, type the URL of the low-res image you want to use.**

   If you don't remember the URL, click the B̲rowse button to display the Select Alternate Image dialog box. The dialog box lists all the files and folders in your Web site. Double-click the file you want to select. If the image is stored inside a folder, double-click the folder to open it and then double-click the image to select it. After you select the image, the dialog box closes, and the image's URL appears in the Lo̲w-Res text box of the Image properties dialog box.

5. **Click OK to close the dialog box.**

Although nothing appears to have changed in your page, FrontPage has added a low-res tag to your page's HTML. To see the low-res effect in action (assuming that the Web browser installed on your computer can display low-res images), preview your page by clicking the Preview In Browser button or choosing F̲ile⇨Preview in B̲rowser.

Setting alternative text

Some Web surfers, desperate to save seconds, turn off their browsers' capability to automatically display the images in a site. Instead of a graphically exciting Web site, as embodied in the example shown in Figure 7-7, the result is a no-nonsense, fast-loading, text-only site, with empty placeholders where the images normally sit, as shown in Figure 7-8.

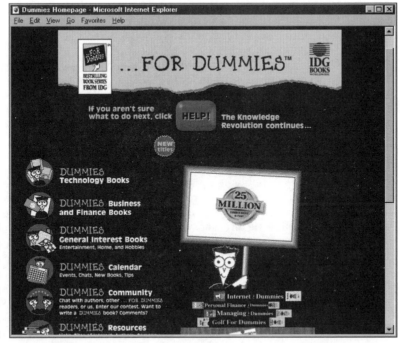

Figure 7-7:
The
Dummies
Home Page,
as seen in
full regalia.

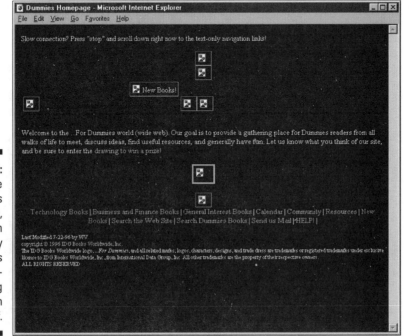

Figure 7-8:
The
Dummies
Home Page,
as seen
with my
browser's
image-
loading
function
turned off.

Visitors who want to dispense with pretty pictures to get just the facts love this feature. But what about you? You painstakingly designed your site's graphics only to discover that some of your visitors never even see them!

This situation is a sad fact of Web publishing life, but one you must accept. All you can do is give each of your images *alternative text.* Alternative text appears inside the placeholder where the original graphic *would* appear if image loading were turned on. Generally, you use alternative text to label the graphic, giving visitors an idea of what the graphic contains (and enabling visitors to decide whether the graphics are worth the load time).

I have, however, seen more . . . um, shall we say *creative*? . . . alternative text treatments. Bold Web publishers use their alternative text labels to urge visitors (with varying degrees of subtlety) to load the site's images. I once visited a Web site (with my browser's image-loading function turned off), where every graphic had the following alternative text: "Unless you're viewing this site's graphics, you're experiencing only half the excitement!" The ploy was a clever trick, although *I* didn't fall for it.

If you decide to use a similar trick on your site, make sure that your graphics are truly dazzling — or your visitors are going to feel duped. *Not* a pretty sight.

To give an image alternative text, follow these steps:

1. **Right-click the image and choose Image Properties.**

   Or click the image and choose Edit⇨Image Properties or press Alt+Enter.

   The Image Properties dialog box appears, with the General tab visible.

2. **Type an alternative text label in the Text box.**

3. **Click OK to close the dialog box.**

   Although nothing appears to have changed in your page, FrontPage has inserted the alternative text into your page's HTML.

Creating a Background Image

You can use an image as the background of your page, with the page's text sitting on top. How the background image appears as viewed with a browser depends on the dimensions of the image file itself. The Web browser *tiles* the image — repeating the image over and over until it fills the browser window — which creates a consistent background for the text.

You also may use the Editor to turn your background into a *watermark.* Watermarks are the same as regular backgrounds, except that watermarks appear fixed in place if viewed with a Web browser — when a visitor scrolls around the screen, the text appears to float above the fixed background. With regular background images, the background and text move together whenever a visitor scrolls around the page. As of this writing, Microsoft Internet Explorer is the only browser that can display watermarks.

The FrontPage clip-art collection contains ready-made background patterns you can use in your pages, or you can download backgrounds from the World Wide Web. You can also create your own in an image-editing program.

Yahoo is your entry to tons of background archives on the Web. Visit `http://www.yahoo.com/Computers_and_Internet/Internet/World_Wide_Web/Page_Design_and_Layout/Backgrounds/`.

If you decide to use a background image, choose one that harmonizes with the image and text colors in your site. If the image is too busy, the background may obscure the text, making the page difficult to read. Additionally, background images, as do inline images, add time to your page's total download speed. The smaller and simpler your background image is, the faster the page loads.

To create a background image, follow these steps:

1. **With a page open in the Editor, choose F̲ormat⇨Bac̲kground.**

   The Page Properties dialog box appears, with the Background tab visible.

2. **In the Background tab, select the Background I̲mage check box.**

   The text box beneath the check box turns from gray to white, indicating that you can type there.

3. **In the text box, type the URL of the image you want to use.**

   If you don't remember the URL, click the B̲rowse button to display the Select Background Image dialog box. As with the Image dialog box (which appears if you add an inline image to a page), the Select Background Image dialog box enables you to select an image in your Web site, an image stored elsewhere on your computer or on the Web, or a FrontPage clip-art image. (Refer to the steps outlined in the section "Adding an image to your page," earlier in the chapter, if you're not sure how to select an image from this dialog box.) After you select the image, the dialog box closes, and the image's URL appears in the Background Image text box of the Image Properties dialog box.

4. **If you want the background to appear fixed, select the W̲atermark check box.**

5. **Click OK to close the dialog box.**

   The background image appears in your page.

If the background image is from a file or FrontPage clip art, on saving the page, FrontPage offers to import the image file to your Web site. Click Yes to import the file.

You can choose a solid color as your page background instead of an image. Solid background colors load instantly and are often easier to coordinate with the color scheme of the page. To specify a background color, choose Format⇨Background to display the Background tab of the Page Properties dialog box. Select the color of your choice from the Background drop-down list and click OK. Alternatively, you can base the page's background color or image on that of another page in your Web site. For instructions on how to do so, refer to the section "Basing hyperlink colors on another page," in Chapter 6.

Deleting an Image

Erasing an image from your page hardly takes a thought. Just follow these steps:

1. **Click the image.**

2. **Press the Backspace or Delete key.**

   It's gone!

Browser offsets — what these things are and why you should care

If you intend to line up images and text in your page's foreground with the page's background image, you need to find out about pesky things called *browser offsets*.

If you place a word or image at the top of your Web page, where the element actually appears on-screen depends on which Web browser you use. Each browser nudges these elements (text, images, and tables) a few pixels over from the left edge of the browser window and a few pixels down from the top of the browser window. The problem is that the *amount* of offset varies depending on the browser. If you want to precisely place an element over a specific spot on your page's background image, this variation wreaks havoc, because the alignment is usually a few pixels off if viewed with another browser.

Right now, Microsoft Internet Explorer is the only browser that enables you to control the amount of offset by setting the margins in your Web page. (You may do so by choosing File⇨Page Properties to display the Page Properties dialog box, clicking the Margins tab, typing pixel values for the top and left margin of your page, and clicking OK.)

Web designer David Siegel discusses browser offsets in detail and has even invented a simple test that you can use to see different browser offsets in effect. Visit http://www.dsiegel.com/tips/wonk14.

Chapter 8
Creating an Image Map

• •

In This Chapter

▶ What's an image map?

▶ Choosing an image map style

▶ Choosing the best image

▶ Creating hotspots

• •

*I*mage maps are the stuff of which Web designer's dreams are made. Image maps look just like regular images, except that visitors can click different parts of the image to go somewhere else. Image maps pack a big visual punch while retaining the utility of a bunch of text hyperlinks. In this chapter, I show you how easy it is to transform a regular image into an image map.

What Is an Image Map?

An image map is simply a regular image that contains several invisible hyperlinks. Unlike a regular linked image, which leads to only one destination, an image map can lead to several. Visitors activate different hyperlinks by clicking different places inside the image (see Figure 8-1).

The clickable areas of the image are called *hotspots*. Similar to a regular hyperlink, a hotspot may link to another page in the Web site or to a location on the Internet.

The FrontPage Editor contains a nifty image map tool that enables you to turn regular images into image maps by drawing hotspots on the image of your choice using simple drawing tools (I show you how this is done in the section "Drawing hotspots," later in this chapter).

If you use an image map in your Web site, consider adding a list of matching text hyperlinks as well (as shown in Figure 8-1). Web surfers who browse the Web with their browser's image-loading function turned off cannot see both regular images and image maps and, therefore, must rely on the text hyperlinks to move around.

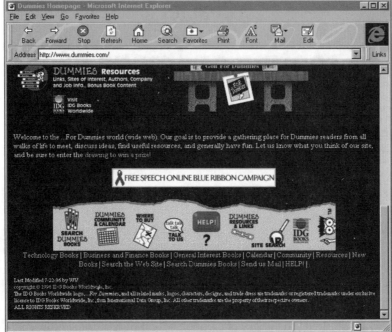

Figure 8-1:
The Dummies Press home page uses an image map to help visitors tour the site.

Choosing an Image Map Style

Before you begin drawing hotspots, you first must tell FrontPage what kind of image map to create. Image maps come in different styles, determined by the type of Web server program running on your host's machine. Each Web server program contains a special miniprogram called a *map program* that's in charge of activating image maps. Each time a visitor clicks an image map stored on that server, the map program springs into action, identifying which hotspot was clicked, matching the hotspot up with the corresponding hyperlink, and sending the visitor to that destination, all within the blink of an eye.

If you're publishing your Web site on a Web server that has FrontPage Server Extensions installed, you're in the clear. (See Chapter 18 for details on publishing your Web site.) FrontPage knows how to create and process its own special style of image map.

If you're publishing your Web site on a Web server that doesn't support FrontPage Server Extensions, you need to speak to the techie-in-charge to find out what type of map program the server uses. All servers use one of three types of map programs: *NCSA, CERN,* or *Netscape* (all corresponding to different types of server programs).

You also need to ask this person the *path,* or the location in the server's internal system of files, to the map program so that after a visitor clicks the image map, the map program can find and activate the image map.

Finally, you need to decide whether to instruct FrontPage to create a *client-side image map.* A client-side image map needs no server-based map program; instead, the Web browser knows how to process the image map information (hence the name *client-side*). Which type of map program you use doesn't really matter to your visitors, but the client-side version puts less of a load on the server, which can now shirk its image map duties. The result is a more nimble image map (and everyone knows how precious speed is).

But (and you *always* find a *but* hiding there somewhere)....

Client-side image maps are relatively new players in the Web-publishing arena, and so older browsers don't know how to process the client-side variety. Have no fear — FrontPage gives you the best of both worlds. You can construct both a client-side *and* a server-side image map at the same time so that every browser remains happy.

To choose an image map style for your Web site, follow these steps:

1. **Open the Web site in the FrontPage Explorer.**

   For details on how to open a Web site, refer to Chapter 1.

2. **Choose Tools⊅Web Settings.**

   The FrontPage Web Settings dialog box appears.

3. **Click the Advanced tab to make the tab visible.**

4. **In the Style drop-down list, select the image map style that's specific to your host Web server.**

   The default setting is FrontPage, so if your server supports FrontPage Server Extensions, leave the default setting alone. If you want to create *only* a client-side image map, select <none>. (I wouldn't make this selection if I were you, however, because if you do, you leave those visitors to your site who use older browsers out in the cold.)

5. **If you selected a style *other* than FrontPage in the previous step, enter the path to your host server's map program in the Prefix text box.**

   FrontPage automatically fills in the common path for each type of image map style. You need to double-check the path with your tech person, however, because each system has its own setup.

6. **Select the Generate client-side image maps check box to have FrontPage generate a client-side image map in addition to a server-side image map.**

   Why not? You may as well create client-side image maps for those among your visitors who can use this variety.

7. **Click OK to close the FrontPage Web settings dialog box.**

   A FrontPage Explorer dialog box pops up, telling you that it needs to recalculate the Web site (that is, to re-retrieve the Web from the server) to put the new settings into effect.

8. **Click Yes to recalculate the Web site.**

   FrontPage recalculates the Web site, and you're all set to create your image map.

If you create non-FrontPage server-side image maps, FrontPage creates a separate file — the *map file* — and places the file in a folder in your Web site called _VTI_MAP. The map file is a text file that lists the coordinates of the image map's hotspots and their associated URLs. When you publish your Web site, you need to transfer the map file along with the rest of the Web's files. For details, jump to Chapter 18.

FrontPage commits a major boo-boo if you use the program to create non-FrontPage image maps. If your image map is server-side; NCSA-, CERN-, or Netscape-style; and part of a "per-user" Web site — that is, one of many Web sites hosted on the same server that are separated by individual accounts (which is how most Internet service providers work) — FrontPage can't set up your image map correctly.

You do, however, have recourse to a simple, but rather tedious, workaround for this problem. The Microsoft Knowledge Base, an extensive online customer-support database, explains the workaround in detail. Point your Web browser to `http://www.microsoft.com/kb` and search for article number Q154598 (the article number for the workaround). Read the article and follow its directions to the letter.

Choosing the Best Image

You don't want to turn just any old image into an image map. Because hotspots are invisible to the visitor, the image you choose should clearly indicate where to click, either with the help of a visual metaphor (buttons, for example) or with text labels (`click here to find out more`).

After you choose your image, in the Editor, open the page in which you want the image map to appear and insert the image. (Refer to Chapter 7 if you're not sure how to insert an image into a Web page.)

Creating Hotspots

Here's the fun part of creating an image map: creating the *hotspots*. Hotspots are areas inside the graphic that contain hyperlinks and can be clicked to go somewhere new.

Drawing hotspots

You use tools available in FrontPage Editor's Image toolbar to draw hotspots; you draw rectangles, circles, and multisided shapes (also known as *polygons*) around the areas you want to make clickable. Hotspots are visible only if the image map is selected in the Editor. If viewed with a browser, hotspots are invisible.

To draw hotspots, follow these steps:

1. **Insert the image map image into your page.**

   Chapter 7 explains how to insert images.

2. **Click the image.**

   The Image toolbar appears.

    3. **Depending on the shape of the area that you want to define, click the Rectangle, Circle, or Polygon tool.**

   If you're not sure which tool to choose, just pick the one you think best approximates the shape of the area you want to turn into a hotspot. You can always move or reshape the hotspot later — or delete the hotspot and start again.

4. **Move the cursor over the image.**

   The pointer turns into a little pencil.

5. **Click the hotspot area and drag the cursor until the resulting hotspot surrounds the area.**

   If you chose the Rectangle, click the corner of your hotspot area and drag the rectangle until the shape surrounds the area. If you chose the Circle, click the center of the hotspot area and drag. (The circle expands from its center point.) If you chose the Polygon, creating a hotspot is like stretching a rubber band between fixed points: Click the first point, release the mouse button, and then drag the mouse pointer. (This action produces a line.) Stretch the line to the second point — click, stretch, click, stretch — until you enclose your hotspot area. After you're finished defining the hotspot, double-click, and FrontPage closes the hotspot for you.

You can overlap hotspots. If you do so, the most recent hotspot is "on top," which means that this hotspot takes priority if you click the over-lapped area.

After you draw the hotspot, the hotspot border appears on top of your image, and the Create Hyperlink dialog box appears, enabling you to attach a hyperlink to the hotspot.

6. **Create a link for the hotspot, just as you would a regular hyperlink.**

   Refer to Chapter 6 if you're not sure how to create hyperlinks.

7. **Keep creating hotspots of any shape until you define all the clickable areas inside the image.**

   Areas not covered by a hotspot can't do anything if clicked unless you specify a default hyperlink. (I show you how in the section "Setting the Default Hyperlink," later in this chapter).

8. **When you're done, click anywhere outside the image to hide the hotspot borders.**

If you later want to change the destination of the image map's hot spots, click the image to make the hot spots visible and double-click the hotspot to open the Edit Hyperlink dialog box. Make any changes you want and click OK to close the dialog box.

Moving hotspots

If the placement of a hotspot isn't just so, move that hotspot — by following these simple steps:

1. **Click the image map to make its hotspots visible.**

   Don't worry — image maps aren't modest.

2. **Click the hotspot that you want to move.**

   You can tell whether you selected a hotspot because *size handles* that look like little square points appear on its border after you select the hotspot.

3. **Drag the hotspot to a new location inside the image and drop it there.**

Resizing hotspots

Hotspots are as malleable as taffy. Adjusting their shapes and sizes is easy. Just follow these steps:

1. **Click the image map to make its hotspots visible.**

2. **Click the hotspot you want to resize.**

   Size handles appear.

3. **Click a size handle and drag the handle until the hotspot is the size or shape you want.**

Size handles act differently depending on the shape of the hotspot. Working with handles, unfortunately, is not yet a precise science. Just keep clicking, dragging, and stretching until you're happy with the results. If you can't bully the hotspot into the right shape or size, delete the little pest and draw a new one.

Deleting hotspots

Sometimes, no amount of coaxing gets a stubborn hotspot into shape. Those times call for drastic action — so delete the recalcitrant hotspot and draw a new one. Just follow these steps:

1. **Click the image map to make its hotspots visible.**

2. **Click the hotspot that you want to delete.**

3. **Press the Backspace or Delete key.**

If you want to replace the deleted hot spot with a new one, refer to the section "Drawing hotspots," earlier in this chapter.

Setting the Default Hyperlink

You can also set up the image map's *default hyperlink*. Visitors jump to the destination of the default hyperlink if they click anywhere on the image map *not* defined by a hotspot. If you forego the default hyperlink, clicking an undefined area does nothing.

To set an image map's default hyperlink, follow these steps:

1. **Right-click the image map and choose Image Properties.**

   Or click the image and select Edit⇨Image Properties or press Alt+Enter.

   The Image Properties dialog box appears, with the General tab visible.

2. **In the Default hyperlink area, type the default hyperlink URL in the**
Location text box.

If you can't remember the URL, click the Browse button to display the
Create Hyperlink dialog box. Chapter 6 contains complete instructions for
using this dialog box.

After you specify the URL, the Create Hyperlink dialog box closes, and the
URL appears in the Location text box of the Image Properties dialog box.

3. **Click OK to close the dialog box.**

The Editor applies the default hyperlink to the image map.

To test drive the image map, click one of the image map hotspots and choose
Tools⇨Follow Hyperlink. The destination page opens in the Editor.

Chapter 9

You Don't Have to Take Wood Shop to Build a Table

● ●

In This Chapter

▶ What's a table good for?

▶ Creating a table

▶ Inserting stuff into a table (including another table)

▶ Selecting part or all of a table

▶ Editing a table

▶ Adding color to a table

▶ Deleting a table

● ●

*P*ut away that hacksaw! True, after you finish this chapter, you can build a table — but not the kind at which one plays cards with buddies. No, in this chapter, I introduce you to the wonders of the *table,* a lovable layout tool that shows up in the best-designed pages on the Web.

What's a Table Good For?

Both left- and right-brained Web publishers *love* tables.

Left-brained, well-organized types use tables to create grids of information, similar to a spreadsheet or a chart. Tables cordon off individual bits of data into *cells,* which are arranged in horizontal rows and vertical columns (see Figure 9-1).

Row   Column

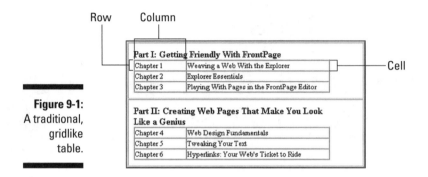

Cell

Figure 9-1:
A traditional,
gridlike
table.

Right-brained, creative types use tables to structure the layout of the page.
Tables without defined borders create an invisible framework into which you
can place chunks of text, images, and even other tables (see Figure 9-2).
The result is a layout similar to what you could achieve by using a desktop-
publishing program — you can place elements anywhere on the page you want.
Invisible tables are a boon for designers who feel constrained by the traditional
one-paragraph-after-another Web page layout.

The HTML tags behind tables are rather cumbersome, causing newbie Web
publishers to shy away from using tables in their pages. FrontPage erases all
cause for alarm because table creation in FrontPage is now a snap. The only
power tool you need is your mouse.

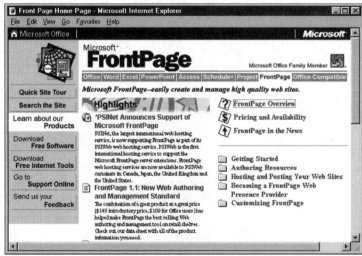

Figure 9-2:
Microsoft
structures
many of
its Web
pages with
invisible
tables.

Sadly, not all Web browsers can display tables. These table-impaired browsers display "tabled" sites as a heap of jumbled paragraphs. Although this problem isn't very common — most people use advanced browsers such as Netscape Navigator and Microsoft Internet Explorer — the situation still exists. Some Web publishers create an alternative set of pages that don't use tables. Others simply include a note that says something such as "You must view this site with a tables-capable browser," along with a link to the preferred browser's download sites. Although you can't always design your pages for the lowest common denominator of browser capabilities, you need to remain aware of how the Web's cross-platform nature affects the look of your site.

Creating an Empty Table

As do most tasks in the FrontPage Editor, creating a table takes the mere click of a button. From that humble beginning, you can add stuff to the table and edit the table's layout as much as you like.

To create a table, follow these steps:

1. **Open a page in the FrontPage Editor.**

2. **Place the cursor wherever in the page you want the table to appear.**

3. **Click the Insert Table button.**

   A grid of white boxes representing table rows and columns appears underneath the button.

   (If you prefer to set the table's layout details — its alignment, border size, and so on — at the same time as you create the table, choose Table⊃Insert Table instead of clicking the Insert Table button. I prefer to create the table first, insert my data, and *then* tinker with the layout. That way, I can see how the table looks with the information inside. I show you how to adjust your table's layout in the sections "Table Tinkering" and "Fiddling with Cells, Columns, and Rows," later in this chapter.)

4. **Click and drag your mouse pointer on the grid until the number of highlighted boxes equals the number of rows and columns that you want your table to contain (see Figure 9-3).**

   As you highlight boxes, the table dimensions appear at the bottom of the grid. If you drag past the last box in a column or row, the grid expands. If you don't know exactly how many rows or columns you need, just pick something close. You can always add rows and columns later.

5. **Release the mouse button.**

   A new, empty table appears in your page.

Figure 9-3:
Highlight the
squares that
correspond
to the
dimensions
you want.

3 by 4 Table

The dashed lines surrounding each table cell tell you that you're working with an invisible table — that is, one with no defined borders. (If you don't see any dashed lines, click the Show/Hide ¶ button.) If you look at your new empty table in a Web browser right now, you won't see a thing. I show you how to add borders in the section called "Setting border thickness," later in this chapter.

FrontPage can convert Word tables and Excel spreadsheets into Web page tables. Just cut and paste portions of a Word or Excel file into an open page in the Editor or open the entire file in the Editor. (I show you how to open non-Web page documents in the Editor in Chapter 3.)

Inserting Stuff into a Table (Including Another Table)

You can insert anything into a table cell that you would add to a regular page: text, images, form fields, WebBots — even other tables. Simply click inside a cell and proceed as usual. The height and width of the cell stretches to accommodate whatever you place inside.

Text entered into a cell *wraps* as you type, which means that, when the text reaches a cell boundary, the word being typed jumps down to a new line. You enter new paragraphs in a cell by pressing Enter and regular line breaks by pressing Shift+Enter. If you're ready to type text in another cell, press Tab until the cursor ends up in your destination cell — and type away.

Table Tinkering

After you plug stuff into your table, you can tinker with the table's layout until the thing looks just the way you want.

Aligning a table on the page

You can left-align, right-align, or center a table on the page. Just follow these steps:

1. **Right-click anywhere inside the table and choose Table Properties from the pop-up menu (or choose Table⇨Table Properties from the menu bar).**

   The Table Properties dialog box appears (see Figure 9-4).

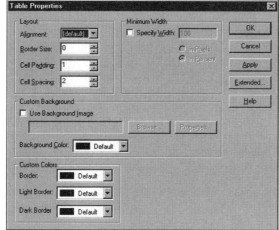

Figure 9-4:
The Table
Properties
dialog box.

2. **Choose an option from the Alignment drop-down list box.**

   Your choices are (default), Left, Center, and Right. The (default) option uses the visitor's default browser alignment setting, which is left aligned.

3. **Click the Apply button to see how the change looks before you close the dialog box; if you like what you see, click OK, and you're on your way.**

   If you don't like what you see, select a new option from the Alignment drop-down list or click Cancel to close the dialog box without making any changes.

   After you click OK, the dialog box closes, and the table alignment changes accordingly.

Setting border thickness

In FrontPage, tables are born without borders. If you add borders, you transform the table into a traditional spreadsheetlike grid, perfect for rows of numbers or a quick game of tic-tac-toe.

Two types of borders are available: those surrounding individual cells and those surrounding the entire table. Cell borders can be only one pixel thick. Table borders, however, can be of any thickness.

To add borders to a table, follow these steps:

1. **Right-click anywhere inside the table and choose Table Properties from the pop-up menu.**

   Or choose Table⇨Table Properties from the menu bar.

   The Table Properties dialog box appears.

2. **In the Border Size text box, type the thickness (in pixels) of your table borders.**

   Whatever number you type only applies to table borders; cell borders are always 1 pixel thick.

3. **Click OK.**

   The dialog box closes, and borders appear in your table.

Borders look different depending on which browser you use. Some browsers display borders as solid black lines. Others display raised lines, similar to what you see in the FrontPage Editor.

Padded cells

What do mental institutions and tables in Web pages have in common? Don't worry: I intend to spare you the answer to that one. Sufficient, I think, to say is that adding space between the contents of table cells and the cell borders is called *padding*. Padded cells open up a table by placing white space around the contents of each cell. Figures 9-5 and 9-6 illustrate the difference a little padding makes.

Figure 9-5:
A table with
no cell
padding.

Chapter 1	Weaving a Web With the Explorer
Chapter 2	Explorer Essentials
Chapter 3	Playing With Pages in the FrontPage Editor

Figure 9-6:
A table with
5 pixels
of cell
padding.

Chapter 1	Weaving a Web With the Explorer
Chapter 2	Explorer Essentials
Chapter 3	Playing With Pages in the FrontPage Editor

To pad cells, follow these steps:

1. **Right-click anywhere inside the table and choose Table Properties from the pop-up menu (or choose Table⇨Table Properties from the menu bar).**

   The Table Properties dialog box appears.

2. **In the Cell Padding text box, type the amount of white space (in pixels) separating cell contents from cell borders.**

3. **Click OK.**

   The dialog box closes, and the table's cell padding changes accordingly.

Adding space between cells

Cell spacing determines how much space exists between cells and also affects the appearance of table and cell borders. Figures 9-7 and 9-8 illustrate how changes in cell spacing affect the look of a table.

Figure 9-7:
A table with
a 1-pixel
border and
no cell
spacing.

Chapter 1	Weaving a Web With the Explorer
Chapter 2	Explorer Essentials
Chapter 3	Playing With Pages in the FrontPage Editor

Figure 9-8:
A table with
a 1-pixel
border and 5
pixels of cell
spacing.

Chapter 1	Weaving a Web With the Explorer
Chapter 2	Explorer Essentials
Chapter 3	Playing With Pages in the FrontPage Editor

To change cell spacing, follow these steps:

1. **Right-click anywhere inside the table and choose Table Properties from the pop-up menu.**

   Or choose T<u>a</u>ble⇨Table <u>P</u>roperties from the menu bar.

   The Table Properties dialog box appears.

2. **In the Cell <u>S</u>pacing text box, type the amount of space (in pixels) separating table cells.**

3. **Click OK.**

   The dialog box closes, and the table's cell spacing changes accordingly.

Setting table width

You can control the width of your table. You have two options: You can give the table an *absolute width* (a fixed measurement), or you can give the table a *proportional width* (based on the width of the visitor's browser window).

Opting for absolute table widths is tempting because you retain total control over the table size. Consider, however, the poor visitor who sees your page using a tiny monitor. That visitor may need to scroll all around the page to see the table in its entirety and may curse the inconsiderate, controlling Web designer who created such a table.

By using a proportional table width, you enable the visitor's browser window to determine the width of the table. You give up precise control, but your visitor gets to see the entire table, no matter what the monitor size used.

Which do you choose? The choice depends on how you use your table. If the overall table structure is more important than the precise placement of its contents, use proportional width. If you require control, use absolute width.

To set table width, follow these steps:

1. **Right-click anywhere inside the table and choose Table Properties from the pop-up menu.**

   Or choose T<u>a</u>ble⇨Table <u>P</u>roperties from the menu bar.

   The Table Properties dialog box appears.

2. **In the Minimum Width area, select the Specify <u>W</u>idth check box.**

   The rest of the area comes into full view.

3. **In the Specify Width text box, type the width of the table.**

   If you are specifying a proportional width, type the width of the table as a percentage of the width of the browser window. For example, if you type 50, FrontPage sets the width of the table at 50 percent, or half the width of the browser window.

   If you are specifying an absolute width, type the table width in pixels.

4. **Select the radio button that corresponds to the measurement you specified in step 3.**

   If you are specifying a proportional width, select the in Percent radio button. If you are specifying an absolute width, select the in Pixels radio button.

5. **Click OK.**

   The dialog box closes, and the table width changes accordingly.

 Want to see how your table looks if viewed though a small monitor or a monitor with low resolution? Choose File⇨Preview in Browser to display the Preview in Browser dialog box, select the 640 x 480 radio button, and click Preview to open the page in your Web browser.

Fiddling with Cells, Columns, and Rows

In addition to tinkering with the table as a whole, you can fiddle with the layout and structure of individual table cells, rows, and columns.

Selecting table parts

Selecting table parts. . . . It sounds like something you do at a hardware store. Well, in this section I don't discuss buying lumber or wood screws; I talk about how to highlight, or select, different parts of your table in order to format those parts in some way.

At times throughout the rest of the chapter, I instruct you to select cells, columns, and rows. Here's how you do it:

✔ **Cells:** To select a cell, choose Table⇨Select Cell. Or you can move the cursor toward the edge of a cell until the cursor turns into a pointer and then double-click to select the cell. To select more than one cell, after selecting the first cell, press and hold the Shift key and click other table cells.

✔ **Columns:** To select a column, choose Table⇨Select Column. Or pass the cursor over the table until the cursor hovers just above a column. The cursor turns into a stubby arrow pointing down. Click once to select the column. To select more than one column, after selecting the first column, press and hold the mouse button and drag until you highlight the area you want.

✔ **Rows:** To select a row, choose Table⇨Select Row. Or pass the cursor over the left side of the table until the cursor hovers just to the left of a row. The cursor turns into a stubby arrow pointing to the right. Click once to select the row. To select more than one row, after selecting the first row, press and hold the mouse button and drag until you highlight the area you want.

Adding new columns

Adding a new column to your table couldn't be easier. To add a new column to an existing table, follow these steps:

1. **Click inside the column next to where you want the new column to appear.**

2. **Choose Table⇨Insert Rows or Columns.**

    The Insert Rows or Columns dialog box appears.

3. **Select the Columns radio button.**

4. **In the Number of Columns text box, type the number of columns you want to add.**

5. **Choose whether you want the new column(s) to appear to the left or right of the selection.**

    Select the radio button next to either Left of selection or Right of selection. The *selection* refers to the spot where you originally clicked in step 1.

6. **Click OK.**

    The dialog box closes, and the new column (or columns) appears inside your table.

Adding new rows

Adding new rows is just as easy as adding columns. To add a new row to an existing table, follow these steps:

1. **Click inside the row next to where you want the new row to appear.**

2. **Choose Table⇨Insert Rows or Columns.**

   The Insert Rows or Columns dialog box appears.

3. **Select the Rows radio button.**

4. **In the Number of Rows text box, type the number of rows you want to add.**

5. **Choose whether you want the new row(s) to appear above or below the selection.**

   Select the radio button next to either Above selection or Below selection. The *selection* refers to the spot where you originally clicked in step 1.

6. **Click OK.**

   The dialog box closes, and the new row (or rows) appears inside your table.

Deleting columns and rows

Want to shave a row or column off of your table? No problem. Just follow these steps:

1. **Select the row(s) or column(s) that you want to consign to oblivion.**

   Refer to the section "Selecting table parts," earlier in this chapter, if you're not sure how to select a row or column.

2. **Press the Backspace or Delete key.**

   The table rows or columns and their contents disappear.

Adding new cells

If want to add a single cell, rather than an entire row or column, you can do that, too. Just follow these steps:

1. **Click inside the cell next to where you want the new cell to appear.**

   If the selected cell is empty, the new cell automatically appears to the right. If the selected cell contains something (text, an image, or a form field), clicking to the *left* of the contents causes the new cell to appear to the left. Clicking to the *right* of the contents causes the new cell to appear to the right.

2. **Choose Table⇨Insert Cell.**

   A new cell appears.

Deleting cells

To delete table cells, follow these steps:

1. **Select the cell(s) that you want to delete.**

   Refer to the section "Selecting table parts," earlier in the chapter, if you're not sure how to select cells.

2. **Press the Backspace or Delete key.**

   Cell(s) all gone.

Aligning cell contents

You can control the horizontal (left and right) and vertical (up and down) alignment of the stuff inside table cells. By selecting several cells, a row or column, or even the entire table, you can apply alignment controls to a group of cells in one fell swoop.

To align cell contents, follow these steps:

1. **Select the cells, rows, or columns that you want to format.**

   Refer to the section "Selecting table parts," earlier in the chapter, if you're not sure how to select a cell, row, or column.

2. **Right-click the selection and choose Cell Properties from the pop-up menu.**

   Or choose Table⇨Cell Properties.

   The Cell Properties dialog box appears (see Figure 9-9).

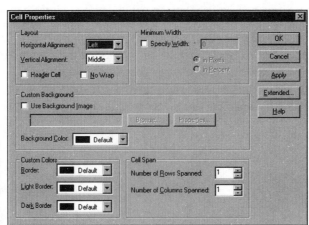

Figure 9-9:
The Cell
Properties
dialog box.

3. **From the Horizontal Alignment drop-down list, select Left, Center, or Right.**

   Left aligns cell contents with the left cell border. Center centers the contents of the cell. Right aligns cell contents with the right cell border.

4. **From the Vertical Alignment drop-down list, select Top, Middle, or Bottom.**

   Top aligns cell contents with the top cell border. Middle centers the contents of the cell. Bottom aligns cell contents with the bottom cell border.

5. **Click OK.**

   The dialog box closes, and cell alignment changes accordingly.

Two options share the Layout area of the Cell Properties dialog box with the Horizontal and Vertical Alignment drop-down lists: the Header Cell check box and the No Wrap check box (refer to Figure 9-9).

✔ The Header Cell check box simply applies a boldface font to whatever text the selected cell contains. If I want bold type, I prefer to use the Bold font format, just to keep things consistent.

✔ The No Wrap check box, when selected, turns off automatic text wrapping inside cells.

Changing cell and column width

Controlling the width of table cells (and by extension, entire columns) is similar to working with table width: You can set an absolute width in pixels or a proportional width based on the width of the entire table. (Refer to the section "Setting table width," earlier in this chapter, for a detailed discussion of the pros and cons of absolute versus proportional width.)

To set an absolute cell/column width, follow these steps:

1. **Select the cells or columns you want to format.**

   Refer to the section "Selecting table parts," earlier in this chapter, if you're not sure how to select a cell or column.

2. **Right-click the selection and choose Cell Properties from the pop-up menu.**

   Or choose Table➪Cell Properties.

   The Cell Properties dialog box appears.

Tables and tribulations

FrontPage contains a nasty bug (or is this quirk actually a feature?) that enables you to set the width of table columns to a number not equal to the total width of the table. If you set the width of a two-column table to 100 pixels, for example, you could set the width of each column to a number totaling more or less than 100.

The Editor's WYSIWYG display also gets confused if you set different widths for individual table cells (as opposed to entire columns of cells), especially if the table is complex.

The solution is to keep your tables relatively simple and to vary the width of entire columns rather than individual cells. And you *must* preview your page in a Web browser (preferably more than one model) to see how your table looks to your visitors.

3. In the Minimum Width area, select the Specify Width check box.

The rest of the area comes into full view.

4. In the Specify Width text box, type the width of the cell or column.

If you are specifying a proportional width, type the width of the cell or column as a percentage of the width of the table. For example, if you type 50, FrontPage sets the width of the cell or column at 50 percent, or half the width of table.

If you are specifying an absolute width, type the width in pixels.

5. Select the radio button that corresponds to the measurement you specified in step 4.

If you are specifying a proportional width, select the in Percent radio button. If you are specifying an absolute width, select the in Pixels radio button.

6. Click OK.

The dialog box closes, and the cell or column width changes accordingly.

Merging and splitting cells

If you merge cells, you erase the borders between these combined cells, creating one big cell. Splitting cells divides one cell into several, arranged in rows or columns.

To merge cells, follow these steps:

1. Select the cells that you want to merge.

Refer to the section "Selecting table parts," earlier in the chapter, if you're not sure how to select a cell.

2. Choose Table⇨Merge Cells.

The cells merge into a single cell.

To split cells, follow these steps:

1. Select the cell or cells that you want to split.

Refer to the section "Selecting table parts," earlier in the chapter, if you're not sure how to select cells.

2. Choose Table⇨Split Cells.

The Split Cells dialog box appears (see Figure 9-10).

Figure 9-10:
The Split
Cells dialog
box.

3. Select the Split into Columns radio button to split the cell(s) vertically or select the Split into Rows radio button to split the cell(s) horizontally.

Depending on which option you select, the box next to the radio buttons shows a representation of how the cell will look after it is split.

4. In the Number of Rows text box, type the number of cells into which you want to divide the cell.

5. Click OK.

The dialog box closes, and the selected cells split.

To return split cells to their previous state, select the split cells and choose Table⇨Merge Cells.

Adding a Caption

You can easily add a *caption* to your table — a bit of descriptive text that sits just above or below the table.

To add a caption, follow these steps:

1. **Click anywhere inside the table.**

2. **Choose Table⇨Insert Caption.**

   The cursor hops to an empty space above the table.

3. **Type the caption text.**

To move the caption underneath the table, follow these steps:

1. **Right-click the caption and choose Caption Properties from the pop-up menu.**

   Or click inside the caption and choose Table⇨Caption Properties.

   The Caption Properties dialog box appears.

2. **Select the Bottom of Table radio button and click OK.**

   The cursor moves to an empty space beneath the table.

Adding Color to a Table

Here's a nifty design effect: You can apply color to the background of your table, down to the individual cell. You can also change the color of table and cell borders.

Changing the background

You can apply a solid background color or a background image to a table or cell, just as you can to an entire page. (I show you how to change your page's background in Chapter 7.)

Unfortunately, advanced browsers are the only ones capable of displaying table background color. And as of this writing, only Internet Explorer (Version 3.0 or later) can display background table images.

Adding background color

To add a background color to a table or cell, follow these steps:

1. **If you're changing the background of the entire table, right-click inside the table and choose Table Properties from the pop-up menu.**

   Or choose Table⇨Table Properties from the menu bar.

   If you're changing the background of selected cells, right-click the selection and choose Cell Properties from the pop-up menu. (Or choose Table⇨Cell Properties from the menu bar.)

   Refer to the section "Selecting table parts," earlier in the chapter, if you're not sure how to select different parts of a table.

   Depending on your choice, the Table Properties or Cell Properties dialog box appears.

2. **Choose a background color from the Background Color drop-down list.**

   If you choose Custom, the Color dialog box appears. The workings of this dialog box are fully explained in Chapter 5.

3. **Click OK.**

   The dialog box closes, and the background color appears in the table or selected cells.

Adding a background image

To add a background image to a table or cell, follow these steps:

1. **If you're changing the background of the entire table, right-click inside the table and choose Table Properties from the pop-up menu.**

   Or choose Table⇨Table Properties from the menu bar.

   If you're changing the background of selected cells, right-click the selection and choose Cell Properties from the pop-up menu. (Or choose Table⇨Cell Properties from the menu bar.)

   Refer to the section "Selecting table parts," earlier in the chapter, if you're not sure how to select different parts of a table.

   Depending on your choice, the Table Properties or Cell Properties dialog box appears.

2. **In the Custom Background area, select the Use Background Image check box.**

   The accompanying text box turns from gray to white, indicating you can type there.

3. **Type the URL of the background image in the text box.**

    If you don't remember the URL, click the Browse button to display the Select Background Image dialog box. This dialog box enables you to select an image in your Web site, an image stored elsewhere on your computer or on the Web, or a FrontPage clip art image. (Refer to the steps outlined in Chapter 7 if you're not sure how to select an image from this dialog box.) After you select the image, the dialog box closes, and the image's URL appears in the text box of the Table Properties (or Cell Properties) dialog box.

    While you're here, select a complimentary background color at the same time. That way, those of your visitors using an advanced browser other than Internet Explorer (who, therefore, can't see the background image) still see a similar effect.

4. **Click OK.**

    The dialog box closes, and the background image appears in the table or selected cells.

Changing border color

You also can change the color of table and cell borders.

As of this writing, however, *only* those of your visitors using Internet Explorer (Version 3.0 or later) can see the color changes. Until more browsers support border color, I recommend using this feature sparingly.

You can use color to create two different visual effects: a flat table with solid borders or a raised table, where you use light and dark colors to simulate shadows. (Figures 9-11 and 9-12 show examples of each table's effect.)

Figure 9-11:
A flat table.

Chapter 1	Weaving a Web With the Explorer
Chapter 2	Explorer Essentials
Chapter 3	Playing With Pages in the FrontPage Editor

Figure 9-12:
A raised table.

Chapter 1	Weaving a Web With the Explorer
Chapter 2	Explorer Essentials
Chapter 3	Playing With Pages in the FrontPage Editor

Changing table border color

To change table border color, follow these steps:

1. **Right-click anywhere inside the table and choose Table Properties from the pop-up menu.**

   Or choose Table➪Table Properties from the menu bar.

   The Table Properties dialog box appears.

2. **Select a border color from the drop-down lists in the Custom Color area.**

   To create a flat table, select a color from the Border drop-down list. To create a raised table, leave the Border color on the Default setting and choose colors from the Light Border and Dark Border drop-down lists.

   If you choose Custom, the Color dialog box appears. The workings of this dialog box are fully explained in Chapter 5.

3. **Click OK.**

   The dialog box closes, and the table borders change color.

Changing cell border color

To change cell border color, follow these steps:

1. **Select the cells that you want to format.**

   Refer to the section "Selecting table parts," earlier in the chapter, if you're not sure how to select cells.

2. **Right-click the selection and choose Cell Properties.**

   Or choose Table➪Cell Properties.

   The Cell Properties dialog box appears.

3. **Select a border color from the drop-down lists in the Custom Color area.**

   As with table border color, you may select *either* a full border color *or* light and dark border colors.

4. **Click OK.**

   The dialog box closes, and the cell borders change color.

Deleting a Table

To delete a table, follow these steps:

1. **Select the entire table.**

   Do so by double-clicking the blank area to the left of the table or by choosing Table⇨Select Table.

2. **Press the Backspace or Delete key.**

   Your table goes off to table heaven.

Chapter 10

Forms Aren't Only for the IRS

● ●

In This Chapter

▶ What's a form?

▶ Creating a form

▶ Working with form fields

▶ Submitting form data

▶ Creating a confirmation page

● ●

*W*hat is the first thing that pops into your mind when I say "forms"? Let me guess: bureaucracy-perpetuating pieces of paper, or worse, multipage monstrosities in triplicate. Well, put those thoughts aside for a moment, because I'd like to introduce you to the wonders of the *interactive form.*

Interactive forms transform your Web site from a showpiece into a workhorse. Here are a few of the amazing things you can do with forms:

✔ Survey your visitors and ask their opinions about things.

✔ If you're hosting a conference, enable attendees to register for the event online.

✔ Enable visitors to search the contents of your site for key words.

✔ Host an interactive discussion forum, where visitors post their thoughts on a continuously updated Web page.

✔ Promote community by creating a guest book that visitors "sign" by submitting a form.

And you don't need to hire an accountant to help you.

How Do Forms Work?

As do paper forms, interactive forms collect different types of information. Web site visitors fill in *fields*, either by entering information or selecting an item from a list (see Figure 10-1). After the visitors complete the form, they click a button to submit the information.

The information submitted from forms is organized into a list of *name/value pairs*. The *name* is a unique identifying label assigned to each field in your form. The field name is invisible to your visitors; it exists inside the form's HTML and is only visible to the person receiving the information submitted from the form. The labels you see in Figure 10-1 — Name, Your favorite ice cream flavor, and so on — are regular Web page text and simply prompt the visitor to fill in certain information.

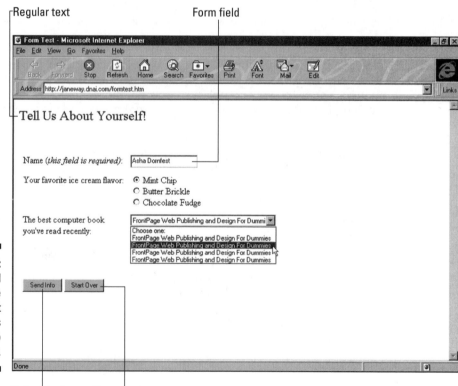

Regular text   Form field

Figure 10-1:
A typical Web page form, as it appears in a Web browser.

Submit button   Reset button

The *value* is the information submitted by the visitor. Depending on the type of field, the value is either the stuff the visitor types or an item the visitor chooses from a list you define. (In Figure 10-1, the value of the first field is Asha Dornfest.)

What happens to that information after a visitor submits the completed form depends on the type of *form handler* assigned to the form. A form handler is a Web server-based program that receives the form data and then does something with it. Depending on the type of form handler, the program may save the data (also known as the *form results*) in a text file or format the results as a Web page.

If this procedure sounds difficult or overly technical, don't worry. The FrontPage Editor takes care of all the hard stuff. All you need to do is decide how you want to use forms in your Web site.

All FrontPage forms use form-related WebBots — special components that add interactive capabilities to FrontPage Webs. (I talk more about form-related WebBots in the section "Choosing a form handler," later in this chapter, and about other WebBots in Chapter 12.) For form-related WebBots to work, you must publish your Web site on a server that supports FrontPage Server Extensions. If your Web server doesn't support FrontPage Server Extensions, you can still use FrontPage form templates, but you need to select a form handler that works with your server. I reveal all in the section "Choosing a form handler," later in this chapter.

Creating a Form

After that rah-rah introduction, no doubt you're pumped up and ready for some serious form creation. The FrontPage Editor is happy to oblige.

You have three choices in creating a new form: You can use a prefab form-page template; you can tag along with the FrontPage Form Page Wizard; or you can add your own form to an existing Web page.

After you finish your form, you must preview the page in a Web browser to get an accurate picture of how the form will look and act after your Web site is published. Form fields, as displayed in the Editor, look somewhat different when seen with a Web browser. More importantly, the only way to test a form (by filling out the form and submitting it) is to do so using a Web browser. To preview your form page, click the Preview in Browser button (or, choose File⇨Preview in Browser) to view and test the form in a Web browser.

Using a template

The trusty Editor contains templates for the most common types of forms that show up in Web sites, as described in the following list:

- ✔ **Feedback Form:** The Feedback Form template creates a form visitors use to send comments, questions, or suggestions.

- ✔ **Guest Book:** The Guest Book template also collects comments but, in its case, saves the submissions in a public Web page that other visitors can read.

- ✔ **Product or Event Registration:** This template creates a registration form that attendees can use to sign up for an event or that customers can use to register a product.

- ✔ **Search Page:** This template works with the Search WebBot to create a searchable key-word index of your FrontPage Web. You find out how to use this feature in Chapter 12.

- ✔ **Survey Form:** The Survey Form template creates a multisection survey, perfect for collecting focused product feedback, marketing information, or public opinion.

- ✔ **User Registration:** The User Registration template creates a registration page that enables visitors to choose a unique user name and password to gain access to a members-only section of the Web site. You discover how to use this feature in Chapter 14.

I also include a custom-designed feedback form template on the CD that comes with this book. (Between you and me, the custom template is *much* more attractive than the Editor's built-in Feedback Form template.) For instructions on how to access the custom template, see Appendix C.

To create a form by using a form page template, follow these steps:

1. **In the Editor, choose File⇨New (or press Crtl+N).**

   The New Page dialog box appears.

2. **From the Template or Wizard list, double-click the name of the template that you want to use.**

   A new page based on the template opens in the Editor.

3. **Customize the page to suit your needs.**

   The purple comments at the top of the page give you hints as to how to proceed with this task (but, then again, so do the sections "Working with Form Fields" and "Submitting Form Results," later in this chapter).

Inside the page, the form consists of all the stuff contained within a box surrounded by dashed borders, as shown in Figure 10-2. (If you don't see this box, click the Show/Hide ¶ button.) The rest of what appears on-screen is a regular old Web page. Treat the entire page (including text inside the form) just as you would any Web page: format the text, insert a few graphics — whatever you want.

Using the Form Page Wizard

The Form Page Wizard possesses magical powers — at least, that's what *I* thought when I saw how easy this Wizard makes creating a form. The Wizard walks you through the entire process of creating a customized form, including choosing form fields, suggesting questions to include for different types of information, setting up the layout of the page, choosing a form handler, and deciding how to format form results.

 Unless you have a Web form or two under your belt, you may not understand some of the Form Page Wizard's options at first glance. For that reason, I recommend skimming this entire chapter first to familiarize yourself with forms and only then activating the Wizard. Not only does everything make sense after you do so, but you also realize just how ingenious the Form Page Wizard really is.

The form consists of the stuff inside this box

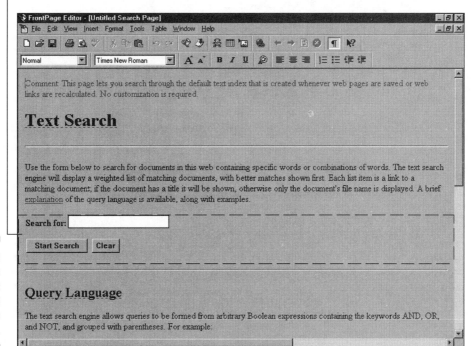

Figure 10-2:
The Search Form template, as it appears in the Editor.

To create a form with the help of the Form Page Wizard, follow these steps:

1. **In the Editor, choose File⇨New (or press Crtl+N).**

   The New Page dialog box appears.

2. **From the Template or Wizard list, double-click Form Page Wizard.**

   The Wizard opens (as shown in Figure 10-3). The opening dialog box explains what the Wizard is about to do. As you can with all Wizards, you can click the Next button to advance to the next screen or the Back button to return to a previous screen. At any time, click the Cancel button to close the Wizard.

Figure 10-3:
The Form
Page
Wizard.

3. **Click Next.**

   The next screen appears. Here, the Wizard generates a URL and a title for the new Web page it is about to create.

4. **If you don't like the URL or title generated by the Wizard, type a new page URL in the Page URL text box and a new title in the Page Title text box and click Next.**

   The next screen appears. Here, you decide what kind of information to include in your form. (This part has all the fun stuff.)

5. **Click the Add button.**

   In the list box at the top of the dialog box, the Wizard lists several categories of information commonly collected with forms (as shown in Figure 10-4). Scroll down the list to see all your options. For details on what each category contains, click its name in the list. A description appears, along with the text question that prompts visitors to fill in the field.

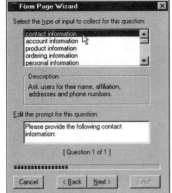

Figure 10-4:
You can
choose
what kind of
information
to collect.

6. Click the category of information that you want to include and then click Next.

The screen that appears next depends on the category you selected. In this screen, you choose the specific types of information that you want the form to collect (see Figure 10-5). If some options don't seem to make sense to you yet, keep this book close at hand as you work and skim the relevant sections of this chapter to clear things up.

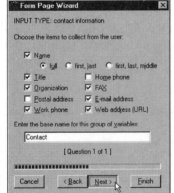

Figure 10-5:
Specify the
information
you want.

7. After you choose the items that you want the form to contain, click Next.

You return to the section of the Wizard where you add more questions to the form. The question you chose in the previous steps appears inside the list box (as in Figure 10-6). To add more questions to your form, click the

Add button and repeat steps 5 and 6. You may rearrange the order questions appear in the form by selecting an item in the list and clicking the Move Up or Move Down buttons. You may also modify or remove any item in your form by selecting the item and clicking the Modify or Remove buttons. To erase everything and start again, click the Clear List button.

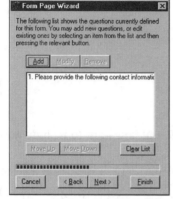

Figure 10-6:
From here,
you can
add more
questions to
your form.

8. **When you finish adding questions, click Next.**

   The Presentation Options screen appears. Here, you decide how you want FrontPage to arrange the questions and form fields on the page: as a series of paragraphs or as a list of items. (Refer to Chapter 5 for a description of each type of list.) You can include in the form page a Table of Contents that contains links to all the pages in your Web site. (You find out how to use the Table of Contents WebBot in Chapter 12.) Finally, you can choose to use an invisible table to align form fields. (Chapter 9 tells you everything you ever wanted to know about tables.)

9. **Select the radio button next to the presentation option that you want to use and click Next.**

   The Output options screen appears. Here, you decide what happens to the information contained in form submissions. (Each option is explained in detail in the section "Choosing a form handler," later in the chapter.) You also select a filename for the form results file.

10. **Choose your output options and click Next to advance to the final screen of the Form Page Wizard.**

11. **Click Finish to create the form page.**

    The Wizard generates a form page based on your specifications.

Adding a form to an existing page

A form is nothing more than a special type of HTML that sits inside a page. You can, therefore, add a form to *any* Web page. To do so, you can rely on the assistance of the Form Page Wizard, or you can create your own form from scratch.

Using the Form Page Wizard

If you want the help of the Form Page Wizard, but want to add the resulting form to an existing page (instead of creating a new page), follow these steps:

1. **Open the page in which you want to place the form.**

2. **Choose File⇨New (or press Ctrl+N).**

   The New Page dialog box appears.

3. **In the Template or Wizard list box, double-click Form Page Wizard.**

   The Form Page Wizard opens.

4. **Create a new form page using the Wizard.**

   For details, refer to the previous section, "Using the Form Page Wizard."

5. **In the new page generated by the Wizard, pass the cursor over the left margin of the form until the pointer turns into a left-pointing arrow that points toward the page margin.**

6. **Double-click to select the entire form.**

 7. **Click the Cut button.**

   Or choose Edit⇨Cut or press Ctrl+X.

   The form disappears from the page. (Actually, it is whisked away to the Clipboard.)

8. **Switch to the page into which you want to place the form by choosing Window⇨*Page title* (where *Page title* is the title of the destination page).**

   The page becomes visible.

9. **In the destination page, place the cursor where you want the form to appear.**

 10. **Click the Paste button.**

   Or choose Edit⇨Paste or press Ctrl+V.

   The form appears in the destination page.

Building your own form

If the Editor's form templates and the Form Page Wizard don't create the kind of form you want, you can easily build your own form. The following section, "Working with Form Fields," shows you how.

Working with Form Fields

Form fields are the collection plates into which visitors drop bits of information. The kinds of fields you include in your form depend on the kinds of information that you want to gather. Do you want visitors to select from a predefined list of choices? Would you rather they fill in whatever information they like? The answers to these questions determine the types of fields to use in your form.

Creating your own form involves adding one or more fields to a page and then customizing the fields so that they look and act how you want. As you customize a field, you give the field a name (a label that identifies the type of information inside) and, in some cases, a value (the information contained in the field), and you adjust how the field looks. Refer to the section "How Do Forms Work?" earlier in the chapter, for more information about field names and field values.

The first time you add a form field to a page, the FrontPage Editor sets aside a space for the form (indicated by a box with dashed borders). You add fields to the form by inserting the fields anywhere within the dashed box. You can cut, copy, and paste fields. You can also drag and drop fields to different locations.

You can use FrontPage to set up rules to *validate* the information visitors enter into the form fields. Specifically, you can specify the format of text or numbers someone enters into a field, or you can make certain fields mandatory — so that visitors cannot submit the form until they fill in all the required fields.

If you intend to validate form data, the form must be part of a page contained in a FrontPage Web site. Also, you must select a validation script language in the FrontPage Explorer. See the sidebar "How does FrontPage validate form data?" later in this chapter for more information.

As you create your form and after the form is complete, be sure to preview the page in a Web browser to test the form. To do so, click the Preview in Browser button or choose File⇨Preview in Browser.

The FrontPage Editor simplifies form field creation through the Forms toolbar (see Figure 10-7). To make the toolbar visible on-screen, choose View⇨Forms Toolbar.

Figure 10-7:
The Forms
toolbar.

One-line text boxes

One-line text boxes are plain vanilla fields into which visitors enter a single line of text. Use a text box when you want to collect small bits of information, such as a name or e-mail address. Figure 10-8 shows a filled-in one-line text box, as seen with a Web browser.

Form design tips

Here are a few simple tricks to make your home-grown forms easy for visitors to fill out:

✔ **Place descriptive text labels next to each field.** If, for example, you include a field in your form for the visitor's e-mail address, use the text label E-mail address (username@domain.com) to make absolutely clear what information you want.

✔ **Help visitors provide you with the correct information.** If your form contains mandatory fields or fields that require that information be entered in a certain way, include a note that demonstrates the correct format or at least that reads This field is required. And identify in which language the validation script is written so that visitors know whether their browser can understand the script.

✔ **Use an invisible table to keep the form's layout neat and tidy.** Insert the first form field, create a two-column table *inside* the dashed box, and drag and drop the field into the top right table cell. Next, place text

labels in the left column and more form fields in the right column. (Refer to Chapter 9 to see how to build a table.) The layout of the custom feedback form template (included on this book's CD) is structured with a table. (See Appendix C for more information about this and other custom templates available on the CD.)

✔ **Pay attention to the order of the fields.** Many browsers enable visitors to use the Tab key to advance to the next field. Fields should, therefore, be arranged in chronological order.

✔ **Use initial text in text box fields to save visitors time and typing effort.** For example, if your form asks the visitor's country of origin, and most of your visitors are American, use USA as the field's initial text.

✔ **Consider rewarding visitors for taking the time to fill out the form.** Enter them in a drawing or give them access to a free downloadable goodie.

Figure 10-8:
A one-line text box.

Name *(this field is required)*: [Asha Dornfest]

Creating a text box

To add a one-line text box to your page, follow these steps:

1. **In the Forms toolbar, click the One-Line Text Box button.**

   Or choose Insert⇨Form Field⇨One-Line Text Box from the menu bar.

   A one-line text box appears in your page.

2. **To customize the text box, double-click the text box in your page or right-click the text box and choose Form Field Properties from the pop-up menu.**

   The Text Box Properties dialog box appears.

3. **In the Name text box, type the field name for the text box.**

   Choose a brief, generic name that describes the information collected by the text box. If, for example, you're creating a text box to collect a visitor's e-mail address, type the name E-mail or E-mail address.

4. **If you want the text box to appear with text inside (instead of empty), type the text in the Initial value text box.**

   Use the initial value to save your visitors' time by entering the most common response to a question. If, for example, the text box asks for the country in which the visitor lives, and most of your visitors are American, type USA as the initial value.

5. **In the Width in characters text box, type the visible width of the text box.**

   The number you type affects the visible size of the text box, not the amount of text a visitor can enter in the text box. To limit the amount of text, use a validation option, as described in the following section.

   If you prefer to adjust the width of a text box manually, skip this step. Instead, after you are finished defining the text box's properties, click the text box in the page and drag the size handles that appear until you're satisfied with its new width.

6. **Specify whether the text box is a password field.**

   Password fields are no different from regular text boxes except that, if viewed with a browser, text someone types into a password field appears on-screen as dots or asterisks — so that nosy passers-by can't see what's typed (which would compromise the password).

Including a password field in your form does not automatically add password protection. To do so, you must coordinate with your Internet service provider or system administrator, as this capability is possible only in conjunction with a special server-based program. Without the server program, a password field works just like a regular text box.

7. **To restrict the type of information visitors can enter into the text box, click the Validate button.**

   If you don't want to restrict the information visitors can enter, skip step 7. (The following section explains how to use validation options.)

8. **Click OK to close the Text Box Properties dialog box.**

   Any initial text you specified appears inside the text box. If you changed the width of the text box, it stretches or shrinks accordingly.

Validating information entered into a text box

FrontPage enables you to make certain form fields mandatory (unless visitors complete these fields, they can't submit the form). You can also control the format of information that visitors type into text boxes. This control is especially helpful if form results will eventually go into a database and must be of a standard format.

After you click the Validate button in the Text Box Properties dialog box, the Text Box Validation dialog box appears (see Figure 10-9).

The FrontPage validation features work only on forms that you initially create as part of a FrontPage Web site. If you later want to use the form as part of a Web site created in another program, you can export finished forms to a separate file, and the validation features remain intact.

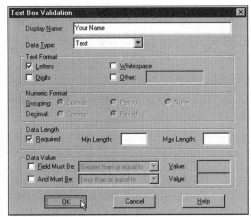

Figure 10-9:
The Text Box Validation dialog box.

To validate information entered into text boxes, follow these steps:

1. **To restrict the type of data that can be entered into the text box, select an option from the Data Type drop-down list.**

   Select one of the following options: No Constraints (no restrictions on data type), Text (letters, characters, or numerals), Integer (whole numbers only), or Number (all numbers, both whole and decimal).

2. **Depending on the option you selected in step 1, select an option from either the Text Format or the Numeric Format area of the Text Box Validation dialog box.**

   • If you selected the Text data type, select options from the Text Format area of the dialog box.

   The Letters check box creates a text box that can contain only alphabetic characters. The Digits check box creates a text box that can contain only numeric characters. The Whitespace check box creates a text box that can contain white space (such as spaces, tabs, and line breaks). If you want to allow other types of characters (such as commas or hyphens, for example), select the Other check box and type the characters in the corresponding text box.

   • If you selected the Integer or Number data type, select options from the Numeric Format section.

   The Grouping radio buttons enable you to control how visitors must punctuate numbers greater than or equal to 1,000: with a comma, as in 1,000; with a period, as in 1.000; or with no punctuation, as in 1000. The Decimal radio buttons enable you to choose which punctuation character visitors can use as a decimal point: a period or a comma.

   The Grouping and Decimal characters must be different.

3. **To control the amount of information typed into a text box or to make a text box mandatory, select options from the Data Length section.**

   Select the Required check box to make the text box mandatory.

   Type a number of characters in the Min Length and Max Length text boxes to control the length of information entered into the text box.

4. **To place restrictive conditions on the content of text box data, choose options from the Data Value area.**

   If you selected the Text or No Constraints data type, these options compare the information visitors type into the text box against the order of the alphabet. If you specify that the field must be greater than *E,* for example, all information entered into the text box must start with the letter *F* or any other letter later in the alphabet (such as *H, Q,* or *Z* — but not *A, C,* or even *E*).

If you selected the Integer or Number data type, these options make a numerical order comparison. If you specify that the field must be less than or equal to 10, for example, a visitor may type 10 or any lesser number in the text box.

5. Click OK to close the dialog box.

If a visitor enters information that doesn't stick to the validation rules, the Web browser pops up a *validation warning message.* The warning message identifies the field by the name you entered in the Name field of the Text Box Properties dialog box. If the name you used wouldn't make sense to a visitor (say, the field collects phone numbers and you named the field phon_num), you can specify a friendlier display name (such as Phone Number) for the purposes of the validation warning. To do so, type the display name text in the Display Name text box at the top of the Text Box Validation dialog box.

Scrolling text boxes

Scrolling text boxes are just like one-line text boxes, except that this type of field holds more than one line of text (see Figure 10-10 for an example of how a filled-in scrolling text box looks as seen with a Web browser). Scrolling text boxes are perfect for verbose visitors who want to send lots of comments.

How does FrontPage validate form data?

If you use the FrontPage validation feature, FrontPage takes down all the rules you specify in a *validation script.* The validation script sits inside the HTML of your Web page and waits for someone to access it with a Web browser. If someone visits your Web site and fills out a form, the browser notices that the form contains a validation script and refers to the script for the data rules for each field. If the visitor enters something into a field that's not allowed or if the visitor leaves a mandatory field empty, the browser pops up a pesky dialog box until the visitor enters the appropriate information.

FrontPage writes validation scripts in one of two scripting languages: VBScript and JavaScript. The language you choose depends on your preference and on the browsers your readers use

because only recent versions of advanced browsers can interpret either language. As of this writing, Internet Explorer (Version 3.0 or later) is the only bilingual browser. Other browsers, including recent versions of Netscape Navigator, understand JavaScript. If a visitor fills in your form who isn't using a JavaScript- or VBScript-compliant browser, the validation features don't work.

To choose a validation script language for your Web site, in the FrontPage Explorer, choose Tools⇨Web Settings to display the FrontPage Web Settings dialog box. Click the Advanced Tab and select a language from the Language drop-down list. For more information about using scripts in your Web pages, read Chapter 13.

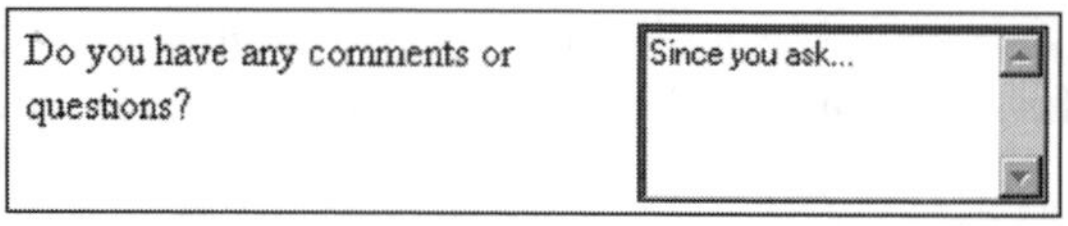

Figure 10-10:
A scrolling
text box.

Do you have any comments or questions?	Since you ask...

To create a scrolling text box, follow these steps:

1. **In the Forms toolbar, click the Scrolling Text Box button (or choose Insert⇨Form Field⇨Scrolling Text Box).**

   A scrolling text box appears in the page.

2. **Double-click inside the scrolling text box in your page to customize it.**

   Or right-click the scrolling text box and choose Form Field Properties from the pop-up menu.

   The Scrolling Text Box Properties dialog box appears.

3. **In the Name text box, type the scrolling text box's field name.**

4. **If you want the scrolling text box to appear with text inside (instead of empty), type that text in the Initial value text box.**

5. **In the Width in characters text box, type the visible width of the scrolling text box.**

6. **In the Number of lines text box, type the number of lines of text the scrolling text box can hold.**

   Effectively, this option controls the height of a scrolling text box. You can also manually adjust the height and width of a scrolling text box (after you finish defining its properties) by clicking the text box in the page and dragging the size handles until the text box is the size you want.

7. **To restrict the type of information that visitors can type into the scrolling text box, click the Validate button.**

   Refer to the preceding section, "Validating information entered into a text box," for details on how to use validation options. If you don't want to restrict this information, skip step 7.

8. **Click OK to close the Scrolling Text Box Properties dialog box.**

   Any initial text you specified appears inside the scrolling text box. If you changed the size of the scrolling text box, it stretches or shrinks accordingly.

Check boxes

Check boxes are like tough teenagers: autonomous but preferring to hang around in groups all the same. (Figure 10-11 shows how a group of check boxes looks as seen with a Web browser.) Use check boxes if you want visitors to select as many items from a predefined list as they want. You can include one check box or several in your form.

Figure 10-11:
A gang of check boxes.

Check the items about which you want more information:	☑ This week's bubble gum flavors ☐ Candy factory tours ☐ Nutritional analysis of Choco-Bombs ®

To insert a check box, follow these steps:

1. **Click the Check Box button or choose Insert⇨Form Field⇨Check Box from the menu bar.**

   A check box appears in your page.

2. **Double-click the check box in your page to customize it (or right-click the check box and choose Form Field Properties from the pop-up menu).**

   The Check Box Properties dialog box appears.

3. **In the Name text box, type the check box's field name.**

4. **In the Value text box, type a label that describes what the marked check box means.**

   Suppose that you're using a check box to enable visitors to tell you whether they want more information about a particular product (as in the example shown in Figure 10-11). Using the first check box as an example, Bubble gum flavors is a good name choice and Info is a good value choice because if visitors mark that check box, their choice means "I want more information about bubble gum flavors."

5. **If you want the check box to appear initially marked, select the Checked radio button.**

6. **Click OK to close the Check Box Properties dialog box.**

To add more check boxes, repeat steps 2 to 5 until you have all the check boxes you want.

Radio buttons

If check boxes are independent teens, *radio buttons* are a giddy high school clique. Radio buttons are never seen alone and base their identity solely on the others in the group.

Use a group of radio buttons to present visitors with a list of options, only one of which may be chosen. Figure 10-12 shows how a group of radio buttons looks, as seen with a Web browser.

Figure 10-12:
A gathering
of radio
buttons.

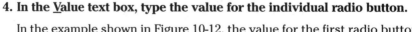

Your favorite ice cream flavor: ● Mint Chip
   ○ Butter Brickle
   ○ Chocolate Fudge

To create a radio button group, follow these steps:

 1. **Click the Radio Button button (or choose Insert⇨Form Field⇨Radio Button from the menu bar).**

   A single radio button appears in your page.

2. **Double-click the radio button in your page to customize it (or right-click the radio button and choose Form Field Properties from the pop-up menu).**

   The Radio Button Properties dialog box appears.

3. **In the Group Name text box, type a name that applies to the entire group (even though you've only created one radio button so far).**

   In the example shown in Figure 10-12, the Group Name is Favorite Flavors.

   The group name you choose does not need to match the text label you insert in the page to identify the list of radio buttons to visitors.

4. **In the Value text box, type the value for the individual radio button.**

   In the example shown in Figure 10-12, the value for the first radio button is Mint Chip.

5. **If you want the radio button to appear empty initially, select the Not Selected radio button.**

   (By default, the first radio button in a group appears selected.)

6. **To require visitors to choose one of the items in the list of radio buttons, click the Validate button.**

   (In this case, validation applies only to a radio button group where *none* of the radio buttons appears initially selected.)

   The Radio Button Validation dialog box appears.

7. **Click the Data Required check box.**

8. **Type a display name in the Display Name text box if you want the validation warning message to identify the radio button group by a name other than the group name.**

   The tip at the end of the "Validating information entered into a text box" section (earlier in the chapter) explains the purpose of the Display Name.

9. **Click OK to close the Radio Button Validation dialog box.**

10. **Click OK to close the Radio Button Properties dialog box.**

Now you must create at least one more radio button to complete the group. To do so, follow these steps:

1. **Click the Radio Button button (or choose Insert⇨Form Field⇨Radio Button).**

   A second radio button appears in your page, to the right of the first one.

2. **Double-click the second radio button in your page to customize it (or right-click the radio button and choose Form Field Properties from the pop-up menu).**

   The Radio Button Properties dialog box appears. The Group Name is the same as for the first radio button. (I told you they stick together.) All you need to do is give the second radio button a unique value. In the example in Figure 10-12, the value for the second radio button is Butter Brickle.

3. **Choose the radio button's initial state.**

   If you want the second radio button to appear initially selected, select the Selected radio button (by default, the first radio button in a group appears selected; because only one radio button may be selected at any given time, if you choose this option, the first radio button in the group appears initially empty). If you want the second radio button to appear empty, select the Not selected radio button.

4. **Click OK to close the Radio Button Properties dialog box.**

   Validation options apply to the entire radio button group, so whatever you specify for the first radio button applies to all radio buttons.

Drop-down menus

Drop-down menus are so named because, after you click the field, a list of choices "drops down." Figure 10-13 shows how a drop-down menu works when viewed with a Web browser. Drop-down menus are similar in function to radio button groups — the option enables visitors to choose from a predefined group of options. The differences between radio buttons and drop-down menus are as follows:

✔ Drop-down menus save space in your document by popping open only after a visitor clicks the down-pointing arrow next to the option.

✔ You can set up a drop-down menu to accept more than one choice at a time.

Figure 10-13:
A drop-down menu.

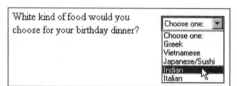

To create a drop-down menu, follow these steps:

1. **Click the Drop-Down Menu button or choose <u>I</u>nsert⇨Form Fiel<u>d</u>⇨Drop-Down Menu from the menu bar.**

   A drop-down menu field appears in your page.

2. **Double-click the drop-down menu in your page to customize it (or right-click the drop-down menu and choose Form Field Properties from the pop-up menu).**

   The Drop-Down Menu Properties dialog box appears (as in Figure 10-14).

Figure 10-14:
The Drop-Down Menu Properties dialog box.

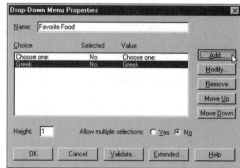

3. **In the Name text box, type the group name.**

   In the example in Figure 10-14, the name is Favorite Food.

   The name you choose does not need to match the text label you insert in the page to identify the form field to visitors.

4. **To add menu choices, click the Add button.**

   The Add Choice dialog box appears.

5. **In the Choice text box, type the text that you want to appear in the menu.**

   In the example in Figure 10-13, the choices are Greek, Vietnamese, and so on. (Although Choose one appears in the drop-down menu in Figure 10-14, it isn't a valid menu choice; I explain how to disallow the first item of a drop-down menu as a choice in step 12.)

6. **If you want the choice's value to be something other than the information you type in the Choice text box, select the Specify Value check box and type the value in the accompanying text box.**

   For example, if you transfer the form results from the example in Figure 10-13 into a database, and the database is unable to process the / character (as in the Japanese/Sushi menu choice), you can instead specify a value of **Japanese_Sushi**. That way, visitors select an item that reads Japanese/Sushi, while the database receives the value Japanese_Sushi.

7. **If you want the choice to appear initially selected, select the Selected radio button.**

8. **Click OK to close the Add Choice dialog box.**

9. **Repeat steps 1 through 8 to add more menu choices until the menu is complete.**

   You can rearrange, modify, or remove menu items by selecting the item in the list and then selecting the Move Up, Move Down, Modify or Remove buttons.

10. **In the Height text box, type the number of menu choices visible before a visitor clicks the drop-down menu and causes it to "drop down."**

    You can also manually adjust the height and width of a drop-down menu (after you're finished defining its properties) by clicking the drop-down menu in your page and dragging the size handles.

11. **To enable visitors to select more than one item from the list, select the Yes radio button in the Allow multiple selection area.**

    As visitors view the form with a Web browser, they select more than one option by pressing and holding the Ctrl key as they click their selections.

12. **Optionally, click the Validate button.**

    The Drop-Down Menu Validation dialog box appears.

    To require that visitors choose an item from the list, select the Data Required check box. (In the case of multiple selection menus, you can specify a minimum and maximum number of choices.) To disallow the first menu choice as a valid selection, select the Disallow First Item check box (in the example in Figure 10-14, Choose one: isn't a valid selection option). Click OK to close the Drop-Down Menu Validation dialog box.

13. **Click OK to close the Drop-Down Menu Properties dialog box.**

    The first menu choice becomes visible in the drop-down menu in your page. (If you specified that more than one menu choice is initially visible, the drop-down menu expands to display the specified number of choices.)

Hidden fields

Hidden fields enable you to include static information in your form that is invisible to visitors. If, for example, the results of several forms appear in the same text file, and you want to track from which form each submission originates, you can place a hidden field inside each form to identify the form's location. When a visitor submits a form, the hidden field information tags along and appears along with the rest of the form results.

To add a hidden field to your form, follow these steps:

1. **Right-click inside the form and choose Form Properties from the pop-up menu.**

    The Form Properties dialog box appears.

2. **In the Hidden Fields area, click the Add button.**

    The Name/Value Pair dialog box appears.

3. **Type the hidden field's name and value in the Name and Value text boxes and click OK to close the Name/Value Pair dialog box.**

    The name/value pair appears inside the list box in the Hidden Felds area of the Form Properties dialog box.

4. **Click OK to close the Form Properties dialog box.**

As hidden fields are, well . . . hidden, your page does not appear to change when you add a hidden field. Don't worry — it's there.

Submitting Form Results

Here's where all the action occurs — after a visitor submits the form results. What happens to the form results is up to you; you get to decide how to handle form results and where the information eventually ends up. FrontPage contains brilliant built-in form handlers that format the results and dump the information into a text file or a Web page. You can also use a form to communicate with a database hooked up to the Internet. If, for some reason, the FrontPage form handlers don't fit the bill, you can use FrontPage to hitch your form to a custom form-handling script.

Inserting Submit and Reset buttons

The *Submit button* is the linchpin of the entire form-submission operation. All forms must contain a Submit button. After visitors click this powerful little tool (usually sitting patiently at the bottom of the form), their browser activates the form handler, which takes over from there, processing the form results. Figure 10-15 shows you how a Submit button looks when seen with a Web browser.

The Submit button is one of a generic group of form fields called *push button fields.* Clicking a push button field activates some sort of server-based program, whether the program is a form handler or another type of server program.

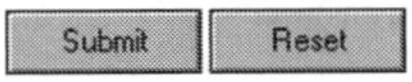

Figure 10-15:
Submit and
Reset
buttons.

| Submit | Reset |

The *Reset button* (also shown in Figure 10-15) is another type of push button field. After visitors click the Reset button, the action clears all the information they entered into the form so, in case they want to change information they've entered, that they can start over fresh.

If gray buttons are too boring for your taste, you can replace the buttons with *image fields.* Rather than a staid button, you can insert a snazzy GIF or JPEG image that, after you click the image, submits the form results, just as a Submit button does (see Figure 10-16).

Alas, image fields can replace any type of button except the Reset button, which is fated always to look like a little gray rectangle.

Go image

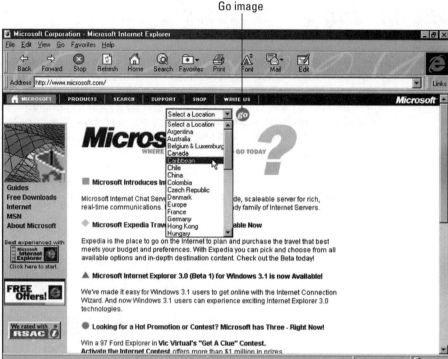

Figure 10-16:
The
Microsoft
home page
uses an
image field
(the Go
image) in
place of a
boring
Submit
button.

Inserting a Submit button

To insert a Submit button, follow these steps:

1. **Click the Push Button button from the Forms toolbar (or choose Insert⇨Form Field⇨Push Button).**

   A Submit button appears in your page.

2. **Double-click the button in your page to customize it (or right-click the button and choose Form Field Properties from the pop-up menu).**

   The Push Button Properties dialog box appears.

3. **Optionally, type a field name in the Name text box.**

   Because the Submit button exists only to activate the form handler, this button doesn't need a field name.

   A button name is useful, however, if you have more than one button in your form and want to process form data based on which button a visitor clicks (this is an advanced operation, however, requiring coordination with your Internet service provider or system administrator).

4. **If you want the text label on the button to read something other than Submit, type a new label in the Value/Label text box.**

How about something vivid, such as Come to Mama!

5. **Click the Form button to choose and set up a form handler.**

The following section shows you how to set up a form handler.

6. **Click OK to close the Push Button Properties dialog box.**

Inserting an image field

To use an image field to submit form data, follow these steps:

1. **Choose Insert⇨Form Field⇨Image.**

The Image dialog box appears. Any image can be transformed into an image field. You can choose an image from your Web site, an image located elsewhere on your computer or the World Wide Web, or you can pick an image from the FrontPage Clip Art collection.

2. **Insert the image of your choice into your page.**

If you're not sure how to insert an image using this dialog box, refer to Chapter 7.

The image appears in your page.

3. **Double-click the image field to customize it (or right-click the image field and choose Form Field Properties from the pop-up menu).**

The Image Form Field Properties dialog box appears.

4. **Optionally, type a field name in the Name text box.**

5. **Click the Form button to choose and configure a form handler.**

I show you how to work with form handlers in the following section, "Choosing a form handler."

6. **Click OK to close the Push Button Properties dialog box.**

Inserting a Reset button

To insert a Reset button, follow these steps:

1. **Click the Push Button button from the Forms toolbar (or choose Insert⇨Form Field⇨Push Button).**

A Submit button appears in your page.

2. **Double-click the button to customize it (or right-click the button and choose Form Field Properties from the pop-up menu).**

The Push Button Properties dialog box appears.

3. **Optionally, type a field name in the <u>N</u>ame text box.**

4. **In the Button type section, select the <u>R</u>eset radio button.**

   (Because <u>S</u>ubmit is the default type of push-button field, you need to specifically tell FrontPage to create a Reset button.)

5. **If you want the text label on the button to read something other than** Reset**, type a new label in the Value/Label text box.**

   Suggestions: **Start Over**, **Undo**, **I Changed My Mind**, or **Forget It**.

6. **Click OK to close the Push Button Properties dialog box.**

In the Push Button Properties dialog box, you may have noticed another push button field type: the *Normal* push button. You can program these types of buttons to do just about anything. You can, for example, include a button in your Web page, that, after a visitor clicks the button, plays a sound clip or opens a new Web page.

For such a feature to work, however, you need to write the custom program to perform the operation and then store the program on the Web server. This task requires advanced programming expertise, plus coordination with your Internet service provider or system administrator. If you want to proceed, speak to your Internet gurus first.

Choosing a form handler

The form handler you choose governs how FrontPage processes form results and where the results eventually end up. FrontPage contains built-in form handlers that deal with form results in a number of ways. In the following sections, I describe what each form handler does and also show you how to customize the form handler to fit your needs.

FrontPage form handlers rely on WebBots to operate. Unless your dedicated Web server supports FrontPage Server Extensions, however, these WebBots don't work. To submit form data, you need to work with your Internet service provider or system administrator to set up a custom form-handling script. See the section "Custom ISAPI, NSAPI, or CGI script," later in this chapter, for more information.

The Save Results WebBot

The *Save Results WebBot* is the default form handler for all FrontPage forms. This WebBot processes form results by listing the name/value pairs in a text file or Web page — or both — using a format you choose. Each time a new visitor submits a form, the WebBot adds the new form results to the file.

The Save Results WebBot also generates a *confirmation page* (a page that tells visitors that the form is successfully submitted) or a *validation failure page* (a page that appears if data entered into the form is invalid).

To use the Save Results WebBot form handler, follow these steps:

1. **Right-click inside the form and choose Form Properties from the pop-up menu.**

   You open the same dialog box by clicking the Form button in the Push Button Properties dialog box while customizing a Submit button or image field.

2. **Select WebBot Save Results Component from the Form Handler drop-down list.**

3. **Click the Settings button to set up the form handler.**

   The Settings for Saving Results of Form dialog box appears, with the Results tab visible (see Figure 10-17).

4. **In the File for results text box, type a filename.**

   FrontPage stores the information submitted from the form in this file (which is called the *results file*). You can choose an existing file in your Web site, or you can enter a new filename, in which case FrontPage creates the file the first time someone submits a form.

   Be sure to type the correct three-letter file name extension corresponding to the file type you choose in step 5: .htm for an HTML file, or .txt for a text file.

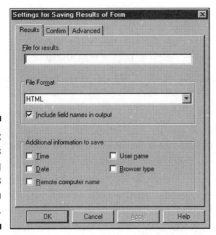

Figure 10-17:
The Settings
for Saving
Results
of Form
dialog box.

To keep the results file hidden from Web browsers, add _private/ to the beginning of the filename (so that the name reads _private/filename). This addition tells FrontPage to save the results file in your Web site's _PRIVATE folder. (Documents stored in that folder aren't visible to Web browsers.)

The _PRIVATE folder is only private if the Web site is published on a Web server that supports FrontPage Server Extensions. For more information, see Chapter 18.

5. Select a format for the results file from the File Format drop-down list.

You can save the results file as an HTML file (that is, as a Web page) or as a text file. You can format HTML files as definition lists, bulleted lists, numbered lists, or formatted text. (Refer to Chapter 5 for descriptions of each type of list.) You can save text files as formatted plain text (a nicely laid-out list of name/value pairs) or as a file with commas, tabs, or spaces separating names and values. (This latter format is handy if you want to import the data into a database or spreadsheet).

6. In the Additional information to save section of the Results tab, select the check boxes next to the other types of information that you want to include in the results file.

The Save Results WebBot can track the time and date the form was submitted, the visitor's Internet user name, the name of the computer from which the form was submitted, and the type of Web browser the visitor was using at the time.

7. In the Settings for Saving Results of Form dialog box, click the Confirm tab to make the tab visible.

Use the options in the Confirm area to specify custom confirmation and validation failure pages (which you discover how to create in "Creating a Confirmation Page" later in this chapter). If you leave this section empty, the Save Results WebBot creates generic pages automatically.

8. Type the confirmation page URL in the URL of confirmation page text box.

Or click the Browse button to display the Current Web dialog box. The dialog box lists the files and folders in your Web site. In the dialog box, select the file that you want to use as your confirmation page and click OK. The dialog box closes, and the page's URL appears in the URL of confirmation page text box.

9. Type the validation failure page URL in the URL of validation failure page text box.

Or click the Browse button to display the Current Web dialog box. The dialog box lists the files and folders in your Web site. In the dialog box, select the file that you want to use and click OK. The dialog box closes, and the page's URL appears in the URL of validation failure page text box.

10. **In the Settings for Saving Results of Form dialog box, click the Advanced tab to make the tab visible.**

11. **If you want to save form results to a second file, type the filename of the second file in the Second file for Results text box.**

    This option is handy if you want FrontPage to generate one file for import into, say, a database and another file for viewing on the Web.

12. **Select the second file's format from the Format of second file drop-down list.**

13. **If you only want the results of certain form fields to appear in the second results page, type the field names into the Form fields to include text box.**

14. **Click OK to close the Settings for Saving Results of Form dialog box.**

15. **Click OK to close the Form Properties dialog box.**

WebBot discussion component

This form handler is the juice that fuels a FrontPage *discussion group*. In a discussion group, visitors post articles that appear inside a public Web page and reply to articles others have posted. In Chapter 16, I take you through the process of creating a FrontPage discussion group from the ground up.

WebBot registration component

This form handler is used in conjunction with a FrontPage *registration system* that enables visitors use to gain access to a members-only section of a Web site. I show you how to create a registration system in Chapter 15.

Custom ISAPI, NSAPI, or CGI script

If your dedicated Web server doesn't support FrontPage Server Extensions, or if you need special data-processing capabilities that FrontPage form handlers can't accommodate, you can process form results by using a *custom form-handling script*. A custom script works just the same as a FrontPage form handler: The script receives and processes form data and then outputs the results. Unlike with a FrontPage form handler, however, you don't control the format of the form results; the script's internal programming determines how form results are formatted and where they are stored.

The chances are good that your Internet service provider or system administrator has a form-handling script already in place on the Web server. (After all, folks have been submitting Web forms since long before FrontPage was born!) Speak to your provider or administrator to discover the script's capabilities and where the script's located on the server (that is, the script's absolute URL).

(To write a custom form-handling script, you need programming experience or, better yet, a brilliant programmer friend who owes you a *big* favor.)

Custom form-handling scripts reside on the Web server and require coordination with the server's administrator to create and use. Validation scripts (and other types of JavaScripts or VBScripts), on the other hand, live inside the Web page and are activated by the visitor's Web browser, with no server involvement at all. You can write these scripts yourself (assuming that you understand JavaScript or VBScript) without needing to confer with the tech gurus first. In Chapter 13, I discuss these kinds of scripts in more detail.

If you must know, *ISAPI* stands for *Internet Server Application Programming Interface;* *NSAPI* stands for *Netscape Server Application Programming Interface;* and *CGI* stands for *Common Gateway Interface.*

To use a custom server script as your form handler, follow these steps:

1. **Right-click inside the form and choose Form Properties from the pop-up menu.**

   You open the same dialog box by clicking the <u>F</u>orm button in the Push Button Properties dialog box while customizing a Submit button or image field.

   The Form Properties dialog box appears.

2. **Select Custom ISAPI, NSAPI, or CGI Script from the Form <u>H</u>andler drop-down list.**

3. **Click the <u>S</u>ettings button to set up the form handler.**

   The Settings for Custom Form Handler dialog box appears.

4. **In the <u>A</u>ction text box, type the absolute URL of the form handler.**

   If you don't know the URL, ask your Internet service provider or system administrator.

5. **If not already visible, select POST from the <u>M</u>ethod drop-down list.**

   The POST method tells the Web browser to send the name/value pairs straight from the form to the script. The majority of Web forms use this method to submit data to a script.

6. **Leave the Encoding <u>t</u>ype text box alone.**

7. **Click OK to close the Settings for Custom Form Handler dialog box.**

8. **Click OK to close the Form Properties dialog box.**

Internet database connector

With this form handler, you can use a form in your Web site to submit queries to a database connected to the Internet. To do so, you must first create a *database connector file* with the help of the Database Connector Wizard in the FrontPage Explorer. This procedure requires that you know how to write database queries using *SQL,* or *Structured Query Language* (a big, fat topic that is beyond the scope of this book).

After you create a database connector file, you can use that file as a form handler. After a visitor submits the form, the database connector file translates the form information into a language the database can understand and then sends the information to the database. When the database returns results based on the query, the database connector file receives the information and formats it as a special Web page called a *database results file*. The FrontPage Editor contains a Database Results template, which you use to set up and format the file.

Using FrontPage in conjunction with an Internet database is an advanced operation (as if you couldn't tell by reading the preceding paragraphs!), requiring coordination with your Internet service provider or your system administrator. The FrontPage Help system contains detailed information on how to use the Database Connector Wizard, as well as how to set up a Database Results page.

Creating a Confirmation Page

A *confirmation page* is the Web page that automatically appears after visitors submit a form. This page lets visitors know that the form submission was successful and (depending on how you set up the page) confirms the information they entered in the form. A confirmation page is a nice way to reassure visitors that the information they just sent didn't simply float off into the ether after they clicked the Submit button.

The Save Results, Registration, and Discussion WebBots all generate their own, plain-Jane confirmation pages. If you want your confirmation page to blend in nicely with the rest of your site's design, create your own page.

The confirmation page can be as simple as a polite acknowledgment and a link back to the Web site's home page ("Thank you for filling out our survey. Click here to return to the Acme home page."), or the page can display some or all of the information visitors entered into the form so that they can note the information for future reference. How does the confirmation page know to display visitors' form entries? Because the confirmation page contains little jewels called *confirmation fields*.

Confirmation fields are simply references to the existing fields in your form. If used as part of a Web page, confirmation fields display the information the visitor typed into the corresponding form fields. Think of this type of field as the Web equivalent of a mail merge.

As always, the FrontPage Editor steps in to help with a handy Confirmation Form template. I include a custom confirmation form template on the CD that comes with this book. (See Appendix C for instructions on how to access the CD contents.) You can also create your own confirmation form by adding confirmation fields to an existing Web page.

To use a custom confirmation page, you must specify its URL as you set up the form handler. Refer to the section "Choosing a form handler," earlier in this chapter. Additionally, you may use confirmation fields only if your dedicated Web server supports FrontPage Server Extensions.

Using the Confirmation Form template

The Confirmation Form template is a good place from which to begin building your own confirmation page.

Before you begin, you must know the names of the form fields that you want to confirm.

To create a confirmation page based on this template, follow these steps:

1. **Choose File⇨New (or press Ctrl+N).**

   The New Page dialog box appears.

2. **In the Template or Wizard list box, double-click Confirmation Form.**

   A page titled Feedback Confirmation appears in the Editor. This page is a boilerplate confirmation page for a feedback form.

3. **In the Editor, change the page to suit your needs.**

   This Web page is just like any other; you can format and rearrange the page any way you like. Add or change text, change the color scheme, and add your own graphics.

   The words that appear inside brackets (such as [UserName] and [UserTel]) are the page's confirmation fields. The word inside the brackets corresponds to the name of a form field. (The confirmation fields in this template correspond to the field names in the form created using the Editor's Feedback Form template.)

4. **To change a confirmation field so that it corresponds to a field in your form, double-click the confirmation field in the page.**

   The WebBot Confirmation Field Component Properties dialog box appears.

5. **In the Name of Form Field to Confirm text box, type the name of the field you want to confirm.**

   Pay attention to upper- and lowercase letters while typing the field name.

6. **Click OK to close the dialog box.**

   The word inside the selected confirmation field changes to the specified field name.

Adding confirmation fields to an existing page

You can add confirmation fields to any page in your Web site and use that page as your form's confirmation page.

To do so, follow these steps:

1. **In the Editor, open the Web page that you want to use as your confirmation page.**

2. **Place the cursor at the point in the page where you want the first confirmation field to appear.**

 3. **Click the Insert WebBot Component button, (or choose Insert⇨WebBot Component).**

   The Insert WebBot Component dialog box appears.

4. **Double-click Confirmation Field in the Select a component list box.**

   The WebBot Confirmation Field Component Properties dialog box appears. (Such a long name for such a tiny dialog box!)

5. **In the Name of form field to confirm text box, type the name of the field that you want to confirm.**

   Pay attention to upper- and lowercase letters while entering the field name.

6. **Click OK to close the dialog box.**

   The confirmation field appears in the page.

Chapter 11

I've Been Framed!

● ●

In This Chapter

▶ What are frames?

▶ Creating a framed Web site

▶ Tweaking a frame

● ●

*O*f all the newfangled design effects to arrive on the Web publishing scene, *frames* are the most exciting. Frames don't just make something happen on a page — frames, in fact, change the way that visitors experience the Web site as a whole.

In this chapter, I show you how to create a framed Web site.

What Are Frames?

Frames are dividers that separate the Web browser's viewing window into sections. Each section contains a separate Web page, enabling you to display more than one page at the same time, as shown in Figure 11-1.

In this example, the browser window contains two frames, each of which displays a separate page. The frame on the left contains a table of contents, and the frame on the right contains the main content of the site. A third page, the *frame set,* defines the layout of the frames themselves.

Sure, frames look slick. Looks are nothing, however, compared to frames' navigational power. Behold — in the site shown in Figure 11-1, clicking a hyperlink in the left frame displays the destination page in the right frame. In this way, frames enable you to display elements such as navigation menus and company logos that remain visible all the time (as the table of contents does in Figure 11-1), while the rest of the site content changes based on where the reader wants to go (as the main content page in Figure 11-1 changes based on which hyperlink someone clicks in the table of contents).

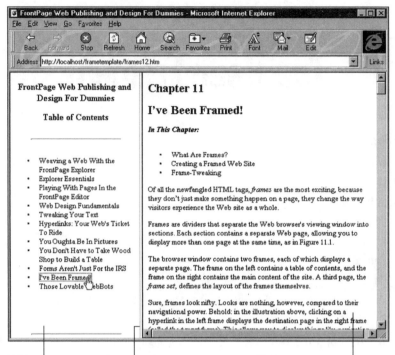

Figure 11-1:
A framed
Web site.

Table of contents   Frame border   Main content page

The main drawback to using frames is that not all Web browsers can display frames. As of this writing, the only frames-capable browsers are Netscape Navigator (Version 2.0 or later) and Microsoft Internet Explorer (Version 3.0 or later). Other browsers can't even display an approximation of a framed site — all the visitor sees is a blank page. The good news is that FrontPage sidesteps the problem by enabling you to specify an alternative, nonframed page for those of your visitors who still use frame-challenged browsers.

The Netscape Frames reference contains an excellent demonstration, full of examples and directions. Visit http://www.netscape.com/comprod/ products/navigator/version_2.0/frames/ to see how a framed site looks and acts in real life. You find another good frames reference at the Microsoft Site Builder Workshop at http://www.microsoft.com/workshop. (Check out the Authoring section for links.)

Creating a Framed Web Site: The Game Plan

Creating a framed site involves the following three basic steps:

- Creating the frame set
- Filling the frame set with content pages
- Modifying the content pages, if necessary, to work inside frames

A *frame set* is a special type of Web page that defines the size and placement of the site's frames. A frame set can display as many frames, in whatever layout, as you want. The FrontPage Editor contains a Frames Wizard that guides you through the entire process.

After you build a frame set, you need to fill the frame set with *content pages.* Content pages are regular, old Web pages that appear inside each frame as a visitor views the frame set with a Web browser. (The frame set itself is transparent, except for the placement of each frame.) *Default content pages* are the first ones visible as a visitor views the frame set with a Web browser. The Frames Wizard can either generate empty content pages while creating the frame set, or it can simply create the frame set, which you later fill with your own existing Web pages.

The final step is to specify a *target frame* for each content page. The target frame is the frame in which hyperlink destination pages appear. By default, hyperlink destination pages appear in the same frame as the page that contains the hyperlink. You can, however, specify a different target frame. In Figure 11-1, for example, if a visitor clicks a link in the table of contents page (inside the left frame), the corresponding page appears in the right frame. The right frame, therefore, is the target frame for the links in the table of contents page.

 After you finish creating the framed site, you must preview the whole package in a frames-capable browser (such as Internet Explorer) to see how the site works and to test that the links work correctly. I explain how to preview your site in the section "Previewing a Framed Web Site," later in this chapter.

Ah, but I get ahead of myself. The easiest place to begin is at the beginning: with the Frames Wizard.

Using the Frames Wizard

With the assistance of the Frames Wizard, you can create an entire framed site in a matter of minutes. The Wizard enables you to choose the layout of your frame set and even creates empty content pages for you to customize later. If you have existing content pages, the Frames Wizard helps you to build the frame set and fit the existing pages inside.

Choosing a frame set template

The easiest way to build a framed site from the ground up is to use a template. The Frames Wizard contains templates for six popular frame set layouts. After you choose a template, the Editor creates empty content pages, which you can modify later on.

To set up a framed site by using the Frames Wizard to choose a frame set template, follow these steps:

1. **In the FrontPage Editor, choose File⇨New (or press Ctrl+N).**

   The New Page dialog box appears.

2. **In the Template or Wizard list box, double-click Frames Wizard.**

   The Choose Technique dialog box appears. Here, you choose how you want to create the frame set.

   As is the case with all Wizards, you must click the Next button to advance to the next screen and Back to go back to a previous screen to change information you entered there. To exit the Wizard at any time, click the Cancel button.

3. **Select the Pick a Template radio button and then click Next.**

   The Pick Template Layout dialog box appears (as shown in Figure 11-2). Here you choose the size and placement of the frames in the frame set.

4. **Select one of the options in the Layout list box and then click Next.**

   A description of the frame set appears in the Description area, and the sample page illustrates the layout of the finished frame set. Each frame is identified by a *name*. (I talk more about frame names in the section "Working with Content Pages," later in this chapter.)

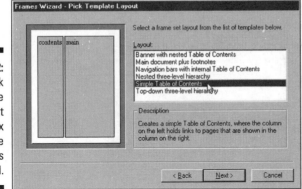

Figure 11-2:
The Pick
Template
Layout
dialog box
of the
Frames
Wizard.

To resize frames, pass the mouse pointer over the frame borders in the sample page until the pointer turns into a double-sided arrow. Click the border and drag it to a new position. (If you'd rather set up the frame set and adjust the frames after you see the setup with content pages inside, that's okay, too. See the section "Tweaking the Frame Set," later in this chapter.)

After you click Next, the Choose Alternate Content dialog box appears.

5. **Click the Browse button to choose the Web page that appears to visitors using a Web browser that can't display frames.**

The Choose Source URL dialog box appears, listing all the pages in your Web site. You can display your site's home page, or you can create a page specifically for this purpose. Click the page that you want to designate as an alternative page and click OK to close the dialog box.

After you click OK, the alternative page's URL appears in the Alternate page URL text box.

(If you want to use an alternative page but haven't yet created the page, click OK to close the Choose Source URL screen and leave the Alternate page URL text box blank. You can create the page later and then edit the frame set to specify the new page as the alternative content page. I describe how to edit frame sets in the section "Tweaking the Frame Set," later in this chapter.)

6. **Click Next.**

The Save Page screen appears. The Wizard generates a page title and URL for the frame set.

7. **If you don't like the title and URL generated by the Wizard, type a new title in the Title text box and a new URL in the URL text box (as shown in Figure 11-3).**

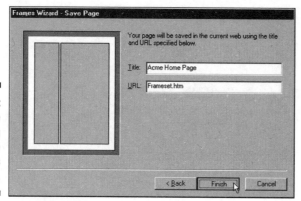

Figure 11-3:
The Save
Page dialog
box of the
Frames
Wizard.

In a framed site, the title of the frame set is the only one visible as a visitor views the site with a Web browser. The titles of the individual content pages don't appear. Make sure that you choose a descriptive title for the frame set.

8. Click Finish to create the frame set and associated content pages.

The Wizard creates the frame set based on your selections, creates corresponding content pages, and saves the frame set and the content pages in your Web site.

9. To start editing content pages, open the pages in the Editor by clicking the Open button, choosing File⇨Open, or pressing Ctrl+O.

The Open File dialog box appears with the Current FrontPage Web tab visible, as shown in Figure 11-4. The title of each content page identifies where the page appears inside the frame set.

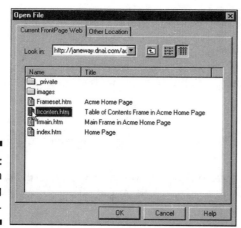

Figure 11-4:
The Open
File dialog
box.

10. Select the page you want to open and click OK.

The content page opens in the Editor (see Figure 11-5). Purple comments inside the page explain how the page works inside the frame set. See the section "Working with Content Pages," later in this chapter, for more information.

To modify the pages that appear in your framed Web site, open and make changes to the *content pages*. If you attempt to open the frame set page in the Editor, the Frames Wizard automatically launches because FrontPage thinks that you want to change the particulars of the frame set page.

If you want to use existing content pages with one of the Wizard's frame set templates, go ahead and follow the preceding steps. Then edit the frame set to use your pages as its content. (The section "Tweaking the Frame Set," later in this chapter, shows you how.) Finally, switch to the FrontPage Explorer (by clicking the Show FrontPage Explorer button or choosing Tools➪Show FrontPage Explorer) and delete the content pages generated by the Wizard. (But leave the frame set page alone!)

Comments

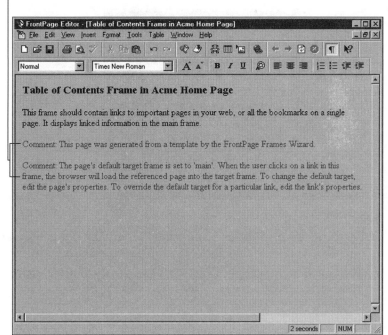

Figure 11-5:
A content
page.

Building your own frame set

The Frames Wizard understands if you'd rather set up your own frame set layout or you have existing pages ready to go inside the frames and you don't want the Wizard to generate its own blank pages.

To build your own frame set, follow these steps:

1. **In the FrontPage Editor, choose File⇨New (or press Ctrl+N).**

   The New Page dialog box appears.

2. **In the Template or Wizard list box, double-click Frames Wizard.**

   The Choose Technique dialog box appears. Here, you choose how you want to create the frame set.

3. **Select the Make a custom grid radio button and then click Next.**

   The Edit Frameset Grid dialog box appears (see Figure 11-6). Here you tinker with the frame set's layout until the frame set looks the way you want.

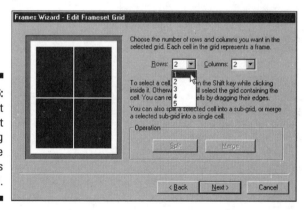

Figure 11-6:
The Edit
Frameset
Grid dialog
box of the
Frames
Wizard.

4. **Select the number of rows and columns contained in the frame set by choosing numbers from the Rows and Columns drop-down lists.**

   The layout of the sample frame set, visible in the box on the left side of the dialog box, changes based on your selections (see Figure 11-7).

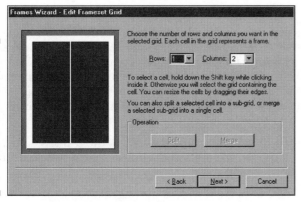

Figure 11-7:
The number
of rows and
columns in
the frame
set changes
based
on your
selections.

- To resize the frames, pass the mouse pointer over the frame borders in the sample frame set until the pointer turns into a double-sided arrow and then click the border and drag it to a new position.

- To split an individual frame into a subgrid, press and hold the Shift key as you click the frame to select it; then click the Split button.

  The frame splits into four individual frames. You can select the subgrid and work with it just as you would the main frame set grid. Click the subgrid to select it and to adjust the number of rows and columns the subgrid contains. To merge the subgrid frames back into one frame, click the Merge button.

5. After you're happy with the layout, click Next.

The Edit Frame Attributes dialog box appears. Here you specify individual settings for each frame in the frame set.

6. Select one of the frames in the sample frame set.

The dialog box options come into full view (see Figure 11-8).

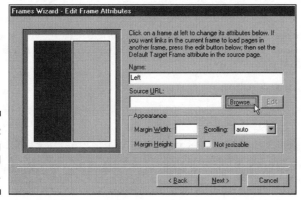

Figure 11-8:
Editing
individual
frames.

7. **In the N͟ame text box, type a frame name.**

   The frame's name acts as an identifying label. The name you choose should be easy to remember because you use the frame name as you specify target frames for the frame set's content pages. (I show you how to do this in the section "Working with Content Pages," later in this chapter.) If the frame is to contain a table of contents page, for example, you could type the name TOC. Or, if you prefer to identify the frame by its position, type a frame name such as Left.

8. **In the Source U͟RL text box, type the URL of the frame's default content page (or click the Br͟owse button to choose a page from a list of all the pages in your Web site).**

   The frame's default content page is the page that's visible the first time a visitor views the frame set.

9. **In the Margin W͟idth and Margin H͟eight text boxes, type the number of pixels that separates the text in the content page from the frame borders.**

10. **Choose a scrolling option from the S͟crolling drop-down list.**

    A framed site automatically adjusts its size based on the size of the visitor's Web browser window. If the browser window is too small to display the contents of each frame, scroll bars appear so that visitors may move around inside the individual frames. You can control the scrolling behavior in your site. The default scrolling setting is auto, which means that, if necessary, scroll bars appear. Yes causes scroll bars to appear even if they're not necessary, and No specifies that scroll bars never appear, no matter what.

11. **If you want to lock the position of frames so that visitors can't resize the frames as they view the site, select the Not r͟esizable check box.**

    By default, whenever visitors view a framed site with a Web browser, they can adjust the positions of frame borders to work with the size of their monitors. By doing so, they don't affect the frame set, just how the framed site appears on-screen. Checking Not r͟esizable turns off that option.

12. **Follow steps 6 through 11 for each frame in the frame set and then click N͟ext.**

    The Choose Alternate Content dialog box appears. Here, you specify the page that appears if a visitor tries to view the frame set with a browser that doesn't support frames.

13. **Click the B͟rowse button.**

    The Choose Source URL dialog box appears, listing the pages in your Web site.

14. **In the list, select the page that you want to use and click OK.**

    The dialog box closes, and the page's URL appears in the Alternate page U͟RL text box.

(If you want to use a custom alternative content page but haven't yet created one, click OK to close the Choose Source URL screen and leave the Alternate page URL text box blank. You can create the page later and then edit the frame set to specify the page as its alternative content page.)

15. **Click Next.**

    The Save Page dialog box appears. The Wizard generates a page title and URL for the frame set.

16. **If you don't like the title and URL generated by the Wizard, type a new title in the Title text box and a new URL in the URL text box.**

    In a framed site, the title of the frame set is the only one visible as a visitor views the site with a Web browser. The titles of the individual content pages don't appear. Make sure that you choose a descriptive title for the frame set.

17. **Click Finish to create the frame set.**

    The Wizard completes its magic and saves the frame set in your Web site.

At this point, you are ready to open the content pages you specified in step 8 and, if necessary, modify the pages to work inside the frame set. I show you how in the section "Editing your own pages to work inside frames," later in the chapter.

Frame set forethought

By default, the FrontPage Frames Wizard creates a frame set page and places that page in your Web site. If you want to give visitors the choice of viewing your site with or without frames, you must place a hyperlink leading to the frame set on another page in your site.

The other option is to specify the frame set as the site's home page so that the frame set page is the first thing visitors see when visiting your site. Because FrontPage automatically sets up an alternative page for browsers that can't handle frames, you're in the clear. Almost.

You need to make sure that those of your visitors viewing the site without frames can still get around. To see what I mean, imagine if the site in Figure 11-1 had no frames and the main body page were used as the alternative content page. How would visitors navigate the site, as no navigational links are on that page?

The solution is to reproduce the links in the table of contents page in the main body page so that visitors can browse the rest of the site. Another option is to create a separate set of pages for browsers that can't display frames. Finally, you can create an alternative content page that specifies that visitors must use a frames-capable browser to view your site and provides links to the Netscape Navigator and Internet Explorer download sites. Whatever you decide, make sure that your site is accessible to *all* your visitors.

Working with Content Pages

As with a fine painting, the frames in your Web site exist only to enhance the contents.

If you used one of the Wizard's frame templates to set up your site, you need to add stuff to the empty content pages the Wizard created. If you built your own frame set, you may need to make a few minor adjustments to your existing content pages so that these pages feel comfy inside their newly framed home.

Editing pages created by the Frames Wizard

To edit the pages generated by the Frames Wizard, simply open those pages in the Editor and make any additions and changes you want. Each page contains purple comments to remind you how the page works inside the frame set. (Comments are visible if the page is open in the Editor but are invisible if the page is viewed with a Web browser. You may delete the comments by clicking anywhere inside the purple text and pressing the Backspace or Delete key.)

Changing the default target frame

As part of the frame set template, the Frames Wizard assigned a *default target frame* to each content page. (The purple comments inside each content page list the default target frame setting.) After you add hyperlinks to the content pages, the hyperlink destination pages appear inside the target frame.

To change a page's default target frame, follow these steps:

1. **Choose File⇨Page Properties (or right-click anywhere inside the page and choose Page Properties from the pop-up menu).**

   The Page Properties dialog box appears with the General tab visible.

2. **In the General tab, type a new frame name in the Default Target Frame text box.**

3. **Click OK to close the dialog box.**

If you don't remember the names of the frames, open the frame set in the Editor. The Frames Wizard launches automatically. Click the Next button until the Edit Frame Attributes dialog box appears and click each frame in the sample frame set to display its name. (While you're there, scribble the names on a sticky note so that you remember them.) Click the Cancel button to close the Wizard and return to work.

Changing the target frame for individual hyperlinks

You can override the default target frame setting for individual hyperlinks inside the page so that their destination pages load in a frame *other* than the page's default frame. To do so, follow these steps:

1. **Create a new hyperlink.**

   The Create Hyperlink dialog box appears, as shown in Figure 11-9. (Refer to Chapter 6 if you're not sure how to create a new hyperlink.)

    Alternatively, select an existing hyperlink and press the Create or Edit Hyperlink button. (Or choose Edit➪Hyperlink, press Ctrl+K, or right-click the hyperlink and choose Hyperlink Properties from the pop-up menu to display the Edit Hyperlink dialog box.)

2. **In the Create or Edit Hyperlink dialog box, type the name of that link's target frame in the Target Frame text box.**

3. **Click OK to close the dialog box.**

Editing your own pages to work inside frames

If you placed your own Web pages into a frame set (as opposed to working with pages generated by the Frames Wizard), the only modification required is to set the pages' default target frames. (I explain how to do so in the section "Changing the default target frame," earlier in this chapter.) If you want, you may specify different target frames for individual hyperlinks inside the page. (Refer to the section "Changing the target frame for individual hyperlinks," earlier in the chapter, for directions.)

Figure 11-9:
You can specify a target frame for individual hyperlinks.

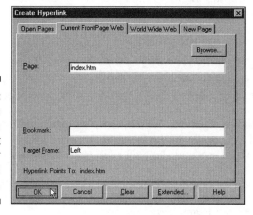

Special target frame names

You can use the following four special target frame names to create different effects. (The underscore character (_) is part of each name):

✔ **_blank:** This name causes the hyperlink destination page to open inside a new Web browser window.

✔ **_self:** This name causes the hyperlink destination page to open inside the same frame in which the hyperlink source page is located.

✔ **_parent:** You can use a second frame set page as the default content page for one or more frames in your site. The result is a *nested frame set,* which is similar in concept to a nested table (which is what you have if you place a table inside a cell of another table). The _parent target frame name causes links in content pages of the nested frame set to load in the *parent frame* — that is, the frame in the original frame set that contains the nested frame set.

✔ **_top:** This name causes the hyperlink destination page to replace the frame set in the browser window.

If your pages contain forms or image maps, you can also specify target frames for form results and image map hotspots.

Setting the target frame for form results

If one of your content pages contains a form, you can specify a target frame for form results. (If you're not familiar with forms, take a look at Chapter 10.) As occurs with hyperlinks, if you specify a target frame for form results, the target frame setting overrides the page's default target frame setting.

To specify a target frame for form results, right-click inside the form and choose Form Properties from the pop-up menu. In the Form Properties dialog box, type a target frame name in the Target Frame text box and then click OK to close the dialog box.

Setting the default target frame for image maps

If one of your content pages contains an image map, you can specify a default target frame for the image map's hotspots. (If you're not sure what an image map is, refer to Chapter 8.) To do so, right-click the image map and choose Image Properties from the pop-up menu. The Image Properties dialog box appears with the General tab visible. In the General tab, type a target frame name in the Target Frame text box and then click OK to close the dialog box.

You can also specify a target frame for individual hotspots inside the image map. To do so, double-click a hotspot to display the Edit Hyperlink dialog box. Type a target frame name in the Target Frame text box, and click OK to close the dialog box. For more details on how to work with image maps, read Chapter 8.

Previewing a Framed Web Site

The only way to see how your framed Web site looks and acts is to preview the site in a Web browser. (Despite its WYSIWYG-ness, the Editor cannot display frames.) Here's the catch: If the frame set is the site's home page, you can't use the Preview in Browser command to open the frame set in a Web browser because opening a frame set in the Editor (so that you can access the Preview in Browser command) automatically launches the Frames Wizard.

To get around this problem, launch your browser separately and type the URL of the frame set in the browser's Location text box. To determine the frame set's URL, switch to the FrontPage Explorer, right-click the frame set's page icon, and choose Properties from the pop-up list. The Properties dialog box appears, and the frame set's URL appears in the Location text box.

Tweaking the Frame Set

You can summon the Frames Wizard whenever you want to edit the frame set itself (say, if you want to change the frame set layout or you want to adjust an individual frame's settings). You can change any of the initial settings you chose while creating the frame set by launching the Frames Wizard again. To do so, follow these steps:

1. **In the Editor, click the Open button (or choose File⇨Open or press Ctrl+O).**

   The Open File dialog box appears with the Current FrontPage Web tab visible.

2. **Select the frame set page from the file list and click OK.**

   The dialog box closes, and the Frames Wizard launches.

3. **Keep clicking the Next button until the dialog box containing the options you want to change appears.**

   All the Frames Wizard options are explained in detail in the section "Using the Frames Wizard," earlier in this chapter.

4. **Make whatever changes you want to these options and keep clicking Next until the final dialog box appears.**

5. **After you reach the final dialog box, click Finish.**

   Unless you rename the frame set, the Wizard confirms that you want the newly changed frame set to overwrite the old version.

6. **Click Yes.**

   The Wizard saves the changes to the frame set.

Chapter 12

Those Lovable WebBots

*A*s if you haven't had to memorize enough FrontPage buzzwords, here comes another: *WebBot*. As soon as you see the wondrous things WebBots can do, however, you shouldn't mind adding a new word to your already-extensive FrontPage vocabulary.

In this chapter, I explain what a WebBot is, I show you what the different WebBots can do, and I demonstrate how you can use them in your Web site.

WebBot Mechanics

A WebBot (known to its friends by the diminutive *Bot*) is a little gizmo you insert in your Web site that simplifies certain Web publishing tasks or adds dynamic features to your site.

WebBots work by teaming up with the FrontPage Personal Web Server. The "gizmo" you add as you insert a WebBot into a page is actually a reference to a special WebBot program, which is built into FrontPage. After you insert a WebBot, the FrontPage Personal Web Server notices the reference and rouses the WebBot program, which springs into action and adds a special effect to your page.

Setting WebBots Loose in Your Web Site

Before the creation of WebBots, adding the following features to your Web site involved lots of mucking around with complicated HTML and server-based programs and coordinating the whole process with the Web server's administrator. Now you accomplish the same thing in a few deft mouse-clicks.

FrontPage contains eight WebBots, each of which performs a different task:

- **Include:** This Bot, added to a Web page, replaces itself with the contents of a second page.

- **Scheduled Include:** This Bot works just like the Include WebBot, except that the inclusion appears only during a specified time period.

- **Scheduled Image:** This Bot works just like the Scheduled Include WebBot, except that it includes an image instead of the contents of a Web page.

- **Search:** This Bot inserts a simple form into a Web page that enables visitors to search for key words throughout your Web site.

- **Substitution:** This Bot enables you to display certain types of standard information in your Web pages.

- **Table of Contents:** This bot generates a Web site table of contents, with hyperlinks leading to each page.

- **Timestamp:** This Bot replaces itself with the time and date the page was last updated.

- **Confirmation Field:** This Bot works in concert with an interactive form to confirm information that visitors enter into form fields. I show you how to use the Configuration Field WebBot in Chapter 10.

In the following sections, I show you how Bots can simplify your life, and I demonstrate how to put the critters to work.

Include WebBot

The Include WebBot simplifies inserting the same information in more than one page in your Web site. After you insert an Include Bot into your page, the Bot is replaced by the contents of a second page.

WebBots and forms

Some WebBots work together with forms. (Chapter 10 talks about forms and form-related WebBots in detail.) These Bots wake up at *runtime,* which means that the Bots activate after a visitor submits form information.

WebBots associated with forms — the Search WebBot, Confirmation Field WebBot, and the form-handling WebBots described in Chapter 10 — work only on a dedicated Web server that supports FrontPage Server Extensions.

Here's an example: I add a copyright notice to the bottom of all the Web pages I create. Instead of typing the copyright notice into each page, I create a separate page that contains only the copyright notice. I then use the Include WebBot to include the contents of the copyright notice page in all the pages in my Web site. If, later, I want to change the wording of the copyright notice, I update the copyright notice page, and the Include Bot reflects the update throughout my Web site.

Inserting the Include WebBot in a page

To use the Include WebBot, follow these steps:

1. **Place the cursor in your page where you want the WebBot to appear.**

 2. **Click the Insert WebBot Component button in the toolbar (or choose Insert⫇WebBot Component).**

    The Insert WebBot Component dialog box appears.

3. **In the Select a component list box, select Include and then click OK.**

    The Insert WebBot Component dialog box is replaced by the WebBot Include Component Properties dialog box.

4. **In the Page URL to include text box, type the URL of the page you want to include.**

    Or click Browse to display the Current Web dialog box. The dialog box lists all the pages and folders in your Web site. Click the page you want to include and click OK. The dialog box closes, and the URL appears in the Page URL to include text box.

5. **Click OK to close the WebBot Include Component Properties dialog box.**

    The contents of the included page appear inside the current page.

 Try passing your mouse pointer over the included information; the pointer turns into a little robot. The robot pointer is a cue that reminds you the text is there courtesy of the Include WebBot. (For more information about the robot pointer, see the sidebar "The robot pointer is more than just cute," later in this chapter.)

To keep included pages hidden from Web browsers, store the pages inside your Web site's _PRIVATE folder. (Refer to Chapter 2 for descriptions of the different FrontPage folders and how to store pages inside them.)

The _PRIVATE folder is private only if you publish the Web site on a Web server that supports FrontPage Server Extensions. For more information, see Chapter 18.

The robot pointer is more than just cute

After you pass your mouse pointer over any text or image displayed with the assistance of a WebBot, the robot pointer appears. Because you can easily forget, for example, that text included by using the Include Bot isn't just plain, old text, the robot pointer serves as a reminder. The robot pointer appears in other situations as well, such as whenever you pass the mouse pointer over purple comments.

Whenever you see the robot pointer, you can double-click to display the appropriate Properties dialog box for that WebBot or element to modify the WebBot's settings. (You can also right-click WebBots and choose WebBot Properties from the pop-up menu.) To delete a WebBot, look for the robot pointer, click to select the WebBot, and then press the Backspace or Delete key.

Updating included pages

To update a page you've included in other pages, simply open that page in the Editor, make your changes, and save the page, just as you would any other Web page. After you save and close the page, FrontPage updates the inclusion throughout the rest of your Web site the next time it recalculates the site's hyperlinks. Recalculating hyperlinks means that the Web Server re-serves the site, integrating any changes made to the site's system of hyperlinks. This usually happens automatically as you update and save the page. (You don't even notice.) To ensure that the Bot updates throughout the site, however, you can specifically tell FrontPage to recalculate your site's hyperlinks.

To do so, open the FrontPage Explorer by pressing the Show FrontPage Explorer button or choosing Tools⇨Show FrontPage Explorer. The Explorer appears. In the Explorer menu bar, choose Tools⇨Recalculate Hyperlinks. The Recalculate Hyperlinks dialog box appears, warning you that recalculating hyperlinks may take several minutes. Click Yes to close the dialog box and proceed with recalculation.

If remembering to recalculate hyperlinks every time you change an included page is a hassle, you can tell FrontPage to remind you whenever an included page has changed, but hasn't yet been updated throughout the site. To do so, choose Tools⇨Options in the Explorer. The Options dialog box appears with the General tab displayed. Click the Warn when included WebBot Components are out of date check box and then click OK to close the dialog box.

Scheduled Include WebBot

The Scheduled Include WebBot functions the same as the Include WebBot, except that the inclusion appears only during a specified time period.

As an example of how the Scheduled Include WebBot can help you, suppose that you use your Web site to announce upcoming events. Instead of keeping track of event dates and making sure that you update your Web site after the event occurs, create a separate page for the announcements. Then use the Scheduled Include WebBot to include the contents of the page in other pages in your Web site, specifying the time period during which the announcements apply. After that time period is over, the announcements automatically disappear.

To use the Scheduled Include WebBot, follow these steps:

1. **Place the cursor in your page where you want the WebBot to appear.**

2. **Click the Insert WebBot Component button in the toolbar (or choose Insert⇨WebBot Component).**

   The Insert WebBot Component dialog box appears.

3. **In the Select a component list box, select Scheduled Include and then click OK.**

   The Insert WebBot Component dialog box is replaced by the WebBot Scheduled Include Component Properties dialog box (see Figure 12-1).

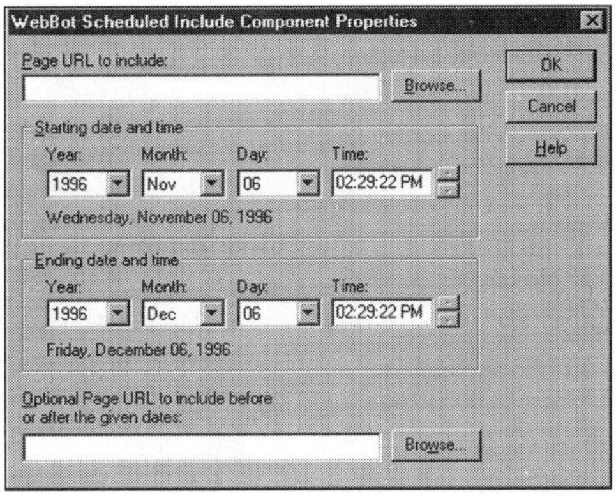

Figure 12-1:
The WebBot
Scheduled
Include
Component
Properties
dialog box.

4. **In the Page URL to include text box, type the URL of the page you want to include.**

   Or click Browse to display the Current Web dialog box. The dialog box lists all the pages and folders in your Web site. Click the page you want to include and click OK. The dialog box closes, and the URL appears in the Page URL to include text box.

5. **In the Starting Date and Time area, select the date and time you want the included page to first appear.**

   Specify the date by selecting options from the Year, Month, and Day drop-down lists. To specify the time, click the time notation inside the Time text box, and click the up- or down-pointing arrows at the right side of the box to adjust the time.

6. **In the Ending Date and Time area, select the date and time you want the included page to disappear.**

   Specify the date by selecting options from the Year, Month, and Day drop-down lists. To specify the time, click the time notation inside the Time text box and click the up- or down-pointing arrows at the right side of the box to adjust the time.

7. **If you want to include a different page before and after the scheduled include time period, type the URL in the Optional page URL to include before or after the given dates text box.**

   Or click Browse to display the Current Web dialog box. The dialog box lists all the pages and folders in your Web site. Click the page you want to include and click OK. The dialog box closes, and the URL appears in the Optional page URL to include before or after the given dates include text box.

   If you don't include an alternative page, nothing appears at the location of the Bot.

8. **Click OK to close the WebBot Scheduled Include Component Properties dialog box.**

   The message [Expired Scheduled Include] appears in your page — unless you specified an alternative URL, in which case the contents of the alternative page appears. The [Expired Scheduled Include] notice appears in the FrontPage Editor only to remind you that the Scheduled Include WebBot is present. If anyone views the page with a Web browser, the notice isn't visible.

If your dedicated Web server is located in another time zone (which is possible if you publish your FrontPage Web sites by using an Internet service provider or company server in another state), the times you schedule must apply to *the server's* time zone, not yours.

Scheduled Image WebBot

The Scheduled Image WebBot works the same as does the Scheduled Include WebBot, except that, instead of inserting another page, this WebBot inserts an image for a limited amount of time. (For more information about using images in your Web site, refer to Chapter 7.)

Scheduled Include caveats

Using the Scheduled Include WebBot and the Scheduled Image WebBot involves a major catch. For the WebBots to work correctly, the FrontPage Explorer must recalculate the Web site's links *during* the scheduled inclusion time. As the Explorer recalculates links, it updates the Web site by asking the Web server to re-serve the site, which updates the display.

Certain events cause FrontPage to recalculate links automatically, such as whether you save a new page containing hyperlinks in your Web site, you edit existing hyperlinks, or a FrontPage form handler automatically adds form results to a page in your site. Unless one of these events occurs during the scheduled include time, however, the include doesn't occur.

You can ensure that the Explorer recalculates your site's hyperlinks during the scheduled include time in one of two ways: by updating your Web site every day or by manually recalculating hyperlinks. To manually recalculate hyperlinks, open your Web site in the FrontPage Explorer. (If the Web site is published on another Web server, open it directly from the server on which it is published; I explain how in Chapter 1.) Choose Tools➪Recalculate Hyperlinks from the FrontPage Explorer menu bar. The Recalculate Hyperlinks dialog box appears, warning you that recalculating hyperlinks may take several minutes. Click Yes to close the dialog box and proceed with recalculation.

This can be very handy if, for example, you flag additions to your Web site with a "New!" icon. Because things are "New!" only for a limited time, you can use the Scheduled Image WebBot to remove the icons after a week or so.

Before you use the Scheduled Image WebBot, be sure to read the accompanying sidebar "Scheduled Include caveats."

To use the Scheduled Image WebBot, follow these steps:

1. **Place the cursor in your page where you want the WebBot to appear.**

2. **Click the Insert WebBot Component button in the toolbar (or choose Insert➪WebBot Component).**

   The Insert WebBot Component dialog box appears.

3. **In the Select a component list box, select Scheduled Image and then click OK.**

   The Insert WebBot Component dialog box is replaced by the WebBot Scheduled Image Component Properties dialog box.

4. **In the Image to include text box, type the URL of the image you want to include.**

   Or click Browse to display the Current Web dialog box. The dialog box lists all the images and folders in your Web site. Select the image you want to include and click OK. The dialog box closes, and the URL appears in the Image to include text box.

5. **In the Starting Date and Time area, select the date and time you want the included image to first appear.**

   Specify the date by selecting options from the Year, Month, and Day drop-down lists. To specify the time, click the time notation inside the Time text box and click the up- or down-pointing arrows at the right side of the box to adjust the time.

6. **In the Ending Date and Time area, select the date and time you want the included image to disappear.**

   Specify the date by selecting options from the Year, Month, and Day drop-down lists. To specify the time, click the time notation inside the Time text box and click the up- or down-pointing arrows at the right side of the box to adjust the time.

7. **If you want to include a different image before and after the scheduled include time period, type the URL in the Optional image to include before or after the given dates text box.**

   Or click Browse to display the Current Web dialog box. The dialog box lists all the images and folders in your Web site. Select the image you want to include and click OK. The dialog box closes, and the URL appears in the Optional image to include before or after the given dates text box.

   If you don't include an alternative image, nothing appears at the location of the Bot.

8. **Click OK to close the WebBot Scheduled Image Component Properties dialog box.**

   The message [Expired Scheduled Image] appears in your page — unless you specified an alternative image, in which case the alternative image appears. The [Expired Scheduled Image]notice appears in the FrontPage Editor only to remind you that the Scheduled Image WebBot is present. If anyone views the page with a Web browser, the notice isn't visible.

If your dedicated Web server is located in another time zone (which is possible if you publish your FrontPage Web sites by using an Internet service provider or company server in another state), the times you schedule must apply to *the server's* time zone, not yours.

Search WebBot

A *key-word search* is to a Web site what a knowledgeable tour guide is to a big city: Both help you bypass the flotsam and get straight to the stuff you want to see. The Search WebBot enables you to add a search function to your Web site in as few as three mouse clicks.

With the Search WebBot nestled in a page in your Web site, visitors enter words or phrases into a text box and then click a button to activate the search. In a moment, a linked list of Web pages matching the search request appears. From there, your visitors need only to click a link to go to a particular page.

You can add the Search WebBot to an existing page or create a separate search page with the help of the Search Page template. To access the template, choose File⇨New to open the New Page dialog box and then double-click Search Page in the Template or Wizard list.

For the Search WebBot to work, the dedicated server on which you publish your Web site must have FrontPage Server Extensions installed. See Chapter 18 for details about publishing your Web site.

To use the Search WebBot, follow these steps:

1. **Place the cursor in your page where you want the WebBot to appear.**

2. **Click the Insert WebBot Component button in the toolbar (or choose Insert⇨WebBot Component).**

   The Insert WebBot Component dialog box appears.

3. **In the Select a component list box, select Search and then click OK.**

   The Insert WebBot Component dialog box is replaced by the WebBot Search Component Properties dialog box (see Figure 12-2).

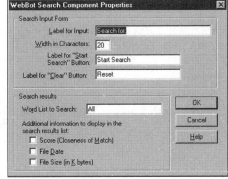

Figure 12-2:
The WebBot
Search
Component
Properties
dialog box.

4. **In the Label for Input text box, type the label that prompts visitors to enter key words.**

   The default label is Search for:.

5. **In the Width in Characters text box, type the width (in number of characters) of the text box into which visitors enter key-words.**

6. **In the Label for "Start Search" Button text box, type the text label that appears on the button that visitors click to start the search.**

   The default label is Search.

7. **In the Label for "Clear" Button text box, type the label that appears on the button that visitors click to erase the contents of the key-word text box.**

   The default label is Reset.

8. **If necessary, specify the scope of the search by typing information in the Word List to Search text box.**

   The default value All causes the search to look through every page in your Web site. To restrict the search to a discussion group in your Web site, type the name of the discussion group directory here. (I show you how to create a discussion group — complete with a search — in Chapter 15.)

   To hide pages from the Search WebBot, stow them away in the _PRIVATE folder. (In Chapter 2, I show you how to move pages into folders.) For example, you may not want the search to extend to index pages that aren't yet complete. The Search WebBot ignores pages in other hidden folders as well (those with names that begin with the underscore character).

   The _PRIVATE folder is private only if you publish the Web site on a Web server that supports FrontPage Server Extensions. For more information, see Chapter 18.

9. **Select the check boxes next to the items you want to appear in the search results list.**

   After a visitor performs a search, the Search WebBot returns a linked list of matching pages. You can tell the WebBot to include additional information by selecting the following check boxes: Score (Closeness of Match) sorts the pages according to the closeness of the match; File Date shows the date the page was last modified; and File Size (in K bytes) shows the page's file size.

10. **Click OK to close the WebBot Search Component Properties dialog box.**

    A search form appears in your page (see Figure 12-3).

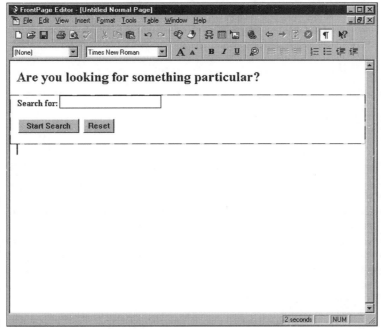

Figure 12-3:
The Search
WebBot
adds a
search form
to your
Web site.

 To test the search form, click the Preview in Browser button (or choose File⇨Preview in Browser). After the search page appears in your Web browser, enter one or a few key words into the text box and click the form's Search button. In a moment, the search results appear.

 If the search results seem out of date, make sure that you save all open pages in the Editor (or choosing File⇨Save All) and recalculate your Web site's hyperlinks in the Explorer. (From the Explorer menu bar, choose Tools⇨Recalculate Hyperlinks.) Now try your search again — it should be fit as a fiddle.

Substitution WebBot

The Substitution WebBot enables you to display placeholders in your page that replace themselves with bits of information called *configuration variables*. Configuration variables describe certain details about the page or contain snippets of information you specify.

Similar to the Include WebBot, which includes in your Web page the contents of another page, the Substitution WebBot includes in your Web page the value of the configuration variable you choose.

Displaying standard configuration variables

FrontPage maintains a standard set of configuration variables for each page, as described in the following list:

- ✔ *Author* is the name of the person who created the page.

- ✔ *ModifiedBy* is the name of the person who most recently edited the page.

- ✔ *Description* is a description of the page.

- ✔ *Page-URL* is the current location of the page.

To see the values for each of a page's standard configuration variables, go to the FrontPage Explorer (if not already there), right-click the page's icon, and choose Properties from the pop-up menu. The Properties dialog box appears, with the General tab visible. Click the Summary tab to make that tab visible (see Figure 12-4). The author's name appears next to Created by in the Summary tab. (If no name appears next to Created by, this omission means that the page was originally created by a program other than FrontPage.) The name of the person who last modified the page appears next to Modified by. The page description appears in the Comments text box. In the General tab, the page's URL appears in the Location box.

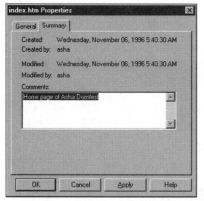

Figure 12-4:
The values
for a page's
standard
configuration
variables
appear
in the
Explorer's
Properties
dialog box.

To use the Substitution WebBot to display standard configuration variables, follow these steps:

1. **In the Editor, place the cursor in your page where you want the WebBot to appear.**

2. **Click the Insert WebBot Component button in the toolbar (or choose Insert⇨WebBot Component).**

   The Insert WebBot Component dialog box appears.

3. **In the Select a component list box, select Substitution and then click OK.**

   The Insert WebBot Component dialog box is replaced by the WebBot Substitution Component Properties dialog box.

4. **Select the configuration you want to display from the Substitute with drop-down list.**

5. **Click OK to close the WebBot Substitution Component Properties dialog box.**

   The value of the configuration variable appears in your page.

If you use the Substitution WebBot to display the Page-URL configuration variable, the URL that appears corresponds to the computer on which the page is currently located. If you later publish the page on another Web server, the URL displayed inside the page reflects the page's old location and is therefore incorrect.

To solve this problem, open the Web site directly from the Web server on which the site is published (refer to Chapter 1 if you're not sure how), and open the page displaying the Page-URL configuration variable. Click the URL and press the Backspace or Delete key to delete the Substitution WebBot. Now reinsert the Substitution WebBot and set it up to display the Page-URL configuration variable. (Follow the steps outlined in this section.) The correct URL appears. Save the page to make the change visible to the rest of the Web.

Creating and displaying your own configuration variables

You can create your own configuration variables to use as placeholders for standard bits of information throughout the Web site. Say, for example, that you want to list your address in several Web pages; instead of typing the address repeatedly, you can create a configuration variable named *Address.* If you use the Substitution WebBot to include the Address configuration variable in your page, your address appears in its place. Even better, if you move down the street, you simply need to update the configuration variable instead of editing your address in every single page.

To create your own configuration variables, follow these steps:

1. **In the Editor toolbar, click the Show FrontPage Explorer button (or choose Tools⇨Show FrontPage Explorer).**

   The Explorer appears.

2. **Choose Tools⇨Web Settings.**

   The FrontPage Web Settings dialog box appears, with the Configuration Tab visible.

3. **Click the Parameters tab to make the tab visible.**

4. **Click the Add button.**

   The Add Name and Value dialog box appears.

5. **In the Name text box, type the name of the configuration variable.**

   Choose a name that is brief and descriptive, such as **Address**.

6. **In the Value text box, type the value of the configuration variable.**

   The value is the text that FrontPage substitutes whenever you display the configuration variable in your page. For the Address configuration variable, for example, you enter your address here.

7. **Click OK to close the Add Name and Value dialog box.**

   The configuration variable's name and value appear in the list box in the Parameters tab (see Figure 12-5).

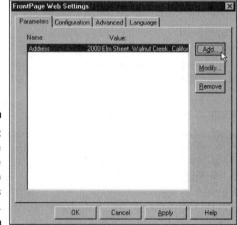

Figure 12-5:
The
FrontPage
Web
Settings
dialog box.

8. **To add more configuration variables, repeat steps 4 through 7.**

   You may modify or remove configuration variables by clicking their names in the list and then clicking the Modify or Remove buttons.

9. **After you finish creating configuration variables, click OK to close the FrontPage Web Settings dialog box.**

To insert the newly create configuration variables in your Web site, follow the steps in the section "Displaying standard configuration variables," earlier in this chapter.

Table of Contents WebBot

One of the best ways to help visitors find their way around your Web site is to include a *table of contents*. A table of contents displays the titles of all your site's pages in a hierarchical list, with links to each page. Despite the usefulness of this feature, however, even the best-intentioned Web publisher dreads creating a table of contents for a Web site that contains many pages, especially if constantly adding and changing pages.

Here's where the Table of Contents WebBot swoops in to the rescue. This WebBot cranks out a fully linked table of contents and keeps the contents list up-to-date even if pages change.

You can use the Table of Contents WebBot to add a table of contents to an existing page, or you can create a new page by choosing File⇨New to display the New Page dialog box and double-clicking Table of Contents in the template or Wizard list.

To use the Table of Contents WebBot, follow these steps:

1. **Place the cursor in your page where you want the WebBot to appear.**

2. **Click the Insert WebBot Component button in the toolbar (or choose Insert⇨WebBot Component).**

   The Insert WebBot Component dialog box appears.

3. **In the Select a component list box, select Table of Contents and then click OK.**

   The Insert WebBot Component dialog box is replaced by the WebBot Table of Contents Component Properties dialog box.

4. **In the Page URL for Starting Point of Table text box, type the URL of the page you want to appear at the top of the table of contents.**

   Or click Browse to display the Current Web dialog box. The dialog box lists all the pages and folders in your Web site. Click the page you want to include and click OK. The dialog box closes, and the URL appears in the Page URL for Starting Point of Table text box.

   By default, the WebBot selects the site's home page as its starting point.

5. **Select the heading size for the first item in the table of contents from the Heading Size drop-down list.**

   Selecting a relatively bold heading (such as Heading 1 or Heading 2) sets the first item apart from the rest so that the item acts as a title for the table of contents. If you'd rather the first item looked like all the others, select none.

6. **If you want each page in your site to appear in the table of contents only once, select the Show each page only once check box.**

   If you don't select this option, pages that link to more than one page in your site appear more than once.

7. **If you want the table of contents to display pages in your site that don't link to other pages, select the Show pages with no incoming hyperlinks check box.**

   If you select this check box, the only access point to the page is through the table of contents, because the page isn't linked to the rest of your Web site.

8. **If you want FrontPage to automatically update the table of contents as you edit pages and add new pages to your Web site, select the Recompute table of contents when any other page is edited check box.**

   If you don't select this option and still want to update the table of contents, you need to recalculate your site's hyperlinks each time a page changes or you add a new page. (To recalculate hyperlinks, choose Tools⇨Recalculate Hyperlinks in the FrontPage Explorer.)

9. **Click OK to close the WebBot Table of Contents Component Properties dialog box.**

   A placeholder table of contents appears (see Figure 12-6).

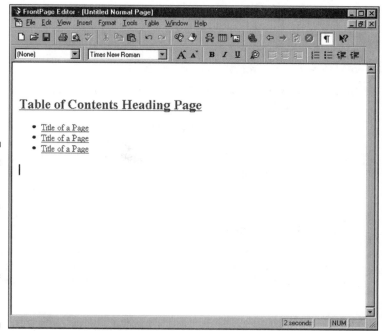

Figure 12-6:
A place-holder table of contents appears in your page after you insert the Table of Contents WebBot.

To see how the actual table of contents looks, click the Preview in Browser button (or choose File⇨Preview in Browser) to view the page.

Timestamp WebBot

The Timestamp WebBot replaces itself with the time and date the page was last modified. This feature is a great way to inform frequent visitors that you've added new stuff to the page since the last time they visited. The presence of this WebBot also tells the world that you're committed to keeping your site's content timely and fresh.

To use the Timestamp WebBot, follow these steps:

1. **Place the cursor in your page where you want the WebBot to appear.**

 2. **Click the Insert WebBot Component button in the toolbar (or choose Insert⇨WebBot Component).**

The Insert WebBot Component dialog box appears.

3. **In the Select a component list box, click Timestamp, and then click OK.**

The Insert WebBot Component dialog box is replaced by the WebBot Timestamp Component Properties dialog box.

4. **Select a display option.**

Select the Date this page was last edited radio button if you want the date to reflect when you last changed the page by hand. Select the Date this page was last automatically updated radio button if you want the date to reflect your edits *and* automatic updates — for example, if a table of contents on the page automatically regenerates.

5. **Select a date format from the Date Format drop-down list (shown in Figure 12-7).**

If you just want to display the time, select (none) from the drop-down list.

Figure 12-7:
The Date
Format
drop-down
list.

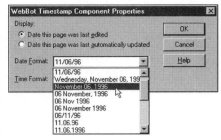

6. **Select a time format from the Time Format drop-down list.**

   If you just want to display the date, select (none) from the drop-down list.

7. **Click OK to close the WebBot Timestamp Component Properties dialog box.**

   The date and/or time the page was last modified appears in the page.

Fixing a broken Bot

Suppose that, while looking over your Web site in the Hyperlink View of the FrontPage Explorer, you notice a page with a red triangle next to it. That triangle means that the page contains a WebBot that's set up incorrectly. To repair the afflicted Bot, follow these steps:

1. **In the Explorer, right-click the page's icon and choose Properties from the pop-up list.**

   The Properties dialog box appears, with the Errors tab visible. In the Description box, you find a detailed description of the problem.

2. **Click OK to close the Properties dialog box and, depending on the problem outlined in the Description box, proceed to repair the WebBot.**

Depending on the type of WebBot, you may need to open the page containing the Bot in the Editor, double-click the Bot to display its associated Properties dialog box, and proceed with repairs there. Or you may need to perform a task in the Explorer, such as correcting a configuration variable. (Refer to the section "Creating and displaying your own configuration variables," earlier in the chapter, for instructions.)

After you complete repairs (and, if necessary, save the page containing the WebBot), return to the Explorer and choose View⇨Refresh to refresh the Web site's display. The red triangles should disappear.

Chapter 13

Eye-Popping Extras: Multimedia, Components, and Scripts

As the Web's popularity grows, resourceful developers are finding ways around the inherent limitations of HTML. No longer satisfied with screenfuls of static text and pictures, software companies are developing ways for surfers to enjoy Web-based sound and animation and even interact with the information they see.

In this chapter, you discover how to take advantage of exciting Web publishing extras. When you use FrontPage, adding multimedia goodies to your page is as simple as inserting a graphic. You also dabble with additions such as ActiveX controls, Java applets, plug-ins, and PowerPoint animations. Finally, you find out how FrontPage simplifies adding scripts to your page.

As sexy as these extras are, they're entirely optional. The most effective Web sites use special effects to enhance already-strong content and good design.

Multimedia Madness

Multimedia — the blending of text, sound, and video — turns your Web page into a sensory event. Movies, music, and words combine to form one heckuva presentation. Use multimedia to add additional effect and to present information in different ways, such as in the form of a rotating slide show or a live interview. FrontPage enables you to easily insert sounds and videos in your Web pages.

Music to your ears

Why not welcome your visitors with a message from the CEO or an aria from *Carmen*? By using the FrontPage Editor, you can embed a *background sound* into your page that plays as soon as someone arrives.

Background sound files must be in one of the following file formats: WAV, MIDI, AIF, AIFC, AIFF, AU, or SND.

Last heard in the Microsoft Web Gallery: a toilet flushing, a train whistle, and various whooshes, bloops, and bangs. Listen for yourself (and download your favorites to use in your own Web site) at `http://www.microsoft.com/ gallery/files/sounds/default.htm`.

To hear background sounds, your visitors must have sound equipment (a sound card and speakers) installed on their computers. Also, as of this writing, Microsoft Internet Explorer (Version 2.0 and later) is the only Web browser capable of playing background sound.

To insert a background sound, follow these steps:

1. In the Editor, choose Insert⇨Background Sound.

The Background Sound dialog box appears. The dialog box contains two tabs: the Current FrontPage Web tab and the Other Location tab (see Figure 13-1).

Figure 13-1:
The Background Sound dialog box.

2. Select the sound file that you want to add:

- If the sound file is a part of your Web site, click the Current FrontPage Web tab. The list box inside this tab displays the sound files and folders stored in your Web site. Click the sound file to select it.

- If the sound file is stored elsewhere on your computer, click the Other Location tab and type the sound file's location in the From File text box or click the Browse button to display a second Background Sound dialog box. This dialog box contains a list of your hard drive's folders and files. Navigate your hard drive until you see the file you want. (If you don't see it, check to see whether the appropriate file type is visible in the Files of type drop-down list.) Then click the file and click OK to close the Background Sound dialog box. The sound's location appears in the From File text box.

- If the sound file is located on the Web, click the From Location radio button and type the sound file's URL (including the `http://`) in the accompanying text box.

3. Click OK to close the Background Sound dialog box.

 To hear the sound, click the Preview in Browser button or choose File➪Preview in Browser. (This action works only if you have sound equipment installed on your computer and you use Internet Explorer.)

If the sound file is located elsewhere on your computer or on the Web, the next time you save the page, the Save File to Web dialog box appears, offering to import the file into your Web site. Click Yes to import the file.

 By default, the background sound plays once as someone views the page with a Web browser. If you want the sound to repeat, choose File➪Page Properties to open the Page Properties dialog box. In the General tab, type in the Loop text box the number of times you want the sound to repeat. If you really want to drive your visitors nuts, click the Forever check box. That way, the sound continues to play until they leave the page.

Fun with video

If a picture says a thousand words, a video clip . . . well, you know. A *video clip* is a bit of animation, or a moving picture, that you insert into your page for added zing. As long as you save the clip in AVI format, it's ready for its debut on the Web.

 You don't need to run out to the corner video store for sample movie clips. Grab a bowl of popcorn and visit `http://www.yahoo.com/Computers_and_Internet/Multimedia/Video` instead.

Only advanced browsers, such as Internet Explorer (Version 2.0 or later) and Netscape Navigator (Version 3.0 or later) can play videos.

To insert a video clip, follow these steps:

1. In the Editor, choose Insert⇨Video.

The Video dialog box appears. The dialog box contains two tabs: the Current FrontPage Web tab and the Other Location tab.

2. Select the video file that you want to add.

- If the video file is a part of your Web site, click the Current FrontPage Web tab. The list box inside this tab displays the sound files and folders stored in your Web site. Click the video file to select it.

- If the video file is stored elsewhere on your computer, click the Other Location tab and enter the file's location in the From File text box or click the Browse button to display a second Video dialog box. This dialog box contains a list of your hard drive's folders and files. Navigate your hard drive until you see the file you want, click the file, and then click OK to close the Background Sound dialog box. The video's location appears in the From File text box.

- If the video file is located on the Web, click the From Location radio button, and type the file's URL (including the `http://`) in the accompanying text box.

3. Click OK to close the Video dialog box.

The first frame of the video appears inside your page.

 To see the video in action, click the Preview in Browser button or choose File⇨Preview in Browser.

If the video clip is located elsewhere on your computer or on the Web, the Save File to Web dialog box appears the next time you save the page. The dialog box offers to import the file into your Web site; click Yes to import the file.

After you insert a video into your page, you can tinker with some of its properties, such as how many times the video repeats and when the video begins playing.

To adjust a video's properties, follow these steps:

1. Right-click the video and choose Image Properties from the pop-up menu.

The Image Properties dialog box appears with the Video tab visible (see Figure 13-2). This tab contains all the FrontPage video-control tools.

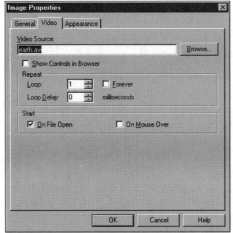

Figure 13-2:
The Video
tab of the
Image
Properties
dialog box.

2. **To display a Play and Stop button below the video, as viewed with a Web browser, check the Show Controls in Browser check box.**

   If you show controls, you enable the visitor to stop and start the video instead of having the video play automatically.

3. **In the Loop text box, specify the number of times you want the video to repeat.**

   If you want the clip to keep playing until the visitor leaves the page, check the Forever check box.

4. **In the Loop Delay text box, specify the number of milliseconds you want the video to pause before repeating.**

   Make sure that you're accurate here. You don't want the video to pause a millisecond more than necessary.

5. **In the Start area, select an option that triggers the video to start playing.**

   Select the On File Open check box to have the video play as soon as a visitor arrives. Select the On Mouse Over check box to have the video play as soon as the mouse pointer passes over the video. Or select both check boxes to have the video begin playing when the visitor arrives and then repeat as soon as the mouse pointer passes over the video.

6. **Click OK.**

   The Image Properties dialog box closes.

Fancy stuff ahead: Proceed with caution

Multimedia, components, scripts, and the Web are relatively new partners and are still in the process of developing a comfortable working relationship. If you use these features in your site, you need to remain aware of the following limitations:

✔ **Speed:** Because they pack so much information, multimedia files and components tend toward chubbiness and, therefore, take a looooong time to load, especially over a slow Internet connection. For an indication of how much load time each addition tacks onto your page, glance at the Estimated Download Time box on the right side of the FrontPage Editor's status bar.

✔ **Compatibility:** Not all browsers know how to deal with multimedia files, components, and scripts. For the most part, visitors need to use the latest version of Internet Explorer or Netscape Navigator — and even then, visitors can't always experience every effect.

If you use multimedia files, components, and scripts in your site, tell your visitors: Insert a note that lists special browser, plug-in, or platform requirements and (if applicable) links to download sites.

Working with Components

If you're ready to position your Web site on the cutting edge, you now need to look beyond HTML to the exciting world of *components*. Components are gizmos that you add to your Web page to give the page extra oomph. As someone visits your page, the visitor's Web browser teams up with the component to produce some kind of special effect. Components can do everything from displaying the day's stock quotes in a scrolling ticker to adding multimedia effects, such as an animated button, to generating a complete Web-based program.

You can add three types of components to your Web site: *ActiveX controls, Java applets,* and *plug-ins.* In this section, I introduce you to each type of component, outline its pros and cons, and show you how to insert each component into your page with the FrontPage Editor.

Throughout the rest of this chapter, I refer to buttons in the Advanced toolbar, as shown in Figure 13-3. You make the toolbar visible by choosing View⇨ Advanced Toolbar.

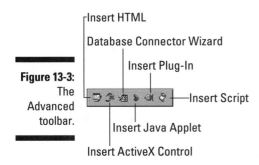

Insert HTML

Database Connector Wizard

Insert Plug-In

Figure 13-3:
The
Advanced
toolbar.

Insert Script

Insert Java Applet

Insert ActiveX Control

In this section, I assume that you have working knowledge of ActiveX controls, Java applets, and plug-ins. If you don't, I refer you to Web sites and other books that help bring you up to speed.

Adding an ActiveX control

An *ActiveX control* is a self-contained program you drop into your page that adds a special feature. What the control does depends on its program; the control may create a simple visual effect, such as rotating text, or the control may perform a task, such as calculating your mortgage. (I haven't yet found an ActiveX control that does dishes, but I continue to search.)

As someone visits a page containing an ActiveX control, the visitor's browser automatically downloads the control, stores it on that person's computer, and runs the control. The next time that person visits a page containing the same control, the Web browser simply refers to the copy of the control on the hard drive, saving precious download time.

You can preview and download tons of ActiveX controls at several excellent Web sites. Microsoft, developer of ActiveX technology, struts its stuff in the ActiveX Control Gallery at `http://activex.microsoft.com`. Two other notable sites to visit: ZDNet's ActiveXfiles at `http://www.zdnet.com/activexfiles` and Activex.com at (where else?) `http://www.activex.com`.

The only problem with ActiveX controls — and it's a biggie — is that, as of this writing, these controls are supported only by Internet Explorer for Windows 95. One ActiveX plug-in approximates ActiveX controls for Netscape Navigator users — those with Version 3.0 or later who use Windows 95, that is — but this plug-in's not as reliable as Internet Explorer's built-in support. (I explain what a plug-in is, by the way, in the section "Partnering with plug-ins," later in this chapter.) ActiveX development for other platforms and browsers is under way, but until these versions become available, I recommend using ActiveX controls sparingly, keeping in mind that the majority of your visitors can't view their effects. (An exception is if you're building a Web site for a corporate Intranet and everyone accessing the site uses Internet Explorer with Windows 95.)

For more information about what ActiveX controls are and how to use them, refer to the Web sites mentioned earlier. (ActiveXfiles' site, especially, has great introductory articles.) Or pick up *ActiveX Internet Programming For Dummies* (IDG Books Worldwide, Inc.), by Kurt Fenstermacher.

To insert an Active X control, follow these steps:

1. **Position the cursor at the location in your Web site where you want to insert the Active X control.**

2. **Click the Insert ActiveX Control button (or choose Insert⇨Other Components⇨ActiveX Control).**

   The ActiveX Control Properties dialog box appears. Everything you need to customize an ActiveX control lives here.

3. **In the Pick a Control drop-down list box, type the filename of the ActiveX control you want to insert (or click the down-arrow at the right side of the list box to open and select a control name from the drop-down list).**

   This drop-down list contains the names of all the ActiveX controls already installed on your computer. (ActiveX control files are identified by the three-letter extension OCX.)

   Some controls in the drop-down list don't work in Web pages because these controls were originally designed to work with non-Internet programs. Unfortunately, you can't tell by looking at the list which controls work and which don't. To be sure, download only those controls that you know are specifically for use in Web pages. After you download a control from the Web — or as you visit a page that contains the control — your Web browser automatically stores the control file in the C:\WINDOWS \ OCCACHE folder. FrontPage looks inside this folder and adds the name of the control to the list of installed controls.

4. **To specify parameters for the ActiveX control, click the Properties button.**

   Depending on the control, one of two things happens, as follows:

   • If the control supports FrontPage editing, the Edit ActiveX Control dialog box appears, along with a Properties dialog box (see Figure 13-4). The Edit ActiveX Control dialog box contains a preview of the control, which changes based on changes you make in the Properties dialog box. (The thing that reads Click here in the Edit ActiveX Control dialog box is a preview of how the control looks in the Web page.) The Properties dialog box lists the names and values of the control's parameters.

Edit a parameter by clicking its name/value with the mouse and typing a new value in the text box at the top of the Properties dialog box; then click the Apply button. Click OK in the Edit ActiveX Control dialog box after you finish. Click OK again to close the ActiveX Control Properties dialog box.

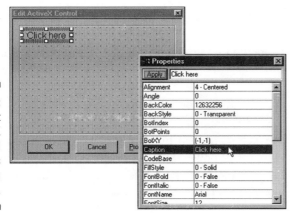

Figure 13-4:
The Edit
ActiveX
Control and
Properties
dialog
boxes.

- If the ActiveX control doesn't support FrontPage editing, the Object Parameters dialog box appears instead. To use this dialog box, you must already know the names of the control's associated parameters. (You should be able to find this information on the Web site from which you downloaded the control.) To define parameters in this dialog box, click the Add button. The Edit Object Parameter dialog box appears. In the Name text box, enter the parameter name. In the Value area, click the radio button next to the value type (Data, Page, or Object) and specify the appropriate value in the accompanying text box. If the value is a page, enter the type in the Media type text box. Click OK after you finish. Click OK again to close the ActiveX Control Properties dialog box.

5. **In the Name text box of the ActiveX Control Properties dialog box, type an optional control name.**

   This action is necessary only if you refer to the control from scripts in your page. (I talk about scripts in the section "Adding Web Page Scripts," later in this chapter.)

6. **Select an option from the Alignment drop-down list.**

   Refer to the section "Aligning an image with surrounding text," in Chapter 7, for a description of each alignment option.

7. **If you want to surround the control with a black border, enter the border thickness in pixels in the Border thickness text box.**

This option is really a waste of time, at least for now, because the border is visible only in Netscape Navigator. Because Netscape supports ActiveX controls only with the help of a separate plug-in (and even then, not all ActiveX controls), what's the point?

8. **In the Horizontal spacing text box, type the number of pixels of white space separating the ActiveX control from text to its right or left.**

9. **In the Vertical spacing text box, type the number of pixels of white space separating the ActiveX control from text above or below the control.**

10. **In the Width and Height text boxes, type the width and height of the ActiveX control, in pixels.**

11. **If you want a message to appear in place of the control in browsers that don't display ActiveX controls, type this message in the HTML text box.**

The message can contain HTML tags. If you want the message to appear bold, add the appropriate HTML tags for bold text — for example, `<b>Your browser does not support ActiveX controls</b>`.

Because I assume in this section that you know how to use ActiveX controls, I also assume that you know the basics of HTML. If you don't, or want to find out more, check out *HTML For Dummies,* 2nd Edition (IDG Books Worldwide, Inc.), by Ed Tittel and Steve James.

12. **If the ActiveX control accepts parameters at runtime, type in the Data Source text box the URL of the file containing the parameters.**

If you don't know the URL, click Browse to display the Select a File dialog box, which contains two tabs: Current FrontPage Web and Other Location.

- If the data source file is a part of your Web site, click the Current FrontPage Web tab. The list box inside this tab displays the sound files and folders stored in your Web site. Click the data source file to select it.

- If the data source file is stored elsewhere on your computer, click the Other Location tab and type the file's location in the From File text box or click the Browse button to display a second Select a File dialog box. This dialog box contains a list of your hard drive's folders and files. Navigate your hard drive until you see the file you want, click the file, and then click OK to close the Background Sound dialog box. The data source file's location appears in the From File text box.

- If the data source file is located on the Web, click the From Location radio button and enter the file's URL (including the `http://`) in the accompanying text box.

13. **If the ActiveX control was created by a third party (that is, the control isn't one of the built-in Microsoft controls), type the control's URL in the Code Source text box.**

    The Code Source URL tells the visitor's Web browser where to go to download the control used in your page. You can either type an absolute URL that points to a specific location on the Web (such as `http://activex.microsoft.com/controls/iexplorer/iepreld.ocx`) or a relative URL that points to a control located inside your Web site. (If you use a relative URL, you must import the control into your Web site. For details on how to import files, refer to Chapter 2.)

14. **Click OK.**

    The dialog box closes, and the ActiveX control appears in your page — or, if the control isn't visible or isn't supported by the Editor, the ActiveX icon appears instead (see Figure 13-5).

Figure 13-5:
The ActiveX
Control icon.

 To see the ActiveX control in action, click the Preview in Browser button or choose File⇨Preview in Browser from the menu bar.

Jammin' with Java applets

On the surface, *Java applets* appear similar to ActiveX controls. As are ActiveX controls, Java applets are small programs you insert in your Web page that download and run as a visitor views the page with a Web browser.

Unlike ActiveX, however, Java applets are *platform independent,* which means that these applets don't rely on a particular operating system to work (Windows 95, for example). The only piece of software necessary to run Java applets is a Java-aware Web browser, such as Netscape Navigator or Internet Explorer.

On the downside, Java applets are not reusable — that is, each time you visit a site containing a Java applet, the browser must redownload the applet to run it. (ActiveX controls download only the first time you visit the site.) This characteristic tacks several seconds to your site's load time, which, as you know, frustrates visitors — especially those with slow Internet connections.

Bottom line: If the effect produced by the Java applet is worth the wait, go for it. If not, can the applet. (I mean, face it — would *you* want to wait 60 seconds for a bit of text that jumps around the page?)

If you want to experiment with Java applets in your site, visit Gamelan (pronounced GAM-a-lahn) at http://www.gamelan.com. Any Java programmer who's anyone displays applets there.

For nuts-and-bolts Java information, check out JavaWorld at http://www.javaworld.com. If you prefer the *...For Dummies* approach to using Java in your Web pages, read *Java For Dummies* (IDG Books Worldwide, Inc.), by Aaron E. Walsh.

To insert a Java applet in your Web page, follow these steps:

1. **Download a Java applet from the Web or, if you know how Java works, create your own applet.**

   (Gamelan is an excellent source of shareware Java applets.)

2. **In the FrontPage Explorer, import the applet to your Web site.**

   Applets are identified by the filename extension CLASS. For details on how to import files, refer to Chapter 2.

3. **From the Explorer, open the Web page into which you want to insert the applet.**

   Chapter 2 also explains the details of opening Web pages from within the Explorer.

   The page opens in the FrontPage Editor.

4. **Place the cursor in the page where you want the applet to appear.**

5. **Click the Insert Java Applet button (or choose <u>I</u>nsert⇨<u>O</u>ther Components⇨<u>J</u>ava Applet).**

   The Java Applet Control Properties dialog box appears.

6. **In the Applet <u>S</u>ource text box, type the name of the applet.**

7. **If the applet is stored inside a folder in your Web site, type the name of the folder in the Applet <u>B</u>ase URL text box.**

   If you store all Java applets in a subfolder of your Web site called APPLETS, for example, type **applets** in the Applet <u>B</u>ase URL text box. That way, as a visitor's browser accesses your page and tries to download the applet to run it, the browser knows to look for the applet inside the right folder.

8. **If you want a message to appear in place of the applet in Java-impaired browsers, type the message in the Message for Browsers without Java Support text box.**

   The message can contain HTML tags. If you want the message to appear bold, add the appropriate HTML tags for bold text — for example, `<b>Your browser does not support Java</b>`.

9. **Click the Add button to add parameter names and values to the text box in the Applet Parameters area of the dialog box.**

   The Set Attribute Value dialog box appears.

10. **In the Name text box, enter the parameter name.**

11. **In the Value text box, enter the parameter value.**

    To leave the Value empty so that the text box may accept the value from another source at runtime, click the Specify value check box to remove the check mark.

12. **Click OK to close the Set Attribute Value dialog box.**

13. **To add another parameter, click Add again and follow steps 10 through 12.**

    To modify existing parameters, click Modify. To remove a parameter, click Remove.

14. **In the Width and Height text boxes, type the width and height of the applet, in pixels.**

15. **In the Horizontal spacing text box, type the number of pixels of white space separating the applet from text to its right or left.**

16. **In the Vertical spacing text box, type the number of pixels of white space separating the applet from text above or below the applet.**

17. **Select an option from the Alignment drop-down list.**

    Refer to the section "Aligning an image with surrounding text," in Chapter 7, for a description of each alignment option.

18. **Click OK.**

    The dialog box closes, and the applet icon appears in the Web page in place of the applet itself (see Figure 13-6).

Figure 13-6:
The Java
applet icon.

To see the applet, click the Preview in Browser button or choose File⇨Preview in Browser. (You must use a Java-capable browser such as Internet Explorer or Netscape Navigator.)

Partnering with plug-ins

A *plug-in* is a file you insert in your Web page that requires the assistance of a separate program (also referred to as a plug-in) for the file to appear on the Web. If you post a Microsoft Word document on the Web, for example, only those visitors with Word installed on their computers can read the file. To get around this problem, Microsoft created the Word Viewer plug-in. This program, if installed, enables visitors to view and print Word documents, even if they don't have Word itself (I talk more about the Word Viewer in Chapter 20).

Some plug-in programs (called *inline plug-ins*) work together with the browser to display files inside the browser window. Other plug-in programs launch and display the plug-in file in a separate window. These types of programs are often referred to as *helper applications*.

 Plug-ins are available for all sorts of file formats. For an overview and links to plug-in download sites, visit Plug-In Plaza at `http://browserwatch.iworld.com/plug-in.html` and Netscape's Plug-In page at `http://home.netscape.com/comprod/mirror/navcomponents_download.html`.

Designers love the plug-in system because plug-ins enable them to use familiar graphic and multimedia tools to create beautiful Web site effects. Web surfers, on the other hand, aren't always so thrilled on running into plug-ins in Web pages.

If you visit a page that contains a plug-in, you can view the file only if you installed the appropriate plug-in program on your computer. If not, you need to go through the tedious process of jumping to the plug-in program's download site, downloading the plug-in (which may take several minutes), installing the program, closing and reopening the browser, going back to the original Web site that contained the plug-in file in the first place, and viewing the file. Frankly, I am rarely willing to jump through so many hoops just to see a flashy effect.

Complication Number 2: Plug-in programs are platform specific, and not all plug-ins come in all platform flavors or work with all browsers.

On the other hand, certain plug-ins, such as the Adobe PDF document format and its associated Acrobat Reader plug-in program, are so widely used that including these files in your Web pages enables you take to advantage of different presentation options with little hassle for visitors. (I talk more about the Adobe Acrobat Reader in Chapter 20.)

Because of all the labor involved, list the plug-ins used in your site on your home page, along with links directly to download sites.

To insert a plug-in in your Web page, follow these steps:

1. **Position the cursor at the location in your page where you want to insert the plug-in.**

2. **Click the Insert Plug-In button (or choose Insert⇨Other Components⇨Plug-In).**

   The Plug-In Properties dialog box appears.

3. **In the Data Source text box, type the URL of the plug-in file (or click Browse to locate the file in your Web site, elsewhere on your computer, or on the Web).**

4. **If you want a message to appear in place of the plug-in in browsers without plug-in support, type the message in the Message for Browsers without plug-in Support text box.**

5. **To adjust the dimensions of the plug-in, type new width and height values, in pixels, in the Height and Width text boxes.**

   By default, the original plug-in file dimensions appear in the Height and Width text boxes.

6. **Select an option from the Alignment drop-down list.**

   Refer to the section "Aligning an image with surrounding text," in Chapter 7, for a description of each alignment option.

7. **If you want the plug-in surrounded by a black border, type the border thickness, in pixels, in the Border thickness text box.**

   As of this writing, borders are visible only in Netscape Navigator.

8. **In the Horizontal Spacing text box, type the number of pixels of white space separating the plug-in from text to its right or left.**

9. **In the Vertical Spacing text box, type the number of pixels of white space separating the plug-in from text above or below the plug-in.**

10. **Click OK.**

    The dialog box closes, and the plug-in icon appears in your page (see Figure 13-7).

Figure 13-7:
The plug-in icon.

To see how the plug-in looks in your Web page, click the Preview in Browser button or choose File➪Preview in Browser. (You must have the appropriate plug-in program installed, and your Web browser must be configured to work with the plug-in.)

If the plug-in file is located elsewhere on your computer or on the Web, the Save File to Web dialog box appears the next time you save the page. The dialog box offers to import the file into your Web site; click Yes to import the file.

Adding a PowerPoint animation

PowerPoint is the Microsoft Office team member in charge of creating many of those snazzy presentations you see at conferences and trade shows. With the addition of the PowerPoint Animation Publisher, you can use PowerPoint 95 to publish animated presentations in your Web site. This addition is big news for the thousands of PowerPoint users who want to share their presentations over an intranet or the Internet.

In addition to the Animation Publisher, Microsoft has created the PowerPoint Player plug-in so that people without PowerPoint can still partake of its presentations. (In case you weren't counting, 11 Ps appear in the preceding sentence. Just for fun, read the sentence out loud.)

I talk more about the PowerPoint Animation Publisher and Player in Chapter 20.

 The PowerPoint Animation Publisher is a free add-on to PowerPoint 95. You can download the add-on and the PowerPoint Player in one fell swoop at http://www.microsoft.com/powerpoint/internet/player/installing.htm. An informative User Guide is available at http://www.microsoft.com/powerpoint/internet/player/userguide.htm.

To insert a PowerPoint animation, follow these steps:

1. **Position the cursor at the location in your page where you want to insert the animation.**

2. **Choose Insert➪Other Components➪PowerPoint Animation.**

   The PowerPoint Animation dialog box appears (see Figure 13-8).

Figure 13-8:
The
PowerPoint
Animation
dialog box.

PowerPoint Animation	▢ ⊠
PowerPoint Animation File:	
	Browse...
Insert As	
⦿ ActiveX Control	
○ Plug-In	
OK Cancel Help	

3. **In the PowerPoint Animation File text box, type the URL of the PowerPoint animation.**

Or click Browse to open the Select PowerPoint Animation File dialog box. This dialog box enables you locate the file in your Web site, elsewhere on your computer, or on the Web.

- If the animation file is a part of your Web site, click the Current FrontPage Web tab. The list box inside this tab displays the sound files and folders stored in your Web site. Click the animation file to select it.

- If the animation file is stored elsewhere on your computer, click the Other Location tab and enter the file's location in the From File text box, or click the Browse button to display a second Select PowerPoint Animation File dialog box. This dialog box contains a list of your hard drive's folders and files. Navigate your hard drive until you see the file you want, click the file, and then click OK to close the Background Sound dialog box. The animation's location appears in the From File text box.

- If the animation file is located on the Web, click the From Location radio button and type the file's URL (including the http://) in the accompanying text box.

Click OK to close the Select PowerPoint Animation dialog box. The animation's location appears in the PowerPoint Animation File text box.

4. **In the Insert As area, choose the method for FrontPage to use to insert the file.**

Select the ActiveX Control radio button to have FrontPage insert the animation as an ActiveX control. (Refer to the section "Adding an ActiveX control," earlier in this chapter, to find out about the pros and cons of ActiveX.) Select the Plug-In radio button to have FrontPage insert the file as a plug-in. (The section "Partnering with plug-ins," earlier in this chapter, tells you all about how plug-ins work.)

5. **Click OK.**

The dialog box closes. If you inserted the animation as an ActiveX control, the ActiveX icon appears in your page. If you inserted the animation as a plug-in, the plug-in icon appears in your page.

 To preview the animation, click the Preview in Browser button or choose File➪Preview in Browser. (You must use Internet Explorer, and if you inserted the animation as a plug-in, you must also have the PowerPoint Player plug-in installed on your computer.)

If the animation is located elsewhere on your computer or on the Web, the Save File to Web dialog box appears the next time you save the page. The dialog box offers to import the file into your Web site; click Yes to import the file.

Adding Web Page Scripts

If the little nerd inside you is looking for something to do, but you're not interested in tackling a programming language, *scripting* is for you. A scripting language, such as JavaScript or VBScript, is much easier to pick up than is a programming language, and the scripting language enables you to write your own custom Web page scripts that produce effects similar to complicated ActiveX controls and Java applets.

Web page scripts are small programs buried in the Web page's HTML tags. After someone opens the page in a Web browser, the browser runs the script.

Unlike components, which are separate objects referenced by the Web page, scripts live directly inside the page. This fact means that you and your visitors get to have fun with spiffy effects, and your visitors don't need to wait for a separate object to download.

FrontPage helps you create two kinds of scripts: *inline scripts* and *event scripts.* Inline scripts run as soon as the page opens in the Web browser. Here are just a few of the effects an inline script can produce:

- ✔ A text banner that scrolls in the browser's status bar (the thin band of space at the bottom of the browser window, where browser messages appear).

- ✔ A button that pops open a new browser window containing another page after someone clicks it.

- ✔ A hyperlink that displays the message of your choice in the browser's status bar after someone passes over the link with the mouse pointer. (I like this effect so much that I use it in my own Web site; try passing your mouse pointer over the hyperlinks in my home page at http://www.dnai.com/~asha.)

Event scripts run after they're triggered by something else, such as an ActiveX control or a Java applet. The combination of a component and an event script is quite powerful because it enables you to add custom features to the component that go beyond its own programming.

Suppose, for example, that you insert into your page an ActiveX control that creates a pop-up menu listing all the pages in your Web site. You want visitors able to select a page from the menu and jump directly to that page. No problem. The ActiveX control is in charge of creating the pop-up menu, but the associated event script actually turns the pop-up menu into a working control.

Are you intrigued? Then follow me so that I can show you how to use the FrontPage scripting features.

As of this writing, Internet Explorer is the only browser capable of running scripts written in VBScript. Both Internet Explorer and Netscape Navigator can run scripts written in JavaScript.

If you're jazzed by the prospect of writing your own scripts but don't know JavaScript or VBScript, plenty of resources are available to get you going. Netscape's JavaScript Guide contains everything you need to get up to speed with JavaScript; visit `http://www.netscape.com/eng/mozilla/3.0/handbook/javascript/index.html`. If VBScript is your language of choice, you can find everything you need, including full documentation, at `http://www.microsoft.com/vbscript`. If you prefer information printed on dead trees, check out *JavaScript For Dummies,* by Emily VanderVeer, and *VBScript For Dummies,* by John Walkenbach. Both are published by IDG Books Worldwide, Inc.

If scripting effects sound neat, but you're not interested in learning a scripting language, that's okay, too. Plenty of public-use scripts are floating around the Web. I found the link overlay script that I use in my home page in the JavaScript area of Addicted2:Stuff at `http://www.morestuff.com`. (While you're there, spend a few minutes poking around — that Web site is *funny.*)

To insert a script in your page, follow these steps:

1. **Position the cursor at the location in your page where you want to insert the script.**

2. **Click the Insert Script button (or choose Insert⇨Script).**

   The Script dialog box appears.

3. **In the Language area, select the radio button next to the language you want to use.**

   Select VBScript or JavaScript. (The Other option is a catch-all in case new scripting languages appear on the scene.)

   You can use only one scripting language per page. Therefore, if the page contains a form that uses a validation script (a script that checks the data visitors enter into form fields), the script language you choose here must be written in the same language. For more information, refer to the sidebar "How does FrontPage validate form data?" in Chapter 10.

4. **Click inside the Script text box and type your script.**

   FrontPage contains a built-in Script Wizard that simplifies building event scripts by listing events and actions that you can select by clicking their icons. To use the Script Wizard, click the Script Wizard button. (For help using the Script Wizard, click the Help button inside the Script Wizard dialog box.)

5. **Click OK.**

   The Script dialog box closes, and FrontPage inserts the script in your page. As a reminder, an icon appears at the location of the script.

To see the script do its thing, click the Preview in Browser button or choose File⇨Preview in Browser. (You must use a Web browser that understands the scripting language you chose.)

 If you prefer, you can add scripts directly to the page's HTML tags. To do so, select View⇨HTML. The View or Edit HTML dialog box appears. Click inside the text box, and script to your heart's content.

Part III
Nifty Web Site Additions

The 5th Wave   By Rich Tennant

"Would you like Web or non-Web?"

In this part . . .

After you build a sturdy, attractive Web site, you may feel the urge to add on to it. Perhaps you want to add a "members-only" section to your site, for example, or attach an interactive discussion group. Both are easy to construct with FrontPage. And you don't even need to hire a contractor.

Chapter 14
Membership Has Its Privileges

. . . .

In This Chapter

▶ Creating a members-only section of a Web site

▶ Creating a registration form

▶ Setting up the registration system

▶ Making sure that the whole thing works

. . . .

*M*uch of the Web's charm is the freedom with which Web surfers can slip in and out of different Web sites as much as they like and with relative anonymity. As a Web publisher, however, knowing a little bit about your visitors can help you develop a better profile of your target audience. (In Chapter 4, I talk about why understanding your target audience is so important.)

FrontPage enables you to place an entry gate in front of certain sections in your Web site. These sections are open to everyone, but to gain access, visitors must register by choosing a unique user name and password, which acts as their key to the rest of the site. You can also require visitors to supply additional information, such as their names, e-mail addresses, and other details about themselves, before they proceed to the protected area of the site.

Some software companies, for example, use their Web sites to distribute free test versions of their products. In some cases, to access the download site, visitors must first complete a registration form. (If you're not sure what a Web form is, read Chapter 10.) The form enables visitors to choose a user name and password to access the site and also collects basic information about them. In this way, the software company exchanges access to free software for valuable marketing information and a contact list of interested customers.

Check out `http://www.microsoft.com/sitebuilder` to see how Microsoft uses a registration system to regulate access to its resource site, the Site Builder Network.

In this chapter, you discover how to add a registration system to your Web site.

How Does a Registration System Work?

To set up a registration system, you must first understand the relationship between the FrontPage *Root Web* (a Web server's top-level Web site) and its *Child Webs* (Web sites stored on the same Web server in a secondary level of folders). If you haven't already, read the sidebar "What is a Root Web?" in Chapter 1 for an introduction.

The Root Web is your main Web site. You can completely contain small Web sites (those with 20 or fewer pages) within the Root Web because keeping a small number of pages organized is usually pretty easy. In a large Web site, however, storing every page inside the Root Web becomes unwieldy and difficult to manage. A better way to organize a large Web site is to create individual Child Webs for each new section and link them to the Root Web (see Figure 14-1). To the visitor, the linked network of the Root Web and Child Webs looks and acts like one big Web site. For you, however, the combination is much easier to manage. (I explain how to create links between the Root Web and Child Webs in Chapter 6.)

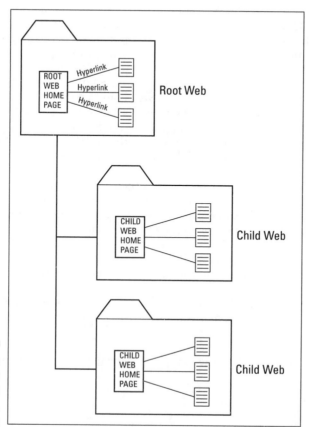

Figure 14-1:
The Root
Web and its
Child Webs.

In a FrontPage registration system, everyone has access to the Root Web but must register to gain access to a particular Child Web. Visitors register by filling out a registration form that, among other things, enables them to select a user name and a password. After visitors submit the form, the Web server stores the names and passwords in a secure file and admits the visitor to the protected Child Web. After a visitor obtains a user name/password key, that person can use the key every time he wants to visit the protected area of the Web site.

To collect additional information about registered visitors, you need only add fields to the registration form. After a visitor submits the form, FrontPage saves the additional data in a file you can access later.

To use a FrontPage registration system, the Web server hosting your Web site must have FrontPage Server Extensions installed. For more information about FrontPage Server Extensions, read Chapter 18.

Creating a Registration System

Adding a registration system to your Web site is a four-part process, as described in the following steps:

1. **Adjust the protected Web site's permissions.**

2. **Add a registration form to the Root Web.**

3. **Configure the registration system.**

4. **Link the registration form to other pages in your Web site.**

In the following sections, I show you how to carry out each step.

Adjusting the protected Web site's permissions

In FrontPage, all Web sites have the same *permissions* as the Root Web. (Permissions are Web server settings that determine who can access the Web site; I talk about permissions in detail in Chapter 17.) Because, in a registration system, visitors choose their own user names and passwords, you must specify that the Child Web you want to protect has its own set of permissions.

To specify permissions for a Web site, follow these steps:

1. **In the FrontPage Explorer, open the Web site you want to protect.**

    If you're not sure how to open a Web site, refer to Chapter 1.

2. **Choose Tools⇨Permissions.**

   The Permissions dialog box appears.

3. **In the Settings tab, select the Use unique permission for this web radio button.**

4. **Click OK.**

   The Permissions dialog box closes, and the Explorer adjusts the Web site's permissions settings.

Adding a registration form to the Root Web

The next step is to add a registration form to the Root Web. Visitors use the form to select a user name and password and to provide additional information about themselves. For a general overview of how Web forms work, read Chapter 10.

If you haven't already copied your main Web site to the FrontPage Root Web, you should do so before proceeding with the steps in this section. Refer to Chapter 2 for instructions.

To add a registration form to the Root Web, follow these steps:

1. **In the FrontPage Explorer, open the Root Web.**

   If another Web site is open in the Explorer, that site automatically closes if you open the Root Web. If you're not sure how to open a Web site, refer to Chapter 1.

2. **Click the Show FrontPage Editor button in the toolbar (or choose Tools⇨Show FrontPage Editor).**

   The FrontPage Editor launches.

3. **In the Editor, choose File⇨New (or press Ctrl+N).**

   The New Page dialog box appears.

Figure 14-2: Choose the User Registration template from the New Page dialog box.

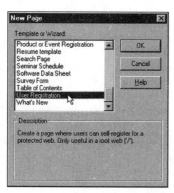

4. From the Template or Wizard list box, double-click User Registration.

A page based on the User Registration template opens in the Editor. The page contains an explanation of how the registration system works, along with a simple form visitors can fill out to choose a user name and a password. (If you prefer, you can build your own registration form from scratch. Refer to Chapter 10 for details on how to create a form.)

5. Customize the registration page to suit your needs.

You can, for example, change the wording of the introductory paragraphs or adjust the design of the page so that this page blends with the rest of your Web site. If you want to collect additional information about registered visitors, you can add the appropriate fields. (Chapter 10 describes each type of form field.)

You can also copy the registration form to an existing page in the Root Web (if, say, you want to place the registration form on your Web site's home page so that visitors see the form as soon as they arrive). To do so, move the mouse pointer to the left margin of the form until the pointer turns into a left-pointing arrow (pointing toward the margin) and then double-click to select the entire form (that is, everything inside the box surrounded by dashed borders). Click the Cut button. Now, open the destination page. Position the cursor where you want the form to appear and click the Paste button.

At this point, you need to configure the registration system itself. In the following section, I show you how.

Configuring the registration system

The WebBot Registration Component *form handler* is the engine that runs the FrontPage registration system. (A form handler is a special server-based program that processes information contained in form submissions.) The WebBot Registration Component does the following things with the information submitted in registration forms:

✔ Passes the user name/password pairs along to the Web server, which stores them in a secure file that only the server can read.

✔ Stores the user name and other information in a separate text file or Web page, which you can access later.

Before you begin, a little reassurance: A lot of steps appear in this section, but they are all easy to follow.

To customize the WebBot Registration Component, follow these steps:

1. **Right-click inside the registration form (anywhere inside the dashed box) and select Form Properties from the pop-up menu.**

   The Form Properties dialog box appears.

2. **If not already visible, select WebBot Registration Component from the Form Handler drop-down list.**

3. **Click the Settings button.**

   The Settings for Registration Form Handler dialog box appears. The dialog box contains four tabs — Registration, Results, Confirm, and Advanced — each of which controls a different aspect of the registration system.

4. **If not already visible, click the Registration tab.**

   The Registration tab becomes visible (see Figure 14-3).

   • In the FrontPage web name text box, type the name of the Child Web that you want to protect.

   • In the User name fields text box, type the name of the form field in which visitors type their user name. (If you used the User Registration template to create the registration form, FrontPage automatically enters the correct field names in the User name fields, Password field, and Password confirmation field text boxes.)

If you want FrontPage to construct a user name out of the contents of more than one field, type both field names in the User name fields text box, separated by spaces or commas. FrontPage then constructs a user name from the values of the fields by placing an underscore character (_) between the values. If, for example, your registration form contains separate fields for the visitor's first name (field name firstname) and last

Figure 14-3:
The Registration tab of the Settings for Registration Form Handler dialog box.

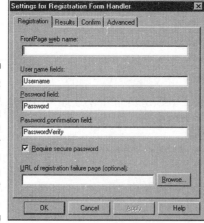

name (field name lastname), type **firstname lastname** in the User name fields text box. If a visitor named Maxwell Goofus fills in the registration form, his resulting user name is Maxwell_Goofus.

- In the Password field text box, type the name of the form field in which visitors enter their passwords.

- In the Password confirmation field text box, type the name of the form field in which visitors re-enter their passwords.

- Select the Require secure password check box to require visitors to choose a secure password. A secure password contains six or more characters and does not partially match the user name.

- Type an optional URL in the URL of registration failure page (optional) text box.

The Registration failure page appears if the visitor selects a user name or password that someone has already taken or (if the Require secure password check box is checked) if the visitor chooses an insecure password. FrontPage automatically generates a simple registration failure page that not only tells the visitor that registration wasn't successful but also explains why and sends the visitor back to the registration form to correct the problem. If you'd rather use your own registration failure page (so that this page blends in nicely with the rest of your site), type its URL here or click Browse to display the Current Web dialog box. The dialog box contains a list of all files and folders in your Web site. Select the file that you want to use and click OK to close the dialog box.

(See the sidebar "Decorating your registration system," later in this chapter, for tips on creating custom registration failure pages.)

5. **Click the Results tab at the top of the Settings for Registration Form Handler dialog box.**

The Results tab becomes visible (see Figure 14-4).

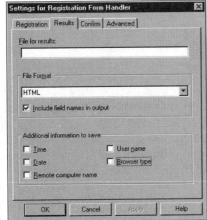

Figure 14-4:
The Results
tab of the
Settings for
Registration
Form
Handler
dialog box.

- In the File for results text box, type the name of the file that you want to contain the form results.

FrontPage stores all the information submitted from the registration form — except for the password — in this file (which is called the *results file*). You can choose an existing file in your Web site, or you can type a new filename, in which case FrontPage creates the file the first time someone submits a form.

(FrontPage stores visitors' passwords in a file accessible only by the Web server, ensuring the privacy of visitors' passwords.)

Make sure that you type the correct three-letter file name extension corresponding to the file type that you choose in the next bullet step: **.htm** for an HTML file or **.txt** for a text file.

To keep the results file hidden from Web browsers, add **_private/** to the beginning of the filename (so that the name reads _private/*filename*). This addition tells FrontPage to save the results file in your Web site's _PRIVATE folder. (Documents stored in that folder aren't visible to Web browsers.)

The _PRIVATE folder is private only if you publish the Web site on a Web server that supports FrontPage Server Extensions. For more information, see Chapter 18.

- Select a file format from the File Format drop-down list.

  You can save registration form results as an HTML file (that is, as a Web page) or as a text file. You can format HTML files as definition lists, bulleted lists, numbered lists, or formatted text. (Refer to Chapter 5 for descriptions of each type of list.) You can save text files as formatted plain text (a nicely laid-out list of form results) or as a file with commas, tabs, or spaces separating names and values. (This latter format is handy if you want to import the data into a database or spreadsheet.)

- Select the Include field names in output check box to save both the name and value of each form field in the results file. Otherwise, FrontPage saves only the field values, which makes the information difficult to sort out later on.

- In the Additional information to save area, select the check boxes next to additional items that you want displayed in the results file. The WebBot Registration Component can track the time and date the form was submitted, the visitor's Internet user name, the name of the computer from which the form was submitted, and the type of Web browser the visitor was using at the time.

6. **Click the Confirm tab at the top of the Settings for Registration Form Handler dialog box.**

   The Confirm tab becomes visible (see Figure 14-5). Here, you specify an optional custom confirmation page (the page that automatically appears after visitors submit the registration form). If you leave this tab empty, the WebBot Registration Component generates its own simple confirmation page. If that's fine for you, jump ahead to step 8.

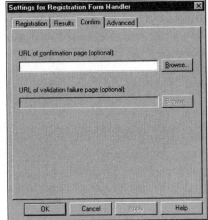

Figure 14-5:
The Confirm
tab of the
Settings for
Registration
Form
Handler
dialog box.

   In the URL of confirmation page (optional) text box, type the URL of the custom confirmation page (or click Browse to locate the confirmation page in your Web site). (For details on how to create your own confirmation page, refer to Chapter 10. For tips on creating a custom confirmation page specifically for registration systems, read the sidebar "Decorating your registration system," later in this chapter.)

7. **Click the Advanced tab at the top of the Settings for Registration Form Handler dialog box.**

   The Advanced tab becomes visible (see Figure 14-6).

   The options on this tab enable you to save registration form results to a second file as well. This capability is handy if you want FrontPage to generate one file for, say, import into a database and another for printing. If you don't want to create a second results file, jump to step 8.

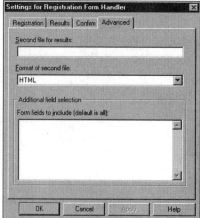

Figure 14-6:
The
Advanced
tab of the
Settings for
Registration
Form
Handler
dialog box.

- In the Second file for results text box, type the name of the second file. Make sure that you include the appropriate three-letter filename extension corresponding to the file format you choose in the following step: **.htm** for an HTML file or **.txt** for a text file.

- Select a file format from the Format of second file drop-down list.

- To select which field values appear in the results file, type the field names, separated by commas, in the Form fields to include (default is all) text box. By default, FrontPage lists in the results file the values of all the form's fields.

8. Click OK to close the Settings for Registration Form Handler dialog box.

Finally!

9. Click OK to close the Form Properties dialog box.

The Form Properties dialog box closes.

Phew! Now that you've set up the registration system's form handler, you simply need to save the page containing the form.

To do so, follow these steps:

1. Click the Save button (or choose File⇨Save or press Ctrl+S).

If you added the registration form to an existing page, FrontPage saves the page's changes. If no dialog box appears, then you're ready to proceed to the following section, "Linking the registration form to the rest of your Web site."

If the registration form is part of a new page, the Save As dialog box appears.

2. In the Page Title text box of the Save As dialog box, type a title for the registration page.

3. **In the File path within your FrontPage web text box, type a filename.**

4. **Click OK.**

    The Save As dialog box closes, and FrontPage saves the registration page to the Root Web.

Linking the registration form to the rest of your Web site

A registration system is useless if visitors can't find the registration form. You need to make sure that the registration form is visible by creating links to the form from other pages in your Web site. Place hyperlinks in logical places throughout your Web site leading to the registration form (such as in your site's home page).

Testing the Registration System

Before you take your Web site on the road, be sure to test your registration system. Verify that everything about the system is in perfect working order. One of the beauties of the FrontPage Personal Web Server is that you can test your registration system on your own computer, but the system acts just as it would live on the Web.

Decorating your registration system

Confirmation and failure pages perform very important functions in a registration system: The confirmation page tells visitors that their registration was successful and leads them to the protected area of the Web site, while the failure page notifies visitors that the registration was unsuccessful and sends them back to the registration form to re-register. If the standard pages produced by FrontPage are a bit too utilitarian for your taste, you can create your own custom pages. The section "Creating a Confirmation Page," in Chapter 10, shows you how. You can also use the custom confirmation page and failure page templates stored on the CD included with this book. (See Appendix C for instructions on how to access the templates.)

In addition to regular confirmation fields, you have access to the following three confirmation fields that apply specifically to registration systems:

- **Registration-Username:** The visitor's user name replaces this confirmation field.

- **Registration-Password:** The visitor's password replaces this confirmation field.

- **Registration-Error:** A brief description of why registration was unsuccessful replaces this confirmation field.

To test your registration system, follow these steps:

1. **With the page containing the registration form open in the Editor, click the Preview in Browser button (or choose File⇨Preview in Browser).**

   The Web browser launches, and the registration page appears.

2. **Fill in and submit the form, just as a visitor would.**

   The registration confirmation page appears. Double-check the wording of the confirmation page. Ensure that the confirmation page contains a link leading to the protected area of the Web site. (After all, that's the entire reason visitors register in the first place.)

3. **After you successfully gain access to the protected area of the Web site, press your browser's Back button to return to the registration form.**

4. **This time, fill in invalid registration information and submit the form.**

   Try filling in duplicate user names or leaving a password field blank. The registration failure page pops up, telling you to re-register. Double-check the wording of the registration failure page and make sure that the page contains a link leading back to the registration form so that visitors can try again.

5. **After you're satisfied that the registration system works, switch to the FrontPage Explorer.**

   Click the Explorer's button on the taskbar or press Alt+Tab. The Explorer appears on-screen.

6. **From the Explorer menu bar, choose View⇨Refresh to update your Web site's display.**

7. **Open the registration form's results page.**

   (If you're not sure how to open a page from within the Explorer, refer to Chapter 2.)

   The results page opens in the appropriate editor. If the page is an HTML file, it opens in the FrontPage Editor; if the results page is a text file, it opens in the Windows 95 Notepad.

8. **Check to see that the results page contains all the information it should.**

   If it does, close the page, sit back, and congratulate yourself on a job well done. If information is missing, return to the open registration page in the FrontPage Editor and double-check the registration form's properties. (Go through the steps in the section "Configuring the registration system," earlier in this chapter.)

Chapter 15

Can We Talk?

*W*eb surfers love new stuff. The surest way to develop a steady stream of new visitors (and a loyal group of fans) is to keep your Web site's content vital and fresh. Add stuff; change stuff; clean out the old stuff. Better yet: Enable surfers *themselves* to contribute to the content of your Web site.

How? By creating a FrontPage discussion group! A discussion group enables visitors to get to know you and each other.

Here are a few things you can do with a FrontPage discussion group:

✔ Start a worldwide conversation about an issue that interests you.

✔ Provide a place for your customers to share opinions about your services.

✔ Create a technical support forum for customers who need help using your product.

✔ Host an ongoing brainstorming session for members of your work group.

In this chapter, you find out how to add a discussion group to your Web site.

What Exactly Is a Discussion Group?

A *discussion group* is a special type of FrontPage Web site that enables visitors to participate in an interactive group conversation.

Visitors view a table of contents that lists all the current posts (called *articles*) related to the discussion topic, as shown in Figure 15-1. To view an article, visitors click the article's hyperlink in the table of contents. At that point, they can either reply to the article or post their own article by filling in a submission form. Visitors can also search the discussion group's articles for key words or phrases.

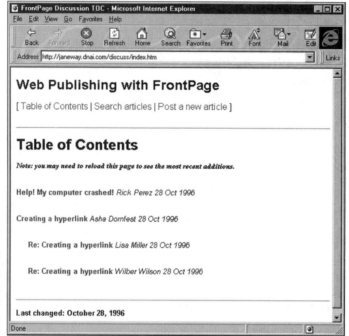

Figure 15-1: A discussion group table of contents.

FrontPage ingeniously combines several individual features — the Include WebBot, the Search WebBot, FrontPage forms, and in some cases, the Registration WebBot and frames — to create a discussion group.

For more information about the components of a FrontPage discussion group, flip through Chapter 10 for an overview of Web forms, look at Chapter 11 if you want to know more about frames, read the "Include WebBot" and "Search WebBot" sections of Chapter 12, and skim Chapter 14 to find out about FrontPage registration systems.

To use a FrontPage discussion group, the Web server on which you publish your Web site must have FrontPage Server Extensions installed. For more information about FrontPage Server Extensions, read Chapter 18.

Creating a Discussion Group

To create a discussion group, simply call on the services of the Discussion Web Wizard, which is accessible from the FrontPage Explorer. The Wizard is in charge of creating the pages and folders that make up the discussion group. After the Wizard does its thing, you open the pages in the FrontPage Editor and customize them however you want.

To add discussion capabilities to your Web site, you then must create a link from your Web site to the discussion group, which is a complete Web site in itself. In Chapter 6, I show you how to create links between FrontPage Web sites. Or, if you prefer, you can copy the contents of the discussion Web site into yours, combining the two. (Chapter 2 shows you how to copy one Web site into another.)

I recommend keeping the discussion group contained within its own Web site. That way, all the discussion articles and pages remain organized in a separate folder, which is easier for you to manage. Furthermore, keeping the discussion group within a distinct Web site enables you to add a registration system. (Chapter 14 explains registration systems in detail.) With a registration system in place, only visitors with a user name and password can participate in the discussion. Because the user name automatically appears within the text of each article, a registration system helps others make reasonably sure that mischievous visitors can't post an article pretending to be someone else.

Firing up the Discussion Web Wizard

Setting up a discussion group is no small task, so FrontPage gives you a Discussion Web Wizard to guide you through the process. This Wizard takes care of everything, from helping you decide on the discussion group's structure to choosing the group's color scheme — and much more.

To create a discussion group by using the Discussion Web Wizard, follow these steps:

1. **From the Explorer toolbar, click the New FrontPage Web button (or choose File⇔New⇔FrontPage Web or press Ctrl+N).**

   The New FrontPage Web dialog box appears.

2. **In the Template or Wizard list box, double-click Discussion Web Wizard.**

   The Discussion Web Wizard dialog box appears. Here, you choose where you want FrontPage to store the new Web site files.

3. **If not already visible, select the name of the Personal Web Server from the Web Server or File location drop-down list.**

4. In the Name of New FrontPage Web text box, type a Web site name and then click OK.

The Name and Password Required dialog box appears.

5. In the Name and Password text boxes, type your administrator name and password and then click OK.

Make sure that you enter the name and password *exactly* as you entered them originally. If you can't remember your administrator name or password, refer to the sidebar "Help! I forgot my password!" in Chapter 1.

After you click OK, FrontPage launches the Discussion Web Wizard. In a moment, the introductory Discussion Web Wizard dialog box appears (as shown in Figure 15-2).

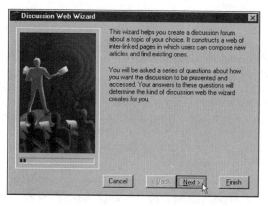

Figure 15-2:
The
Discussion
Web
Wizard.

6. Click Next in the introductory dialog box.

The next Discussion Web Wizard dialog box appears. Here, you choose your discussion group's features.

7. Select the check boxes next to the features that you want to include in your discussion group and then click Next.

Your choices are as follows:

- Table of Contents (which contains links to all the articles posted to the group)

- Search Form (which enables visitors to search the contents of the discussion group)

- Threaded Replies (which groups together replies to current posts instead of simply adding replies to the end of the table of contents)

- Confirmation Page (which tells visitors that their post was added to the discussion group)

After you click Next, the next Discussion Web Wizard dialog box appears.

8. **In the Enter a descriptive title for this discussion text box, type a title.**

   If your discussion centers around Albanian children's literature, for example, type Albanian Children's Literature Discussion Group.

9. **In the Enter the name for the discussion folder, type a folder name and then click Next.**

   FrontPage creates a special folder in your Web site in which the program stores all the articles posted to the discussion group. The folder name must begin with an underscore character (_). After you click Next, the next Discussion Web Wizard dialog box appears.

10. **Select the radio button for the set of fields that you want to include in your submission form and then click Next.**

    Your can choose among three options as follows:

    • Subject, Comments (the simplest type of submission form, with fields for the article's subject line, and the text of the article)

    • Subject, Category, Comments (a Category drop-down list enables visitors to specify an article type, such as comment, question, or complaint)

    • Subject, Product, Comments (If the discussion focuses on a group of products, a Product drop-down list enables visitors to specify which product they're talking about.)

    After you click Next, the next Discussion Web Wizard dialog box appears.

11. **Decide whether your discussion group requires registration by selecting the appropriate radio button and then click Next.**

    Here, you choose whether the discussion group is protected by a registration system. (Refer to Chapter 14 for details on how registration systems work.) If you select Yes, only registered users can post articles, so the Wizard creates a registration form for the discussion group, which you customize after the Wizard finishes. If you select No, anyone can post articles, and the Wizard creates a regular, unprotected discussion Web site. After you click Next, the next Discussion Web Wizard dialog box appears.

12. **Decide on the order in which articles appear in the table of contents by selecting the appropriate radio button and then click Next.**

    Your two choices are Oldest to newest or Newest to oldest. After you click Next, the next Discussion Web Wizard dialog box appears.

13. **Decide whether you want the table of contents to be the Web site's home page by selecting the appropriate radio button and then click Next.**

    If the discussion group is a stand-alone Web site, select Yes. If you intend to copy the contents of the discussion group to an existing Web site, select No; otherwise, the table of contents overwrites that Web site's home page. After you click Next, the next Discussion Web Wizard dialog box appears.

14. If, in step 7, you included a search form in your discussion group, choose the information that you want the search form to display by selecting the appropriate radio button and then click Next.

Your choices are as follows:

- Subject (the article's subject line)

- Subject, Size (the subject along with the article's file size in kilobytes)

- Subject, Size, Date (the subject, size, and the date the article was posted)

- Subject, Size, Date, Score (the subject, size, date, and the closeness of the match)

After you click Next, the next Discussion Web Wizard dialog box appears.

15. If you want to adjust the discussion group's background and text colors, select options in this dialog box and click Next.

Here, you can specify the color scheme of your discussion group. The current color scheme is visible in the box on the left side of the dialog box (see Figure 15-3). If you are satisfied with the color scheme, skip this step. Otherwise, choose new colors, as follows:

- In the Background section, select a background pattern from the Pattern drop-down list or click the Solid button to choose a solid background color from the Color dialog box. In the Color dialog box, click the color swatch corresponding to the color that you want and then click OK to close the dialog box. (For more information about how to use the Color dialog box, refer to Chapter 5.)

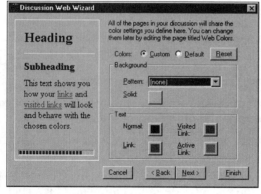

Figure 15-3:
You can
choose your
discussion
group's
color
scheme.

- In the Text section, click the Normal button to change the color of the discussion group's body text. Click the Link, Visited Link, and Active Link buttons to choose new colors for the discussion group's hyperlinks. After you click each button, the Color dialog box appears. In the Color dialog box, click the color swatch corresponding to the color you want and then click OK to close the dialog box. (For more information about changing the color of body text, as well as how to use the Color dialog box, refer to Chapter 5. For more information about changing hyperlink colors, refer to Chapter 6.)

After you click Next, the next Discussion Web Wizard dialog box appears.

16. **Select the radio button next to the layout you want and then click Next.**

    In this dialog box, you decide whether to use frames to structure the discussion group. (If you're not familiar with frames, read Chapter 11.) You have the following four choices:

    - No frames

    - Dual interface — use frames if available, normal pages if not

    - Contents above current article

    - Contents beside current article

    I recommend selecting No frames or Dual interface because the last two options use frames exclusively and not all Web browsers can display frames.

    For a preview of each layout, select one of the radio buttons. The layout appears in the illustration on the left side of the dialog box, as shown in Figure 15-4.

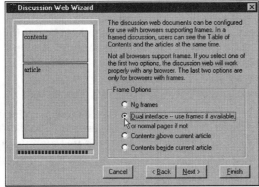

Figure 15-4: You can choose a framed layout for your discussion group.

After you click Next, the final Discussion Web Wizard dialog box appears. This dialog box lists the names of the discussion group's main pages. If you want to change any of the discussion group settings, click the Back button to return to previous Discussion Web Wizard dialog boxes. Otherwise, continue on to step 17.

17. Click Finish.

After you click Finish, the Discussion Web Wizard closes, and after a few moments of hard drive rumbling, the discussion group Web site's pages and folders appear in the Explorer.

At this point, you can take a well-deserved break, or you can start customizing the pages in the discussion group — I show you how in the next section.

Customizing the discussion group's pages

The discussion group pages created by the Discussion Web Wizard are perfectly functional — but they are rather bland. All they need is a little makeover, which you can supply by opening each page in the FrontPage Editor and making whatever cosmetic changes you want. (The chapters in Part II show you how to use the Editor's different page editing tools.)

Many elements in the discussion group pages take advantage of FrontPage WebBots and other FrontPage features. Here are a few tips for working with those elements:

- ✔ **Page headers:** In a nonframed or dual interface discussion group, the text that appears at the top of each discussion group page is actually contained in a separate Web page and included using the Include WebBot (refer to Chapter 12 for details on how the Include Bot works). FrontPage stores these included pages inside the discussion group's _PRIVATE folder. To edit the page headers, open the page titled Included Header for Discussion Name (where *Discussion Name* is the name of your discussion group). If you're not sure how to open a page from within the Explorer, refer to Chapter 2.

- ✔ **Page footers:** Similar to page headers, page footers (the text that appears at the bottom of each page in a nonframe or dual interface discussion group) are also contained in separate Web pages and included with the Include WebBot. To edit page footers, follow the instructions for editing page headers, but open the page titled Included Footer for Discussion Name.

- ✔ **Article headers:** FrontPage attaches a header to each article posted to the discussion group (regardless of whether the discussion group's layout includes frames). To edit article headers, follow the instructions for editing page headers, but open the page titled Included Article Header for Discussion Name.

- **Article footers:** FrontPage also attaches a footer to each article posted to the discussion group. To edit article footers, follow the instructions for editing page headers, but open the page titled Included Article Footer for *Discussion Name*.

- **The color scheme:** FrontPage bases the color scheme for all the pages in the discussion group on a single page. To adjust the color scheme, follow the instructions for editing page headers, but open the page titled Web Colors. (Refer to Chapters 6 and 7 for details about basing the color scheme of several pages on the style of a single page.)

- **The search form:** The discussion group's search form centers around the Search WebBot. To change the Search WebBot's properties, open the page titled *Discussion Name* Search Form. (Unlike the header, footer, and color scheme pages, this page isn't stored in the _PRIVATE folder; the search form is located in the discussion group's main directory.) Refer to Chapter 12 for detailed instructions on adjusting the Search WebBot.

- **The confirmation page:** The confirmation page appears after a visitor submits an article. To edit the discussion group's confirmation page, open the page titled Discussion Name Confirmation. (Unlike the header, footer, and color scheme pages, this page isn't stored in the _PRIVATE folder; the search form is located in the discussion group's main directory.) Refer to Chapter 12 for detailed instructions on adjusting the Search WebBot.

- **The table of contents:** To adjust the layout of the discussion group's table of contents, you need to tinker with the workings of the discussion group itself, which I explain in the following section, "Adjusting how the discussion group works."

Depending on your discussion group's layout, the group may contain other pages as well. If you're curious about the content of any page, simply open the page in the Editor and make whatever changes you want.

If, rather than tweaking the pages generated by the Discussion Web Wizard, you prefer to use your own pages for headers, footers, and color guides, you need to change the properties of the discussion group itself. The following section, "Adjusting how the discussion group works," shows you how.

Adjusting how the discussion group works

Some aspects of a discussion group go beyond cosmetic appearance. If you want to alter how the discussion group actually works, you need to delve into the properties of the WebBot Discussion Component form handler.

A form handler is a server-based program that processes information contained in form submissions. (For more information about what form handlers can do, read Chapter 10.) The WebBot Discussion Component form handler orchestrates everything that happens after a visitor posts an article by using the discussion group's submission form.

The WebBot Discussion Component does the following things:

✔ Formats and maintains the table of contents.

✔ Controls the directory in which FrontPage stores discussion group articles.

✔ Enables you to add descriptive information to articles, such as the time and date visitors post the articles.

✔ Controls which pages FrontPage includes as headers and footers and which page the program uses as the color scheme guide.

✔ Enables you to specify a custom confirmation page that visitors see in place of the standard page as they post articles.

To adjust the WebBot Discussion Component, follow these steps:

1. **Open the page titled Discussion Name Submission Form.**

2. **Right-click inside the form (anywhere inside the box surrounded by dashed lines) and select Form Properties from the pop-up menu.**

   The Form Properties dialog box appears.

3. **Click the Settings button.**

   The Settings for Discussion Form Handler dialog box appears. The dialog box contains three tabs — Discussion, Article, and Confirm — each of which controls a different aspect of the discussion group.

4. **If not already visible, click the Discussion tab.**

   The Discussion tab becomes visible (see Figure 15-5).

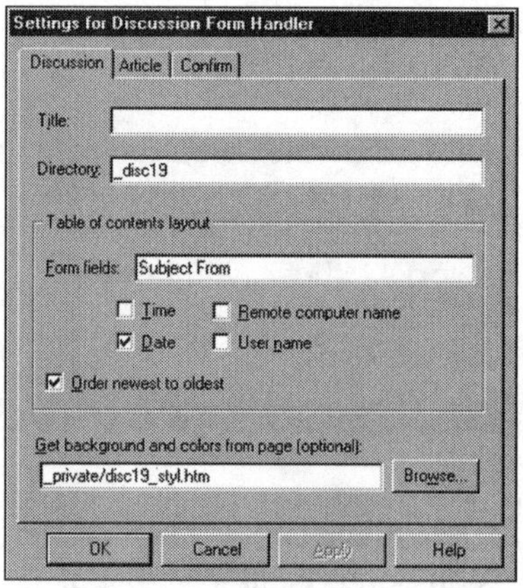

Figure 15-5:
The Discussion tab of the Settings for Discussion Form Handler dialog box.

- In the Title text box, enter an optional article title.

  The title appears inside all discussion group articles.

- In the Directory text box, enter the name of the directory in which FrontPage stores discussion group articles.

Change the contents of this text box only if you want to change the directory originally set up by using the Discussion Web Wizard. Also, the directory name must begin with an underscore character (_).

- In the Form fields text box, enter the names of the form fields (separated by spaces) from which FrontPage constructs the table of contents listing for each article.

  By default, Subject From appears inside this text box, because FrontPage constructs table of contents listings from the article's subject line plus the name of the person who posted the article.

- Select the check boxes for the additional details you want to include in each table of contents listing.

  Your choices are Time (the time the article was posted), Date (the date the article was posted), Remote computer name (the name of the computer from which the article was posted), and User name (the Internet user name of the article's author).

- Select the Order newest to oldest check box if you want to display the most recently posted articles at the top of the table of contents.

  If no check appears in this check box, FrontPage displays the oldest articles at the top of the table of contents.

- In the Get background and colors from page text box, type the URL of the page on which you want to base the discussion group's color scheme.

5. **Click the Article tab at the top of the Settings for Discussion Form Handler dialog box.**

   The Article tab becomes visible (see Figure 15-6).

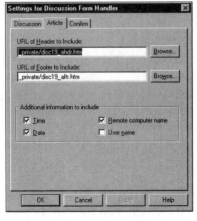

Figure 15-6:
The Article tab of the Settings for Discussion Form Handler dialog box.

- In the URL of Header to Include text box, type the URL of the article header (or click Browse to select the page from a list of files in your Web site).

- In the URL of Footer to Include text box, type the URL of the article footer (or click Browse to select the page from a list of files in your Web site).

- In the Additional information to include area, select the check boxes for the additional items that you want to appear in each article.

The WebBot Discussion Component can include the time and date the article was submitted, the name of the computer from which the article was submitted, and the visitor's Internet user name.

6. **Click the Confirm tab at the top of the Settings for Discussion Form Handler dialog box.**

The Confirm tab becomes visible (see Figure 15-7).

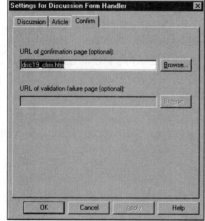

Figure 15-7: The Confirm tab of the Settings for Discussion Form Handler dialog box.

Use the options on the Confirm tab to specify a custom confirmation page. If you leave this tab empty, the WebBot Discussion Component generates its own confirmation page. If that's okay with you, skip to step 7. (For details on why and how to create your own confirmation page, refer to Chapter 10.)

In the URL of confirmation page text box, type the URL of the custom confirmation page (or click Browse to locate the confirmation page in your Web site).

7. **Click OK to close the Settings for Discussion Form Handler dialog box.**

8. **Click OK to close the Form Properties dialog box.**

9. **Click the Save button to save the submission page (or choose File⇨Save or press Ctrl+S).**

FrontPage saves the changes to the submission page.

You are now ready to link your discussion group to the rest of your Web site.

Linking the discussion group to your Web site

The final step necessary to complete the discussion group is to integrate the discussion group with the rest of your Web site so that visitors can access the group. You may perform either of the following actions to accomplish this goal:

- ✔ Create a link from your Web site to the discussion group Web site. (Refer to Chapter 6 for details.)
- ✔ Copy the contents of the discussion group into your Web site, combining the two. (Refer to Chapter 2 for instructions.)

If you protect your discussion group with a registration system, you _must_ keep the discussion group contained within its own Web site.

Talking to Yourself

Your discussion group is complete! Before you throw your doors open to the world, however, make sure that everything works as it should. Preview your discussion group in a Web browser and try out all its functions.

If your discussion group doesn't use frames (or if it is a dual interface discussion group, and you want to see how the nonframe layout looks to those of your visitors using browsers that can't display frames), open the page titled Discussion Name TOC. After the page opens in the Editor, click the Preview in Browser button in the toolbar (or choose File➪Preview in Browser) to open the page in your Web browser.

If your discussion group is laid out using frames, launch your browser separately and type the URL of the discussion group's frame set in the browser's Location text box. To determine the frame set's URL, in the FrontPage Explorer, right-click the frame set's page icon (the page is titled Frameset for Discussion Name) and choose Properties from the pop-up list. The Properties dialog box appears, and the frame set's URL is visible in the Location box.

Check and recheck every feature of your discussion group: Submit an article, scrutinize the confirmation page, view an article you just posted, and review the table of contents. If you're unhappy with any aspect of your discussion group, go back through the steps in this chapter to adjust that segment.

Moderating your discussion group

In certain cases, you may want to retain some editorial control over the content of your discussion group's articles. For example, say you are hosting a technical support forum, and someone posts incorrect information. You want to be able to edit the article so that it contains the correct information. This is called *moderating* a discussion group.

When a visitor posts an article, FrontPage saves a copy of the article in a special folder created by the Discussion Web Wizard. The folder name is different, depending on your choices in step 9 of "Firing up the Discussion Web Wizard" and step 4 in "Adjusting how the discussion group works," earlier in the chapter. Article folders in all discussion groups, however, begin with the underscore character (_). FrontPage classifies folders beginning with underscores as *hidden,* which means that files stored inside this folder are not visible in the Explorer. (The _PRIVATE folder is an exception; it exists simply to keep its pages safe from nosy Web browsers and the Search WebBot. For more information about the _PRIVATE folder, refer to Chapter 2.)

To open the articles stored in the discussion group article folder (which is a hidden folder), you must specifically tell the Explorer to make the articles visible. To do so, in the Explorer, choose Tools⇨Web Settings. The FrontPage Web Settings dialog box appears, with the Configuration Tab visible. Click the Advanced Tab to make that tab visible. Select the Show documents in hidden directories check box and click OK to close the dialog box. The FrontPage Explorer dialog box appears, asking your permission to refresh the Web site's display. Click Yes to close the dialog box and refresh the display. Now, if you switch to the Explorer's Folder View (click the Folder View button, or choose View⇨Folder View) and open the discussion group's article folder, the individual articles are visible. To edit the articles, simply open them in the Editor and make whatever changes you like.

Part IV

Taking Your Web Site to a New Level

The 5th Wave   By Rich Tennant

"Children- it is not necessary to whisper while we're visiting the Vatican Library Web site."

In this part . . .

Web publishing can be a solitary task or can happen as part of a team, with many authors creating different chunks of the Web site. In this part, you discover how FrontPage helps you organize and manage a Web-building team. You find out how to control who can access your Web site. And finally, you discover how to publish your site on the World Wide Web.

Chapter 16

Staying Organized By Using the FrontPage To Do List

*T*he most challenging task for a Web publisher is, ironically, the most mundane: remembering all the details associated with creating and maintaining a Web site. Managing a large-scale Web site involves a bundle of tiny tasks — fixing hyperlinks, updating images, adding content — each of which you must complete if the Web site is to look flawless. If the site is maintained by a team of authors, keeping track of what needs to be done becomes even more complicated.

The creators of FrontPage understand this dilemma and thoughtfully included a little helper called the FrontPage To Do List. The To Do list helps you (and the rest of your Web publishing team) keep track of the tasks that you still need to complete. In this chapter, I show you how to take advantage of the To Do List.

The To Do List Tour

Each FrontPage Web site has its own To Do List (see Figure 16-1). As you work on the Web site, you add *tasks* to your To Do List. A task is a job or detail you need to complete. You give each task a name, a priority, and, if necessary, a detailed description. Some tasks link to specific pages in the Web site. In Figure 16-1, for example, the task "Add the day's headlines" links to the "Newsday Headlines" page. Other tasks are independent and are not associated with a particular page. In Figure 16-1, the task "Add discussion forum" is an example of an independent task.

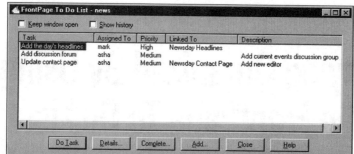

Figure 16-1:
The
FrontPage
To Do List.

After you complete a task, you can either delete the task from the list or you can mark the task as complete, creating a history to which you can refer later.

Keeping track of tasks is certainly helpful, but the real power of the To Do List becomes apparent if you use the list as part of a team. Because the FrontPage Explorer can open Web sites stored on remote Web servers, several authors can make changes to the Web site simultaneously; the different authors simply open the Web site — which is located on another Web server to which they're connected via the Internet — on their own computers to make their changes. If different authors access the same Web site, all can use the Web site's To Do List, adding and completing tasks as they go. In this way, the team members can keep in touch about which tasks they still need to complete and about who is actually responsible for completing the tasks. (I talk more about multiple Web site authors in Chapter 17.)

To share the To Do List with a team, the server on which you publish the Web site must have FrontPage Server Extensions installed.

Using the To Do List

The To Do List is so well-integrated with the FrontPage Explorer and Editor that the list is easier to use than that pad of sticky notes sitting on your desk.

Adding tasks

You can add two types of tasks to the To Do List: tasks linked to pages and independent tasks. *Linked tasks* apply to specific pages, whereas *independent tasks* are more general or apply to the entire Web site.

To add a task to the To Do List, perform one of the following actions:

✔ **Adding a linked task from the Explorer:** Click the icon of the page to which you want to link the task and choose Edit⇨Add To Do Task.

✔ **Adding a linked task from the Editor:** Open the page to which you want to link the task and choose Edit⇨Add To Do Task.

 ✔ **Adding an independent task from the Explorer or the Editor:** Open the To Do List by clicking the Show To Do List button (or choosing Tools⇨Show To Do List). In the To Do List, click the Add button.

Whenever you add a task to the To Do List, the Add To Do Task dialog box appears (see Figure 16-2).

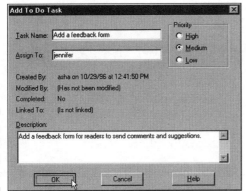

Figure 16-2:
The Add
To Do Task
dialog box.

This dialog box contains descriptive information about the task (such as when the task was created and whether the task is linked to a page). The dialog box also contains spaces where you specify the task's details.

To specify the task's details, follow these steps:

1. **In the Task Name text box, type a brief, descriptive title.**

2. **In the Assign To text box, type the name of the person responsible for completing the task.**

   The name you enter here should appear on the Web site's list of authors. Chapter 17 shows you how to add Web site authors.

3. **In the Priority area, select the radio button for the task's priority level.**

   Your choices are High, Medium, and Low.

4. **If necessary, type detailed information or instructions in the** <u>D</u>**escription text box.**

5. **Click OK.**

The dialog box closes, and the task appears in the To Do List.

You can adjust how the To Do List looks by performing the following tasks:

✔ **Sorting tasks in the To Do List:** Click the descriptive label that sits at the top of each column. To sort tasks by priority, for example, click the Priority label.

✔ **Changing the width of each column:** Move the mouse pointer over the boundary between each label until the pointer turns into a line with little arrows sticking out of each side. Click the label boundary and drag the boundary to the right or left.

Modifying tasks

You can modify or update any task in the To Do List. If you want to include additional directions in the task's description, for example, you can easily do so.

To modify a task in the To Do List, follow these steps:

1. **In the Explorer or the Editor, open the To Do List by clicking the Show To Do List button (or choosing** <u>T</u>**ools⇨Show To** <u>D</u>**o List).**

   The To Do List appears.

2. **Select in the list the task that you want to modify and then click** <u>D</u>**etails.**

   The Task Details dialog box appears. (Except for its title bar, this dialog box looks just like the Add To Do Task dialog box.)

3. **Make whatever changes you want, as described in steps 1 through 4 in the preceding section.**

   Update the task description, for example, or enter a different name in the <u>A</u>ssign To text box.

4. **Click OK.**

   The dialog box closes, and the modified task appears in the To Do List.

Completing tasks

Something intrinsically satisfying is involved in crossing items off a To Do List and watching the list get shorter and shorter.

To complete a task in the To Do List, follow these steps:

1. **If not already visible, open the To Do List by clicking the Show To Do List button (or choosing Tools⇨Show To Do List).**

2. **Select in the list the task that you want to complete.**

   - If the task is linked to a page (which you can determine by checking the Linked To column in the To Do List), click Do Task.

     The linked page opens in the Editor so that you can complete the task.

     To keep the To Do List open while you complete the task, select the Keep window open check box.

   - Independent tasks aren't linked to particular pages. Therefore, if you select an independent task in the To Do List, the Do Task button is dimmed. In this case, close or minimize the To Do List and complete the task in the Explorer or the Editor (or both programs, depending on the task). After the task is complete, continue with step 3.

3. **After you complete the task, if not already visible, click the Show To Do List button.**

   The To Do List appears.

4. **Select the name of the task that you want to mark as complete.**

5. **Click Complete.**

   The Complete Task dialog box appears. Here you specify how to record the completed task in the To Do List.

6. **Select the radio button for the option that you want.**

   If you select Mark this task as completed, FrontPage removes the task from the To Do List and saves the task in the Web site's history. If you select Delete this task, FrontPage deletes the task and does not save a record in the Web site's history.

7. **Click OK.**

   The dialog box closes, and the task disappears from the To Do List.

Viewing completed tasks

Want to make yourself feel good? Take a look at your Web site's history and see all the tasks you (and your team) have completed.

To view your Web site's To Do List history, select the Show history check box in the To Do List. Completed tasks then appear along with the current tasks in the To Do List (see Figure 16-3). You can tell which tasks are complete by noting the date in the Completed column.

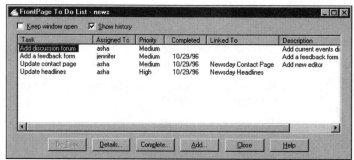

Figure 16-3:
Viewing
completed
tasks.

To remove a completed task from the To Do List history, select the Show history check box to display completed tasks and then click the completed task you want to delete. The Complete button turns into the Remove button. Click Remove to delete the task from the To Do List history.

Chapter 17

Bossing Around Your Web

• •

• •

*W*hen I was a kid, I knew I'd pushed my parents a little too hard if they said, "You live in our house — you live by our rules." To this statement, I could offer no reply — simply acceptance (and a few minutes of serious pouting).

Well, this Web site is *your* home page — which means that *you* get to make the rules. You control who can update or change your Web site and even who can view it. The process is called *adjusting permissions,* and with FrontPage, you can perform the task with ease.

What Are Permissions?

Permissions are simply different levels of Web site access. By using the FrontPage Explorer, you can allow people to have different levels of access to your Web site by assigning people different permissions. This capability is useful if you're part of a site-building team and you want to control authoring privileges or if you want to create a restricted-access Web site. (To browse a restricted-access Web site, visitors must enter a user name and a password that you specify.)

A restricted-access site is different from a site for which visitors can register themselves. In a restricted-access site, you authorize visitors by assigning them specific user names and passwords, which those people then use to gain entry to the Web site. In a Web site outfitted with a registration system, all visitors have access as long as they choose their own user name and password. For more information about registration systems, refer to Chapter 14.

FrontPage provides for the following three levels of access:

- ✔ **Administer:** An administrator can create, edit, and delete Web sites and pages and adjust Web site permissions.

- ✔ **Author:** An author can create, edit, or delete pages, but cannot create or delete Web sites or adjust Web site permissions.

- ✔ **Browse:** A person with Browse access can only view a Web site with a Web browser; that person can't edit the Web site or even open the site in the FrontPage Explorer.

Every Web site must have at least one administrator. When you installed FrontPage, you chose an administrator name and password, which automatically makes you the administrator. If you want to share the administrator mantle with someone else, you can add another administrator to the permissions list. I show you how in the next section, "Authorizing Access to Your Web Site."

Authorizing Access to Your Web Site

To control who may edit your Web site, use the Explorer to specify administrators and authors. If you want your Web site to appear only to authorized visitors, you can also create a list of people with browsing access.

Permissions caveats

As you use the Explorer to adjust your Web site's permissions, the adjustments occur on the Web server on which you stored the Web site. So, if you're creating your Web site by using the FrontPage Personal Web Server but intend to publish the site on another Web server (such as the server maintained by your Internet service provider or company), the permissions you adjust on the Personal Web Server do not carry over to the other server.

To work around this problem, publish your Web site (see Chapter 18) and then follow these steps:

1. **In the Explorer, open the Web site directly from the server on which you just published the Web site.**

In Chapter 1, I explain how to open Web sites stored on remote servers.

2. **Set your Web site's permissions.**

Follow the steps listed in the section "Authorizing Access to Your Web Site," in this chapter.

3. **Choose File➪Exit to close the Web site and exit the Explorer.**

Or, to continue working, do not exit the Explorer; rather, open another Web site. The current Web site closes automatically, saving permissions changes.

By default, all FrontPage Web sites have the same permissions as the Root Web and are visible to anyone with a Web browser. Therefore, if you adjust the Root Web's permissions, you automatically change the permissions of all Child Webs as well. (If you're not sure what a Root Web or Child Web is, refer to Chapter 1.)

To set your Web site's permissions, follow these steps:

1. **Open the Web site in the Explorer.**

2. **Choose Tools⇨Permissions.**

   The Permissions dialog box appears.

   If the Web site is the Root Web, the dialog box contains two tabs: Users and Computers. If the Web site is a Child Web, the dialog box contains a third tab: Settings (see Figure 17-1). The Settings tab enables you to change the default FrontPage permission setting (in which all Child Webs inherit permissions from the Root Web) so that the Web site uses its own set of permissions.

3. **Select the Use unique permissions for this web radio button and then click Apply.**

   FrontPage adjusts the Web site's permissions.

4. **In the Permissions dialog box, click the Users tab.**

   The Users options become available. The administrator name you chose at the time you installed FrontPage appears in the user list. (If the Web site uses a registration system, the user names of registered visitors also appear in the list.)

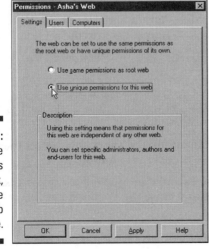

Figure 17-1:
The Permissions dialog box, with the Settings tab visible.

5. **To add a user, click the Add button.**

   The Add Users dialog box appears (see Figure 17-2)

   This dialog box enables you to specify an individual's user name, password, and level of access.

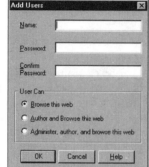

Figure 17-2:
The
Add Users
dialog box.

6. **In the Name text box, type the individual's user name.**

   User names and passwords are case sensitive, which means that FrontPage sees **joe** and **Joe** as two different names.

7. **In the Password text box, type a password.**

8. **In the Confirm Password text box, type the password again.**

9. **In the User Can area, select the radio button for the level of access that you want the individual to have.**

   Your choices are Browse this web, Author and Browse this web, and Administer, Author, and Browse this web. Refer to the section "What Are Permissions?" earlier in this chapter, for an overview of each level of access.

10. **Click OK.**

    The Add Users dialog box closes, returning you to the Users tab of the Permissions dialog box.

11. **To restrict browsing access to authorized users only, select the Only registered users have browse access radio button.**

12. **Click Apply to activate changes and continue adjusting permissions or click OK to activate changes and close the Permissions dialog box.**

TECHNICAL STUFF

Authorizing group access

You can control Web site access based on *IP address* rather than individual user names and passwords. Short for *Internet Protocol Address,* an IP address is a computer's unique address on the Internet. This address consists of four numbers separated by periods. (A typical IP address looks something like the following example: 190.172.112.15.)

If you set permissions based on a computer's IP address, anyone using that computer has the specified level of permission. You can also apply permissions to a range of computers on the same network that share similar IP addresses (for example, their IP addresses all begin with the number 190).

This capability can prove useful if your Web site is part of an *intranet* (that is, an internal company network based on Internet technology but accessible only to company insiders) and you don't want to go through the hassle of authorizing individual users.

To set permissions based on IP address, follow these steps:

1. **With the Web site open in the Explorer, choose Tools⇨Permissions.**

   The Permissions dialog box appears.

2. **Click the Computers tab.**

3. **Click Add.**

   The Add Computer dialog box appears. Here you specify the IP address (or range of addresses, called an *IP mask*) and its associated level of access.

4. **In the IP Mask text boxes, type the four numbers that make up the IP address.**

   If you don't know the computer's IP address, speak to your system administrator.

   If you are using an IP mask, enter only the number common to all IP addresses in the group; enter an asterisk (*) in the other text boxes.

5. **In the Computer Can area, select the radio button for the level of access that you want the computer to have.**

6. **Click OK to close the Add Computer dialog box.**

7. **Click Apply to activate changes and continue adjusting permissions or click OK to activate changes and close the Permissions dialog box.**

Adjusting Permissions

You can easily adjust your Web site's permissions. You can, for example, upgrade an author's access to administrator. Or you can remove a user from the list of people authorized to browse the site.

To edit a user's permissions, follow these steps:

1. **Open the Web site in the Explorer.**

2. Choose Tools➪Permissions.

The Permissions dialog box appears.

3. If it's not already visible, click the Users tab.

4. In the User List, click the name of the user whose permissions you want to adjust.

5. Click Edit.

The Edit Users dialog box appears.

6. In the User Can area, select the radio button for the user's new permission setting.

7. Click OK.

The Edit Users dialog box closes, returning you to the Users tab of the Permissions dialog box.

8. Click Apply to activate changes and continue adjusting permissions or click OK to activate changes and close the Permissions dialog box.

To remove a user from the permission list, follow the instructions in the preceding steps, but in step 5, click the Remove button rather than the Edit button.

Changing Passwords

If you're serious about keeping your FrontPage data secure, changing your password every couple of weeks is a good idea (especially if you're a Web site administrator).

To change your password, follow these steps:

1. In the FrontPage Explorer, choose Tools➪Change Password.

The Change Password for *User* dialog box appears. (*User* is the user name of the person currently accessing FrontPage — presumably that's you.)

2. In the Old Password text box, type your old password.

3. In the New Password dialog box, type your new password.

4. In the Confirm Password dialog box, retype your new password.

5. Click OK.

The dialog box closes, and FrontPage updates your password.

To change another user's password, you must remove the user from the permissions list, add the user again, and choose a new password for the user.

Chapter 18
Making Your Worldwide Debut

● ●

In This Chapter
▶ What "publishing your Web site" means
▶ The skinny on FrontPage Server Extensions
▶ Going public
▶ Keeping your site fresh

● ●

Drum roll, please! It's the moment you've been waiting for . . . time to unveil your painstakingly prepared, lovingly built Web site — and make the site visible to the entire world.

In this chapter, I talk about what it means to publish your Web site. I show you how to use the FrontPage publishing features with different types of Web servers. Finally, I give you tips on how to update your site and keep your Web fresh and interesting.

What "Publishing Your Web Site" Means

In the not-so-distant past, "publishing" meant having your writing printed in a book, magazine, or journal and distributed to others to read. "Getting published" was a big deal, something relatively few people achieved.

Today, anyone with an Internet connection and a little techno-savvy can publish on the World Wide Web. Publishing your Web site means making the site visible on the Web for all to see.

For your site to be accessible on the Web, you must store the site on a Web server. (In Chapter 4, I give you a quick-and-dirty overview of how the Web works.) Although FrontPage comes with its own fully functional Personal Web Server, this server is really meant just for your own personal use — so that you can test the Web sites you create in FrontPage. To publish your site, you need to transfer your Web site to a more powerful Web server that's connected to the Internet 24 hours per day. This type of server is called a *dedicated Web server*.

For most people, this requirement means getting an account with an Internet service provider (or ISP for short) or storing the Web site on a company Web server (with the approval of the company system administrator, of course).

The Skinny on FrontPage Server Extensions

Having access to a dedicated Web server is only part of what you need to publish a FrontPage Web site. For all FrontPage features to work correctly, the Web server must have a set of auxiliary programs called *FrontPage Server Extensions* installed. FrontPage Server Extensions are special programs that act as translators between FrontPage and the Web server program. If someone posts an article to a FrontPage discussion group, for example, FrontPage relies on information generated by the Web server to process the article. (Read Chapter 15 if you're not familiar with FrontPage discussion groups.) Unless the Web server is equipped with FrontPage Server Extensions, which translate the information generated by the Web server into stuff that's usable by FrontPage, the discussion group can't function.

Installing FrontPage Server Extensions is a big job, which is why many ISPs and system administrators have yet to fully support FrontPage. The number of FrontPage-friendly ISPs is growing every day, however, and as FrontPage becomes more widespread, the number is sure to increase. (For tips on finding an ISP to host your FrontPage Web site, read the accompanying sidebar "Finding a FrontPage ISP," later in this chapter.)

The good news is that you can publish a FrontPage-created Web site on *any* Web server — including servers without FrontPage Server Extensions installed — with certain caveats. You can use all FrontPage features except those that rely on FrontPage Server Extensions — namely, those described in the following list:

- ✔ **WebBots associated with forms:** The Confirmation Field WebBot; the Search WebBot; and the Discussion, Registration, and Save Results form handlers.

- ✔ **FrontPage image maps:** Instead, use the image map style specific to your dedicated Web server.

- ✔ **Permissions:** If you want to adjust your Web site's permissions, you need to discuss your options with your ISP or your system administrator.

- ✔ **The FrontPage To Do List:** You can use the To Do List to organize your own tasks, but you can't share the To Do List with a Web-building team.

- ✔ **The _PRIVATE folder:** Pages stored inside the _PRIVATE folder are fully accessible on Web servers without FrontPage Server Extensions installed.

Finding a FrontPage ISP

The benefits of using a FrontPage-friendly ISP are clear. So how do you find one? Microsoft maintains a list of FrontPage ISPs at http://www.microsoft.com/frontpage/wpp/list. To get the lowdown on which providers offer the best service, ask for advice on the FrontPage newsgroup at microsoft.public.frontpage.client. FrontPage users trade stories and share help on this newsgroup, and they have plenty to say about their ISP experiences. To access Internet news groups, you need to use news reader software. Internet Explorer 3.0, which comes with the FrontPage Bonus Pack, installs with a companion news reader. Refer to the program's documentation for instructions on how to access Internet newsgroups.

  ✔ **Opening or creating Web sites directly on remote Web servers:** If you want to use the Explorer to create or open a Web site that's stored on a remote server, the server must have FrontPage Server Extensions installed.

  ✔ **FrontPage Publishing:** Instead of publishing your Web site using the Explorer's built-in publishing capability, you must use the FrontPage Web Publishing Wizard (a companion program that comes with the FrontPage Bonus Pack) or an FTP program. I explain each publishing option in detail in the following section, "Going Public."

Going Public

Okay, time to take this show on the road! In this section, I show you how to publish your Web site.

 Before you publish, just *one* final detail: Make sure that you give your Web site a complete once-over before you take the site live. Click the Editor's Preview in Browser button (or choose File⇨Preview in Browser) to view your site in a Web browser — preferably more than one model. Run through each function — test forms, click image maps, submit discussion articles . . . you get the idea. Give your Web site the white glove test so that the site makes its debut on the Web with style and polish.

After you're sure everything is in perfect working order, how you publish your site depends on whether your dedicated server has FrontPage Server Extensions installed.

Publishing procedures vary widely among ISPs and company Web servers. Although the instructions in this chapter apply to most Web servers, your server may differ. *Before* you publish your Web site, be sure to read your ISP's instructions thoroughly (or speak to your system administrator) for details about specific publishing procedures.

If your Web server has FrontPage Server Extensions installed

If your dedicated Web server supports FrontPage Server Extensions, you can publish your Web site by using the FrontPage Explorer. The Explorer establishes a connection with the Web server and transfers all the Web site's files and folders from your computer to the dedicated Web server.

FrontPage contains a particularly bizarre feature: After you publish a new Web site on a dedicated Web server, your ISP or system administrator must manually restart the server for the server to recognize the Web site. After the server restarts, you need to repeat the publishing procedure to transfer the Web site's files to the Web server. (Restarting the server is simple, but only your ISP or system administrator can do it.) Some ISPs tell you to request a restart whenever necessary, while others restart the server once a day. Whatever the case, you need to find out your provider's policy and then resign yourself to waiting for the server to restart before you can finish publishing a new Web site.

To publish your Web site by using the FrontPage Explorer, follow these steps:

1. **Open the Web site that you want to publish.**

   Refer to Chapter 1 for instructions on how to open a Web site.

2. **Choose File⇨Publish FrontPage Web.**

   The Publish FrontPage Web dialog box appears (see Figure 18-1).

Figure 18-1: The Publish FrontPage Web dialog box.

3. **In the Destination Web Server or File Location text box, type the name of the Web server on which you want to publish your Web site.**

A Web server name looks something like the following example: www.myisp.com. If you don't know the name of your dedicated Web server, check with your ISP or system administrator.

The information that you enter in this dialog box is specific to your Web server and may vary slightly from what is listed here.

4. **In the Name of Destination FrontPage Web text box, type the Web site's name or, if you're publishing the Root Web, leave the text box blank.**

   The Web site's name is the name that you chose at the time you first created the Web site. The Web name is listed in the Explorer's title bar (the stripe at the very top of the Explorer window).

5. **If this is the first time you are publishing the Web site, deselect the Copy changed pages only check box.**

6. **If a Web site with the same name already exists on the Web server, select the Add to an existing FrontPage Web check box.**

   Most FrontPage ISPs create all new accounts with a default Root Web. So although you're publishing your Root Web for the first time, as far as FrontPage is concerned, you're adding on to an existing site.

   If you're publishing a Child Web (that is, any FrontPage Web site other than the Root Web) for the first time, deselect this check box.

7. **If you're publishing the Root Web and want to copy all Child Webs at the same time, click Copy child webs (for Root Web only).**

8. **Click OK.**

   The Publish FrontPage Web dialog box closes. A pause occurs as FrontPage contacts the dedicated Web server. Then the Name and Password Required dialog box appears.

9. **In the Name and Password text boxes, enter the user name and password that you chose at the time you first established your Internet account and then click OK.**

   Depending on the Web site's permission settings, the Name and Password Required text box may appear again, this time requesting your FrontPage administrator name and password. If this occurs, in the Name and Password text boxes, enter your administrator name and password and then click OK.

At this point, different things happen depending on whether you're adding pages to an existing site or creating a new site, as follows:

✔ If you're adding pages to an existing Web site, FrontPage copies all your Web site files to the remote Web server. Depending on the size of your Web site and the speed of your Internet connection, this process may take a few minutes. After the work is done, a FrontPage Explorer dialog box appears, telling you that the transfer was successful. Click OK to close the dialog box and rejoice at being published!

> ✔ If you're creating a new Web site, the FrontPage Explorer dialog box appears, telling you that the Web server must be manually restarted before proceeding. Click OK to close this dialog box and then click Cancel to close the Publish FrontPage Web dialog box. After the server restarts, repeat the entire procedure described in the preceding steps, making sure that you select <u>A</u>dd to an existing FrontPage Web as you reach step 6. This time, FrontPage publishes your Web site without a hitch.

If your Web server doesn't have FrontPage Server Extensions installed

If your Web server doesn't support FrontPage Server Extensions, you have two publishing options: You can use the Explorer together with the Microsoft Web Publishing Wizard (a utility included in the Bonus Pack), or you can transfer your Web site files by using an FTP program. Which option you choose depends on your computer's setup, the size and organization of your Web site, and the method with which you feel most comfortable.

Using the Web Publishing Wizard

The Web Publishing Wizard works with the FrontPage Explorer to publish Web sites on servers without FrontPage Server Extensions. After the Web Publishing Wizard is set up to work with your dedicated Web server, the Wizard integrates so well with the Explorer that you don't even realize you're using a separate program.

Unfortunately, the Web Publishing Wizard works only under the following conditions:

> ✔ Your connection to the dedicated Web server must be via a company network (a local-area network or Intranet) or an Internet connection set up by using Windows 95 Dial-Up Networking. (If you don't know what Dial-Up Networking is or you're not sure whether your Internet connection uses Dial-Up Networking, refer to your Windows 95 documentation and speak to your system administrator or your ISP.)

> ✔ Your Web site must be contained within a single folder: the Root Web or a single Child Web.

> ✔ You must use the English version of Windows 95 or Windows NT.

If any of these conditions don't apply to you, skip this section and instead follow the instructions in the section "Using an FTP program," later in this chapter.

For detailed information about the Web Publishing Wizard, visit the Microsoft Web Publishing Wizard home page at `http://www.microsoft.com/windows/software/webpost`.

To publish a Web site by using the Web Publishing Wizard, follow these steps:

1. **If you haven't already done so, install the Web Publishing Wizard.**

   For instructions, refer to the documentation included with FrontPage.

2. **In the Explorer, open the Web site that you want to publish.**

3. **Choose File⇨Publish FrontPage Web.**

   The Publish FrontPage Web dialog box appears.

4. **In the Destination Web Server or File Location text box, type the name of the Web server on which you want to publish your Web site.**

   A Web server name looks similar to the following example: www.myisp.com. If you don't know the name of your dedicated Web server, check with your ISP or system administrator.

   The information you enter in this dialog box is specific to your Web server and may vary slightly from what is listed here.

5. **Leave the Name of Destination FrontPage Web text box blank.**

6. **If this is the first time you are publishing the Web site, deselect the Copy changed pages only check box.**

7. **Leave the Add to an existing FrontPage Web check box selected.**

   Even though you're publishing your Web site for the first time, FrontPage thinks that you're adding on to an existing site because the destination folder on the Web server already exists (even though it's empty).

8. **Leave the Copy child webs (for Root Web only) check box empty.**

9. **Click OK.**

   The Publish FrontPage Web dialog box closes. A pause occurs as FrontPage contacts the dedicated server. After the program determines that the server does not have FrontPage Server Extensions installed, the Web Publishing Wizard opens (see Figure 18-2).

Figure 18-2:
The Web Publishing Wizard.

10. **Select the radio button that describes how you connect to the dedicated Web server and then click the Next button.**

    If you connect to the server by using a company network, select Use Local Area Network (Intranet). If you connect to the dedicated server by using the Internet, select Use Dial-up Networking to access the Internet. If you selected Use Dial-up Networking, select your connection from the drop-down list underneath Choose a Dial-Up Networking connection to access a server.

    After you click Next, a dialog box appears, which prompts you to click Next again to begin the connection process using the Web Publishing Wizard's default settings.

11. **Click Next.**

    The Gathering Information dialog box appears. FrontPage pauses as the Web Publishing Wizard tries to establish a connection with the Web server.

    If the Web Publishing Wizard can establish a connection, the next Web Publishing Wizard dialog box appears, prompting you to click Finish to publish your Web site. If this happens, skip to step 19.

    If the Web Publishing Wizard can't establish a connection to the Web server, a Web Publishing Wizard dialog box appears, telling you so, and prompts you to review the Web Publishing Wizard's default settings.

12. **Click OK to close the dialog box and then click the Back button until you reach the beginning of the Wizard.**

    You move back through dialog boxes you haven't seen before; this is because the Web Publishing Wizard used its default settings to attempt to establish a connection. By going though each dialog box from the beginning, you can verify each setting, changing settings as necessary.

    You know you're at the beginning of the Wizard when you see the Back button turn gray.

13. **Select the radio button that describes how you connect to the dedicated Web server and then click Next.**

14. **Select your protocol option and click Next.**

    If you connect to an ISP, select FTP. If you're publishing your Web site on a Web server to which you're connected by Windows 95 Networking, select Windows File Transfer.

    If you're not sure about any of the information the Web Publishing Wizard wants, click Cancel to close the Web Publishing Wizard and give your ISP or system administrator a call. After you have the information you need, start again at step 1.

    After you click Next, the next Wizard dialog box appears.

15. **Type your user name in the Underline{U}ser name text box and your password in the Underline{P}assword text box and then click Underline{N}ext.**

    The user name and password that you enter in this dialog box are the ones you chose at the time you signed up with your ISP or, if you're publishing your site on a company server, were assigned to you by the system administrator.

    Some ISPs require you to select *two* user name/password combinations: one to use your account and the other to log onto servers to transfer files. If this is the case, in this dialog box, type the user name and password required to transfer files.

    After you click Underline{N}ext, the next Wizard dialog box appears.

16. **Type the name of the server in the Underline{F}TP Server Name text box and click Underline{N}ext.**

    Here you type the name of the Web server on which you intend to publish your Web site. (The Web Publishing Wizard refers to the server as an FTP server because in addition to serving Web site files, the server must also have the capability to accept files transferred from other computers.)

    After you click Underline{N}ext, the next Wizard dialog box appears.

17. **In the Underline{S}ubfolder containing your Web pages on your FTP server text box, type the name of the Web server folder that contains your Web site's files.**

    All Web servers contain a special folder that holds Web site files. An ISP's Web server, which hosts many users' Web sites, contains an individual folder for each user. (Most Web servers name this folder PUBLIC_HTML, but some servers use other folder names.)

18. **In the Underline{U}RL for your home root on your Web server text box, type your Web site's URL and then click Underline{N}ext.**

    My Web site's URL, for example, is `http://www.dnai.com/~asha`.

    After you click Underline{N}ext, a Wizard dialog box appears, which prompts you to click Underline{N}ext again to verify the updated settings.

19. **Click Underline{N}ext to have the Web Publishing Wizard verify the information you typed.**

    The Gathering Info dialog box appears. If the Web Publishing Wizard still can't establish a connection, the Web Publishing Wizard dialog box appears and asks you to go back through the Wizard again to double-check your choices. Sigh with resignation and then click OK to close this dialog box and either click the Underline{B}ack button to return to the first Web Publishing Wizard dialog box and start again or click Cancel to close the Web Publishing Wizard and publish your Web site by using an FTP program.

If the Web Publishing Wizard can't connect to your Web server even though you entered the correct information, your server program may not know how to communicate with the Web Publishing Wizard. (This problem occurs infrequently, but it does happen.) To solve the problem, your ISP or system administrator needs to make a simple adjustment to the Web server program. Refer the system administrator to the Web Publishing Wizard home page at http://www.microsoft.com/windows/software/webpost for complete information.

If the Web Publishing Wizard is able to connect to the Web server, the final dialog box appears.

20. Click Finish to publish your Web site.

The Transferring Files dialog box appears and stays visible while the Web Publishing Wizard copies your Web site files to the Web server. After the process finishes, the Web Publishing Wizard dialog box appears, telling you that the transfer was successful.

21. Click OK to close the dialog box and the Web Publishing Wizard.

Using an FTP program

If, for any reason, you can't publish your Web site by using the Web Publishing Wizard, you can rely on a trusty FTP program to get the job done. *FTP* stands for *File Transfer Protocol,* which is the standard method used to transfer files to and from computers over the Internet. You use an FTP program to select your Web site files and folders and then transfer them from your computer to the dedicated Web server.

If you sign up for Internet service, most ISPs include an FTP program as part of the software package that they distribute to customers. If you don't have an FTP program, I've included my favorite program, called WS_FTP LE, on the CD that comes with this book. (See Appendix C for help installing the program and setting the program up to work with your Web server.)

Because every FTP program works a little differently, the following instructions are intentionally general. For detailed instructions on how to use your FTP program, refer to the program's documentation.

To publish your Web site by using an FTP program, follow these steps:

1. Launch your FTP program.

2. Establish a connection with the Web server on which you want to publish your Web site.

In most FTP programs, this process involves typing the name of the Web server, typing your access user name and password, and specifying the location of the folder in which you store all your Web site files. If you're not sure how to establish a connection with your dedicated Web server, contact your ISP or system administrator for details.

3. **After you establish the connection, use the FTP program to display the folder on your hard drive that contains your FrontPage Web sites.**

   The default folder for FrontPage Web sites is C:\FRONTPAGE WEBS\CONTENT. This folder stores the Root Web's files and folders and contains all Child Webs within folders. (The names of the Child Web folders are the same as the names of the Child Webs they contain.)

4. **Select the files and folders that you want to transfer to the dedicated Web server.**

   If you're transferring the Root Web, select all the Root Web's pages and any folders containing Web site files (such as the IMAGES and _PRIVATE folders). If you're transferring the Root Web and Child Webs, select the Child Web folders as well.

   Certain files and folders contain FrontPage-specific information, such as folders that begin with _VTI and the file named #HTACCESS.CTL. Do not transfer these files and folders; they are useless on Web servers without FrontPage Server Extensions installed.

   Transfer the CGI-BIN folder if your ISP or system administrator enables you to write your own server-based scripts. (If in doubt, don't transfer the folder until you check with the appropriate techie.)

   Keep in mind, too, that files stored in the _PRIVATE folder are not kept private on servers without FrontPage Server Extensions installed.

   (Each Child Web folder contains its own set of FrontPage-specific files and folders. If you're transferring the Root Web and Child Webs, simply delete FrontPage-specific files and folders from the dedicated Web server after they're transferred.)

   Be aware of one important exception: If your Web site contains an image map created by using the NCSA, CERN, or Netscape style, the folder named _VTI_MAP contains the image map's map file. You must transfer the map file along with the rest of the Web site files. You need only transfer the map file itself — the file has the three-letter filename extension .MAP — not the _VTI_MAP folder. For more information about image maps, refer to Chapter 8.

5. **Start the transfer.**

   The FTP program copies each file and folder from your computer to the dedicated server.

6. **After the transfer finishes, exit the FTP program.**

You're Live!

Congratulations — your Web site has joined the Internet community, and you can now call yourself a true-blue Web publisher! Visit your Web site at its new URL and, just to be safe, give the site one last check. If all is well, set off those fireworks!

If something doesn't work correctly, fix the problem on the local copy of your Web site — the one on your computer — and transfer the changed pages to the dedicated Web server. I show you how in the following section.

Keeping Your Web Site Fresh

Stagnant Web sites are as appealing as day-old pastry. On the Web, freshness counts, so keep your site vital by changing its content, updating its graphics, and adding new features regularly.

Updating your site simply involves making changes on the local copy of your Web site and republishing the Web site on the dedicated Web server. This time, you tell FrontPage to only publish those pages that have changed since the last time you published the Web site. The new pages automatically overwrite the old pages stored on the Web server.

(If you used an FTP program to publish your Web site, follow the steps listed in the section "Using an FTP program," earlier in the chapter, and transfer only those pages and files you've changed.)

To update your site by using the FrontPage Explorer or the Web Publishing Wizard, follow these steps:

1. **Open the Web site that you want to update.**

   Refer to Chapter 1 for instructions on how to open a Web site.

2. **Choose File⇨Publish FrontPage Web.**

   The Publish FrontPage Web dialog box appears.

3. **In the Destination Web Server or File Location text box, type the name of the Web server on which you stored your Web site.**

4. **In the Name of Destination FrontPage Web text box, type the name of the Web site.**

   Even though you're updating an existing Web site, you still must specify the Web site's name so that FrontPage knows where to transfer the new files.

You're open for business!

Now that your Web site is live, you need to let everyone know you're entertaining visitors. Whether your Web site sells products or showcases your Fabio photo collection, the site can benefit from publicity. How do you invite the world to your home page? Here are a few tried-and-true tips:

✔ **Search services:** List the page with popular search services such as Yahoo! (http://www.yahoo.com), Excite (http://www.excite.com), and AltaVista (http://www.altavista.digital.com). (I include links to these sites, as well as the others listed elsewhere in the book, in the Internet Launch Pad. See Appendix C for instructions on how to access this page.)

✔ **Net-happenings:** Net-happenings is one of the oldest and most respected Internet announcement services. Visit the Net-happenings Web site at http://www.gi.net/NET to find out how to submit a description of your Web site.

✔ **Word of mouth:** Invite your friends and colleagues to visit your Web site and encourage them to spread the word.

✔ **Newsgroups:** Post a discreet announcement to newsgroups that discuss related topics.

✔ **E-mail signature:** Include your Web site's URL in the signature line of your e-mail messages. (Most e-mail programs enable you to append one or two lines to the bottom of every message.)

If you're updating the Root Web, leave the text box blank.

5. **Leave the Copy changed pages only check box selected.**

6. **Leave the Add to an existing FrontPage Web check box selected.**

7. **If you're updating the Root Web and want to copy updated pages inside Child Webs at the same time, select the Copy child webs (for Root Web only) check box.**

8. **Click OK.**

   FrontPage pauses as the program contacts the dedicated Web server. In a moment, the Name and Password Required dialog box appears.

9. **In the Name and Password text boxes, type the user name and password that you chose at the time you first established your Internet account and then click OK.**

   Depending on the Web site's permission settings, the Name and Password Required text box may appear again, this time requesting your FrontPage administrator name and password. If this occurs, in the Name and Password text boxes, type your administrator name and password and then click OK.

After you click OK, FrontPage contacts the dedicated server and transfers the pages that have changed since the last time you published the site. In a moment, a dialog box appears, telling you the transfer was successful.

10. Click OK to close the dialog box.

Your site is now fresh as a daisy.

Part V
The Part of Tens

In this part . . .

In the following chapters, I give FrontPage a rest and share some tips that help you expand your Web-publishing consciousness. Don't worry, I don't encourage you to meditate; instead, I list ten things you can do with your Web site, ten must-have shareware tools, and ten Net spots you don't want to miss.

Chapter 19

Ten Things You Can Do with Your Web Site

. . . .

*W*eb sites are like rubber bands; if you put your mind to the task, you can think of a million ways to use them. To get you started, here are ten (minus one) of my favorite ways to use a Web site.

Make a Million Bucks

Some folks see flashing dollar signs as they think of the millions of potential customers surfing the Web. Although Internet commerce has yet to take off (people are still nervous about releasing their credit card numbers in cyberspace), secure transactions and electronic payment technology are giving rise to more and more virtual storefronts. So fire up the Corporate Presence Wizard (as I show you how to do in Chapter 1) and create a slick business Web site. Who knows — maybe you're destined to become the next Net Rockefeller.

Keep in Touch

Your parents settled down in Miami. Your best friend is pursuing her fortune in Paris. Your brother works all the time and has no energy for phone calls. No problem! Use your Web site as a meeting place for friends and family. They can log on and share gossip 24 hours a day. Set up a password-protected chat room that only registered loved ones can enter. (Refer to Chapter 15 for details on setting up a discussion group and Chapter 17 for information about Web site permissions.) Post a family tree online with hyperlinks to the home pages of other wired relatives. Devote a page to everyone's birthdays and anniversaries. Scan snapshots from the last family reunion (including that embarrassing one of Aunt Minnie) and put them online for all to see.

Impress Potential Employers

A Web site is the perfect place to toot your own horn. Post your resume online. (Check out the Resume template on the CD that comes with this book.) List your accomplishments, talk about your goals, and point to the Web sites of past workplaces and your alma mater. Add your Web site's URL to your business card and present the card, along with a firm handshake, to people you want to impress.

Impress Geeky Friends

If you play "my hard drive is bigger than your hard drive" with your friends, use your Web site to become king or queen of the technical hill. Download obscure Java applets and ActiveX controls — or, better yet, write your own — and install them in your Web site. (Check out Chapter 13 to find out how to add Java applets and ActiveX controls to your Web pages.) Create a hot list of favorite Web destinations and include links to the home pages of Sun Microsystems, Microsoft, and the Official Star Trek Fan Club. Cultivate a vocabulary full of Web-publishing buzzwords and use them often. ("Yeah, I added a JavaScript to my IMG tags, but it wonked out after Jim ran it with Netscape 3.4026b and his box crashed.")

"Wire" Your Company

If your employees have Web access or are part of a company *intranet* (an internal network based on Internet technology but accessible only to company insiders), use a Web site as a central information hub. Publish company policies and the employee handbook. (Think of all the paper you save by updating them online.) Set up discussion groups for each of your departments. Start a Web-based company newsletter. Use the FrontPage Editor's Guest Book template to create an employee suggestion box. (Refer to Chapter 3 for instructions on how to create a new Web page by using a FrontPage template.)

Spread the Word about a Good Cause

Can you think of something you want the world to know? A Web site is potentially visible to hundreds of thousands of people, making your Web site one of the most effective ways to spread the word about an important cause. Create that Web site, publicize the site far and wide, and watch interested visitors start pouring in. (Refer to the Chapter 18 sidebar "Open for business!" for promotion tips.) Create a feedback form or a discussion group so that visitors can ask questions. Offer to send more information to those who are interested. Keep your site up-to-date so that your Web site becomes a well-respected resource for information and news.

Indulge Your Artistic Side

If you're a poet, artist, or musician, publishing a Web site is the next best thing to a local reading, a gallery showing, or a concert. Use your Web site to showcase your art. Transform your favorite poems into Web pages and invite feedback. Include sample clips of your music. If your work is on display somewhere else, tell visitors where to go to experience your talent.

Incite World Revolution

The photocopy machine put the power of the press in everyone's hands. Social activists produce reams of flyers and leaflets to help spread the word about important issues. The Web makes broadcasting information even easier — a Web page is visible to millions, and you don't need to staple it to telephone poles or hand it to passers-by. So use your Web site to make a difference. Get on your virtual soapbox and issue a call to action.

Erect a Personal Monument

Something's just inherently thrilling about seeing one's name in print or engraved on a plaque. Perhaps the permanence of writing is the key — the idea that your words are always going to be there. A Web site can be the electronic equivalent of a personal monument — a place where you can immortalize the things most important to you. Scan your favorite vacation snapshots and create an online travel diary. Start an unofficial fan club for someone you admire. Use your Web site as a place to pay tribute to the things that inspire you.

Chapter 20

Ten Must-Have Free Internet Tools

● ●

*T*he Internet is brimming with free software. You can download all sorts of tools that make your time on the Internet more efficient and enjoyable. Here are my picks for the ten free shareware tools that all respectable Web publishers need to have tucked away on their hard drives.

The Internet Launch Pad included on the CD contains links to each Web site mentioned in this chapter (for that matter, every chapter in the book).

VirusScan

I put VirusScan at the top of the list because nobody — and I mean *nobody!* — is immune to computer viruses. You are especially susceptible if you swap files over the Internet and download and install software. Protect yourself with a virus detection utility such as McAfee's well-respected VirusScan. VirusScan is a commercial product, but you can download a free evaluation copy to use for 30 days.

Visit the McAfee home page at `http://www.mcafee.com` to download VirusScan.

Microsoft Office Viewers

Microsoft Office Viewers are free programs that enable unfortunate souls without Microsoft Word, Excel, or PowerPoint to read, browse, and print Office documents. If you include an Office document in your Web site, make sure that you point your visitors to the download site for the appropriate viewer.

For more information or to download Microsoft Office viewers, visit the following Web sites:

  ✔ **Word Viewer:** `http://www.microsoft.com/word/Internet/Viewer/default.htm`

✔ **Excel Viewer:** http://www.microsoft.com/excel/Internet/Viewer/default.htm

✔ **PowerPoint Viewer:** http://www.microsoft.com/powerpoint/Internet/Viewer/default.htm

Microsoft PowerPoint Animation Publisher and Player

The Microsoft PowerPoint Animation Publisher and Player enables you to create PowerPoint animations for use in your Web pages. (I show you how in Chapter 13.) The Publisher and Player are two separate programs bundled into one package: The Publisher works with PowerPoint to optimize PowerPoint files for use on the Internet, and the Player works together with your Web browser to display PowerPoint files.

Find out the details from Microsoft at http://www.microsoft.com/powerpoint/internet/player/default.htm.

Paint Shop Pro

If you want to tinker with your Web graphics but don't need the sophistication of Microsoft Image Composer, JASC Software's Paint Shop Pro is your best bet. Use this feature-packed shareware program to create new images or edit existing graphic files. Paint Shop Pro contains basic drawing, cropping, and painting tools, plus special effects such as drop shadows, chiseling, and tiling.

Paint Shop Pro comes on the CD included with this book. To install the program and get started with Paint Shop Pro, see Appendix C.

Everything you ever wanted to know about Paint Shop Pro is available on the Paint Shop Pro home page at http://www.jasc.com/psp.html.

GIF Construction Set

Animated GIFs are individual GIF graphic files grouped together in a single animation file. (I talk more about animated GIFs in the Chapter 7 sidebar, "Movin' and shakin' with GIF animation.") Alchemy Mindworks' GIF Construction Set is one of the best GIF animation tools around.

Read about and download GIF Construction Set from the Alchemy Mindworks home page at `http://www.mindworkshop.com/alchemy/gifcon.html`.

WS_FTP LE

If your dedicated Web server doesn't support FrontPage Server Extensions and you can't use the Web Publishing Wizard, you need an FTP program to publish your Web site. My favorite FTP program is Ipswitch Software's WS_FTP LE. The program's compact, easy to use, and gets the job done.

WS_FTP LE comes on the CD included with this book. For installation instructions and help getting started, see Appendix C.

You can find more about WS_FTP LE (including a helpful list of frequently asked questions) at the Ipswitch home page at `http://www.ipswitch.com`.

WinZip

I use this indispensable utility every day. WinZip compresses (zips) files into tiny, easy-to-transport packages. I use WinZip to archive files on my hard drive that I no longer use but don't want to recycle. I also zip the files I attach to e-mail messages so that they're as small as possible and therefore download quickly. In fact, every word in this book was, at one point, zipped up and sent to my editor via e-mail.

To download the program (or find out more about it), visit the WinZip home page at `http://www.winzip.com`.

This Isn't Shareware, But It's Helpful Anyway

If the prospect of downloading and installing software from the Internet sounds intimidating, read the Beginner's Guide to Download.com at `http://www.download.com`. (The Beginner's Guide is located in the Toolkits section of the Web site.) This site contains links to many of the most popular shareware programs around. The Download.com staff wrote this extremely helpful step-by-step guide to downloading and installing software to help folks use their service.

Chapter 21

Ten Net Spots You Don't Want to Miss

*T*hroughout the book — and in the Internet Launch Pad included on the CD —
I point you to Net sites that I've found particularly helpful. In this chapter, I
highlight ten must-see spots you really shouldn't miss.

The Microsoft FrontPage Home Page

This site is the place to go for all things FrontPage. Here you find FrontPage tips
and information, plus links to the home pages of all the Bonus Pack programs.
Most important, you can access online support and FrontPage help, including
FrontPage newsgroups, a FAQ list (a list of frequently asked questions), and
much more.

Go to `http://www.microsoft.com/frontpage` to visit the Microsoft
FrontPage home page.

The Microsoft Site Builder Workshop

This complex Web site can keep enthusiastic Web publishers occupied for
several hours; the site contains information on everything from basic Web page
creation to design tips to planning a large-scale Web site. I find myself returning
for information again and again, and I rarely need to look elsewhere. For
maximum browsing enjoyment, use a frames-capable browser such as Internet
Explorer (which comes with the Bonus Pack) to view this site.

Go to `http://www.microsoft.com/workshop` to see the Microsoft Site
Builder Workshop.

The Microsoft Knowledge Base

Got a question? The Microsoft Knowledge Base has answers. This mammoth online database contains thousands of articles that answer common software questions or explain annoying bugs. The Knowledge Base contains articles pertaining to all Microsoft products, including FrontPage.

Check out the Microsoft Knowledge Base at `http://www.microsoft.com/kb`.

The Netscape Home Page

Huh? Why am I pointing you to the home page of Microsoft's sworn enemy, you ask? Because Netscape Navigator is still the most popular Web browser in use today, and if you want to design pages that look good to all your visitors, you need to stay abreast of Netscape developments. Better yet, download and install Netscape Navigator. Even if you don't use the program to browse the Web, use Netscape in combination with the FrontPage Editor's Preview in Browser button to preview your Web pages. The more browsers you use to preview your pages, the better you know how they appear to your visitors.

Browse the Netscape home page at `http://www.netscape.com`.

The Beginner's Guide to HTML

The surest way to beef up your Web publishing savvy is to learn HTML, the language behind every Web page. Plenty of good books on the subject are out there, but if you're fired up to get started, check out this legendary Web site. The Beginner's Guide to HTML has been around since the Web first got popular and continues to be a straight-forward, easy-to-take introduction to HTML basics.

You find the Beginner's Guide to HTML at `http://www.ncsa.uiuc.edu/General/Internet/WWW/HTMLPrimer.html`.

The World Wide Web FAQ

If you just want to know how the Web *works*, visit this Web site. The World Wide Web FAQ answers the most common questions about the Web and covers information on the Web itself, Web publishing, Web servers, and more.

The World Wide Web FAQ is available at `http://www.boutell.com/faq`.

Search.com

The Web contains information about the current political climate, pictures of African wild dogs, and several online dating services — the trick is finding these sites. By using Search.com, you can find just about anything, with links to the Web's most popular search utilities, an online Yellow Pages, an e-mail address directory, maps, flight information. . . . You name it — it's here.

Start your Internet exploration at `http://www.search.com`.

Download.com

Everyone keeps talking about the gigabytes of free software available on the Net, but where do you get all that stuff? In Chapter 20, I direct you to several download sites, but if you prefer to browse a listing to see what's available, take a look at Download.com. This way-cool site groups shareware offerings into categories such as Business, Multimedia and Design, and Internet. Or you can look at a list of top picks or the most popular titles.

Surf on over to Download.com at `http://www.download.com`.

The Web Style Manual

This Web site goes into detail about the principles behind designing a Web site that is attractive and easy to use. The information you find here is pretty dense but well-worth a read if you're interested in how to best use the Web as a publishing and communication medium.

Go to `http://info.med.yale.edu/caim/StyleManual_Top.HTML` to check out the Web Design Manual.

Addicted2Stuff

If FrontPage is driving you batty and you just want a little comic relief, visit this hilarious Web site. The witty writers of Addicted2Stuff poke fun at our collective obsessions, including cheesy TV shows, cars, and food. Between guffaws, bone up on Web publishing skills in the sections on HTML, JavaScript tricks (I use one of these tricks in my home page), imagemaps, and GIF animation.

You find Addicted2Stuff at `http://www.morestuff.com`.

Appendix A

The FrontPage Bonus Pack

● ●

*Y*ou got a bonus when you bought FrontPage — the FrontPage Bonus Pack, that is. The Bonus Pack consists of four individual programs that work together with FrontPage to extend FrontPage's capabilities as a Web publishing dynamo.

Because everyone loves bonuses, I tell you in this appendix a bit about each Bonus Pack program. I don't go into detail; if I did, I'd end up writing four entire books. Instead, I give you a little teaser about each program and graciously pass you on to the programs' Web sites for more information. For installation instructions, refer to the documentation that comes with FrontPage.

Microsoft Internet Explorer with Mail and News

Microsoft Internet Explorer is a powerful Web browser that you can use to surf the Web or preview the Web sites you build by using FrontPage. Internet Explorer boasts support for just about every cutting-edge Web publishing effect, including text formatting and color effects, tables, frames, ActiveX, Java, Web page scripts, and much more. Internet Explorer also comes with a built-in e-mail program and a news reader so that you can easily send and receive e-mail messages and read and post articles to Usenet newsgroups, all from within the same tightly integrated program.

Everything you ever wanted to know about Internet Explorer and its associates is available at http://www.microsoft/com/ie.

Microsoft Image Composer

If you want to create good-looking images for your Web site, look no further than the Microsoft Image Composer. This potent image-editing program carries a learning curve but is well worth the time. By using the Image Composer, you can create your own images (called *sprites*), or you can assemble images out of the sprites included with the program. You embellish images with text and art effects, such as charcoal sketch, embossing, or neon glow. Best of all, Image Composer ties in nicely with FrontPage so that you can easily switch between the two programs while you create your Web sites pages and graphics.

Visit the Image Composer Web site at `http://www.microsoft.com/imagecomposer` for more information, more free sprites, and general inspiration.

Microsoft Web Publishing Wizard

If you intend to publish your Web site on a Web server that doesn't support FrontPage Server Extensions, definitely install this program. The Web Publishing Wizard works inside FrontPage to automate transferring Web site files from your computer to your Web server. I show you how to use the Web Publishing Wizard in Chapter 18.

The Web Publishing Wizard home page at `http://www.microsoft.com/windows/software/webpost` contains lots more information.

Microsoft Personal Web Server

FrontPage comes with its own built-in Web server — the FrontPage Personal Web Server — so that you can both build and test FrontPage Web sites on your own computer. Although the FrontPage Personal Web Server is a fully functional Web server program, it can't handle the amount of traffic buzzing around the Internet or a corporate intranet. Folks who want a more powerful Web server to use with FrontPage can instead try the Bonus Pack's Microsoft Personal Web Server. Use this Web server as the basis for a small-scale intranet, to share files with other Web site authors, or to host a low-traffic Web site.

Visit `http://www.microsoft.com/ie/isk/pws.htm` for more info about the Microsoft Personal Web Server.

Appendix B

Installing FrontPage

● ●

*I*f installing FrontPage on your computer seems like a gargantuan task, help is here. In this appendix, I take you step-by-step through the FrontPage installation process. (For information about how to install each Bonus Pack program, refer to the documentation included with FrontPage.)

To install FrontPage, follow these steps:

1. **Turn on your computer and CD-ROM drive.**

    If your computer is already on, exit any programs that are currently open.

2. **Insert the FrontPage 97 CD-ROM into your CD-ROM drive (make sure that the writing on the CD is facing up).**

    In a moment, the opening screen of the Microsoft FrontPage 97 with Bonus Pack installation program appears.

    If no opening screen appears, double-click the My Computer icon on your Windows 95 Desktop to open a window that contains icons for each of your computer's drives. Double-click the CD-ROM icon to launch the installation program.

3. **In the opening screen, click the FrontPage 97 Installation button.**

    The FrontPage 97 Setup Wizard launches, and the Welcome dialog box appears (see Figure B-1).

4. **Click the Next button.**

    The FrontPage Registration dialog box appears.

5. **Enter your name and your company name in the Name and Company text boxes and click Next.**

    The Confirm FrontPage Registration dialog box appears.

6. **If the registration information is correct, click Yes.**

    To change the registration information, click No to return to the FrontPage Registration dialog box. Enter a new name and/or company name in the appropriate text box and click Next to advance to the Confirm FrontPage Registration dialog box. Click Yes to accept the new registration information.

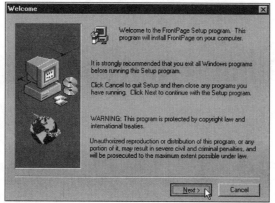

Figure B-1:
The
Welcome
dialog box
of the
FrontPage 97
Setup
Wizard.

After you click <u>Y</u>es, The Destination Path dialog box appears. Here you specify the folder where you want FrontPage installed on your computer.

7. **To accept the FrontPage default destination directory setting (which is C:\PROGRAM FILES\MICROSOFT FRONTPAGE), click <u>N</u>ext.**

I recommend using the FrontPage default destination directory, just to keep installation simple. If, however, you'd rather install FrontPage in a different folder, click the B<u>r</u>owse button to display a list of your computer's folders, choose the one you want and click OK to return to the Destination Path dialog box.

You can, at any time, return to a previous dialog box to change your settings by clicking the <u>B</u>ack button or exit the Setup Wizard by clicking the Cancel button.

After you click <u>N</u>ext, the Setup Type dialog box appears, as shown in Figure B-2.

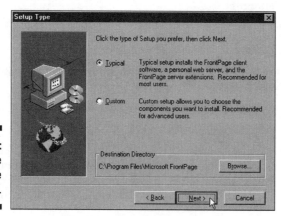

Figure B-2:
The
Setup Type
dialog box.

8. Click the Typical radio button.

The Typical option installs everything you need to get started with FrontPage. I recommend this option if you're installing FrontPage on your computer for the first time or if you're replacing an older version of FrontPage with FrontPage 97. If you prefer to select each component individually, click the Custom radio button.

The Destination Directory area in the Setup Type dialog box displays the folder you chose in step 7. If you want to change the folder at this point, you may do so by clicking the Browse button to display a list of your computer's folders, choosing the one you want, and clicking OK to return to the Setup Type dialog box.

9. Click Next.

If you chose Typical in step 8, the Choose Microsoft FrontPage Personal Web Server Directory dialog box appears. Here you specify the folder where you want the FrontPage Personal Web Server installed on your computer.

If you chose Custom in step 8, the Select Components dialog box appears. Check the check boxes next to the components you want to install; your choices are Client Software, Microsoft Personal Web Server, and Server Extensions. Then click Next to advance to the Choose Microsoft FrontPage Personal Web Server Directory dialog box.

10. To accept the FrontPage default destination directory setting (which is C:\FRONTPAGE WEBS), click Next.

If you'd rather install the Personal Web Server in a different folder, click the Browse button to display a list of your computer's folders, choose the one you want, and click OK to return to the Choose Microsoft FrontPage Personal Web Server Directory dialog box; then click Next.

After you click Next, the Start Copying Files dialog box appears. The Current Settings box contains a list of all the components the Wizard is about to install on your computer, along with the components' destination directories. Review the contents of this box . If you want to change the settings, click the Back button to return to previous dialog boxes, where you can choose different options. Otherwise . . .

11. Click Next to start copying files to your computer.

The dialog box closes, and two progress bars appear, indicating the progress of the installation procedure. Installation takes several minutes, so sit back and relax.

When installation is almost complete, the Administrator Setup for FrontPage Personal Web Server dialog box appears. Here you choose an administrator name and the password you need to access the Web sites you create using FrontPage.

12. **In the Name text box, enter an administrator name; in the Password text box, enter an administrator password; in the Confirm password text box, enter the password again, exactly.**

Administrator names and passwords are case-sensitive (meaning that FrontPage sees Asha and asha as two different names).

Don't forget your administrator name and password! You need your administrator name and password each time you launch FrontPage.

13. **Click OK.**

The Administrator Setup for FrontPage Personal Web Server dialog box closes, and the Setup Complete dialog box appears.

14. **Click Finish to complete the setup process.**

The FrontPage Explorer launches, and a FrontPage dialog box appears stating that it will determine your computer's hostname and IP address. (In essence, the hostname and IP address are names that your computer uses to identify itself on the Internet or company network.)

15. **Click OK.**

The dialog box closes, and in a moment, a second FrontPage dialog box appears, listing your computer's hostname.

FrontPage uses your computer's hostname to identify the FrontPage Personal Web Server — you use this information as you create, open, and publish FrontPage Web sites.

16. **Click OK.**

The dialog box closes, and the Getting Started with Microsoft FrontPage dialog box appears, as shown in Figure B-3. This dialog box leads you straight to ongoing Web publishing adventures!

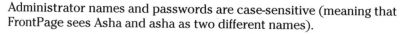
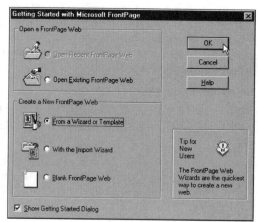

Figure B-3:
The Getting Started with Microsoft FrontPage dialog box.

Appendix C

Using the Stuff on the CD-ROM

● ●

*T*he CD-ROM included with this book contains treats that make Web publishing with FrontPage easier or more fun. In this appendix, I show you how to install and use the stuff on the CD-ROM.

Custom-Designed Web Page Templates

The FrontPage Editor page templates are good starting points for Web pages, but the templates aren't particularly attractive. So I designed a set of custom templates especially for readers of this book. Examples include an online resume, a personal home page, a feedback form, and more.

To use the custom templates (or to open them in the FrontPage Editor to take a look-see), you must copy all the folders stored inside the TEMPLATES folder on the CD-ROM to the C:\PROGRAM FILES\MICROSOFT FRONTPAGE\PAGES folder on your hard drive. (If you originally installed FrontPage in a different destination directory, the PAGES folder is located there.)

This process is most easily accomplished by using the Windows 95 Explorer. (I assume that you know how to use the Windows 95 Explorer; if you don't, refer to your Windows 95 documentation.)

To copy the template folders from the CD to your hard drive, follow these steps:

1. **Launch the Windows 95 Explorer.**

2. **In the left pane, expand the outline of your computer's files and folders until the PAGES folder is visible.**

   To do so, click the plus icon next to your hard drive. A list of the folders on your hard drive becomes visible. Click the plus icon next to the FrontPage destination directory (PROGRAM FILES\MICROSOFT FRONTPAGE — unless you chose a different destination directory at the time you installed FrontPage). Continue expanding folders until you see the PAGES folder in the outline. (The PAGES folder needs only to be visible; you don't need to open the folder.)

   3. While still in the left pane, click the CD-ROM drive icon (you may need to scroll down the left pane to see the icon, as it is located near the bottom of the outline).

   The contents of the CD-ROM become visible in the right pane of the Windows 95 Explorer.

   4. In the right pane, double-click the TEMPLATE folder to open it.

   The folders stored inside the TEMPLATES folder appear in the right pane. If necessary, in the left pane, drag the scroll bar until the PAGES folder is visible again.

   5. Select all the folders in the right pane, drag the selected folders over to the left pane, and drop them into the PAGES folder.

   The Windows 95 Explorer copies each folder to the PAGES folder.

   6. After Explorer copies all the folders, close the Windows 95 Explorer.

Now that you've stored the templates in the right place on your hard drive, you can open them in the FrontPage Editor. To do so, simply follow the steps outlined in the section "Creating a New Web Page from a Template," in Chapter 3.

Internet Launch Pad

Throughout the book, I refer you to helpful and interesting sites on the Internet. The *Internet Launch Pad* is a Web page that contains hyperlinks to every site (plus a few bonus hyperlinks) so that you don't need to type obscure URLs into your Web browser. To view the Internet Launch Pad, simply open the page in any Web browser. If you want to open the page without inserting the CD every time, copy the page (LAUNCH.HTM) to your hard drive before you open it.

NETCOLPC.GIF

This image file contains swatches of each of the "browser-safe" colors; these are the colors that you should use in your Web graphics. (I talk about browser-safe colors in Chapter 7.) Most image-editing programs, including Microsoft Image Composer and Paint Shop Pro, enable you to open an image and then save the colors in the image as a *palette*. Later, you can apply the colors in the palette to other images open in the program, or you may use the palette to select colors for new images you create. For details, refer to your image-editing program's documentation.

Paint Shop Pro

If Microsoft Image Composer is too sophisticated for your taste (or if you don't have enough hard drive space to install the big bruiser), use Paint Shop Pro to create and edit your Web graphics.

To install Paint Shop Pro, follow these steps:

1. **Insert the CD-ROM into your CD-ROM drive.**

2. **On your Windows 95 Desktop, double-click the My Computer icon to open a My Computer window containing icons for each computer drive.**

3. **Double-click the CD-ROM drive icon to display the CD-ROM contents.**

4. **Double-click the PSP folder to open it.**

5. **Double-click SETUP.EXE to launch the Paint Shop Pro installation program.**

   The installation program begins. Follow any prompts that appear on the screen to complete the installation.

To run Paint Shop Pro, click the Windows 95 Start button. Then choose Programs➪Paint Shop Pro➪Paint Shop Pro Shareware 3.12 - 32 Bit.

Because Paint Shop Pro is shareware, you need to pay for it if you decide to keep the program. For more information on registering, click the Help button on the program's initial message box or choose Help➪Purchasing.

To look at graphics files in Paint Shop Pro, follow these steps:

1. **Choose Start➪Programs➪Paint Shop Pro➪Paint Shop Pro Shareware 3.12 - 32 Bit to run Paint Shop Pro; click OK.**

2. **Choose File➪Open to display the Open Image dialog box.**

3. **Choose the drive that contains the file that you want to display by clicking the Drives box; if the drive you want is already selected; go to step 4.**

4. **Choose the folder that contains the file that you want to display by double-clicking the drive letter at the top of the Directories box.**

5. **Double-click the folder you want.**

   A list of files appears.

6. **Double-click the file you want.**

7. **To exit Paint Shop Pro, click the Close button.**

WS_FTP

If you must use an FTP program to publish your Web site, WS_FTP is the best program around. This program enables you to transfer files between your computer and computers on the Internet.

To install WS_FTP, follow these steps:

1. **Insert the CD-ROM into your CD-ROM drive.**

2. **On your Windows 95 Desktop, double-click the My Computer icon to open a My Computer window containing icons for each computer drive.**

3. **Double-click the CD-ROM drive icon to display the contents of the CD-ROM.**

4. **Double-click the WS_FTP folder to open it.**

5. **Double-click INSTALL.EXE to launch the WS_FTP installation program.**

   The installation program begins. Follow any prompts that appear on the screen to complete the installation.

To run WS_FTP, click the Windows 95 Start button and choose Programs➪Ws_ftp➪WS_FTP95LE.

Because this version of WS_FTP is a limited edition, it's free for noncommercial use. But if you want to use the program commercially, you need to register it. For more information, click the <u>A</u>bout button and the About WS_FTP Pro button.

Index

• F •

• G •

• H •

IDG BOOKS WORLDWIDE, INC.

END-USER LICENSE AGREEMENT

Read This. You should carefully read these terms and conditions before opening the software packet(s) included with this book ("Book"). This is a license agreement ("Agreement") between you and IDG Books Worldwide, Inc. ("IDGB"). By opening the accompanying software packet(s), you acknowledge that you have read and accept the following terms and conditions. If you do not agree and do not want to be bound by such terms and conditions, promptly return the Book and the unopened software packet(s) to the place you obtained them for a full refund.

1. **License Grant.** IDGB grants to you (either an individual or entity) a nonexclusive license to use one copy of the enclosed software program(s) (collectively, the "Software") solely for your own personal or business purposes on a single computer (whether a standard computer or a workstation component of a multiuser network). The Software is in use on a computer when it is loaded into temporary memory (i.e., RAM) or installed into permanent memory (e.g., hard disk, CD-ROM, or other storage device). IDGB reserves all rights not expressly granted herein.

2. **Ownership.** IDGB is the owner of all right, title, and interest, including copyright, in and to the compilation of the Software recorded on the disk(s)/CD-ROM. Copyright to the individual programs on the disk(s)/CD-ROM is owned by the author or other authorized copyright owner of each program. Ownership of the Software and all proprietary rights relating thereto remain with IDGB and its licensors.

3. **Restrictions on Use and Transfer.**

   (a) You may only (i) make one copy of the Software for backup or archival purposes, or (ii) transfer the Software to a single hard disk, provided that you keep the original for backup or archival purposes. You may not (i) rent or lease the Software, (ii) copy or reproduce the Software through a LAN or other network system or through any computer subscriber system or bulletin-board system, or (iii) modify, adapt, or create derivative works based on the Software.

   (b) You may not reverse engineer, decompile, or disassemble the Software. You may transfer the Software and user documentation on a permanent basis, provided that the transferee agrees to accept the terms and conditions of this Agreement and you retain no copies. If the Software is an update or has been updated, any transfer must include the most recent update and all prior versions.

4. **Restrictions on Use of Individual Programs.** You must follow the individual requirements and restrictions detailed for each individual program in Appendix C, "About the CD," of this Book. These limitations are contained in the individual license agreements recorded on the disk(s)/CD-ROM. These restrictions may include a requirement that after using the program for the period of time specified in its text, the user must pay a registration fee or discontinue use. By opening the Software packet(s), you will be agreeing to abide by the licenses and restrictions for these individual programs. None of the material on this disk(s) or listed in this Book may ever be distributed, in original or modified form, for commercial purposes.

5. **Limited Warranty.**

   (a) IDGB warrants that the Software and disk(s)/CD-ROM are free from defects in materials and workmanship under normal use for a period of sixty (60) days from the date of purchase of this Book. If IDGB receives notification within the warranty period of defects in materials or workmanship, IDGB will replace the defective disk(s)/CD-ROM.

(b) IDGB AND THE AUTHOR OF THE BOOK DISCLAIM ALL OTHER WARRANTIES, EXPRESS OR IMPLIED, INCLUDING WITHOUT LIMITATION IMPLIED WARRANTIES OF MERCHANTABILITY AND FITNESS FOR A PARTICULAR PURPOSE, WITH RESPECT TO THE SOFTWARE, THE PROGRAMS, THE SOURCE CODE CONTAINED THEREIN, AND/OR THE TECHNIQUES DESCRIBED IN THIS BOOK. IDGB DOES NOT WARRANT THAT THE FUNCTIONS CONTAINED IN THE SOFTWARE WILL MEET YOUR REQUIREMENTS OR THAT THE OPERATION OF THE SOFTWARE WILL BE ERROR FREE.

(c) This limited warranty gives you specific legal rights, and you may have other rights which vary from jurisdiction to jurisdiction.

6. <u>Remedies</u>.

(a) IDGB's entire liability and your exclusive remedy for defects in materials and work-manship shall be limited to replacement of the Software, which may be returned to IDGB with a copy of your receipt at the following address: Disk Fulfillment Department, Attn: *FrontPage Web Publishing and Design For Dummies,* IDG Books Worldwide, Inc., 7260 Shadeland Station, Ste. 100, Indianapolis, IN 46256, or call 1-800-762-2974. Please allow 3–4 weeks for delivery. This Limited Warranty is void if failure of the Software has resulted from accident, abuse, or misapplication. Any replacement Software will be warranted for the remainder of the original warranty period or thirty (30) days, whichever is longer.

(b) In no event shall IDGB or the author be liable for any damages whatsoever (including without limitation damages for loss of business profits, business interruption, loss of business information, or any other pecuniary loss) arising from the use of or inability to use the Book or the Software, even if IDGB has been advised of the possibility of such damages.

(c) Because some jurisdictions do not allow the exclusion or limitation of liability for consequential or incidental damages, the above limitation or exclusion may not apply to you.

7. <u>U.S. Government Restricted Rights</u>. Use, duplication, or disclosure of the Software by the U.S. Government is subject to restrictions stated in paragraph (c) (1) (ii) of the Rights in Technical Data and Computer Software clause of DFARS 252.227-7013, and in subparagraphs (a) through (d) of the Commercial Computer-Restricted Rights clause at FAR 52.227-19, and in similar clauses in the NASA FAR supplement, when applicable.

8. <u>General</u>. This Agreement constitutes the entire understanding of the parties and revokes and supersedes all prior agreements, oral or written, between them and may not be modified or amended except in a writing signed by both parties hereto which specifically refers to this Agreement. This Agreement shall take precedence over any other documents that may be in conflict herewith. If any one or more provisions contained in this Agreement are held by any court or tribunal to be invalid, illegal, or otherwise unenforceable, each and every other provision shall remain in full force and effect.

Installation Instructions

To install, please see Appendix C, "About the CD."

IDG BOOKS WORLDWIDE REGISTRATION CARD

RETURN THIS
REGISTRATION CARD
FOR FREE CATALOG

Title of this book: FrontPage™ Web Publishing & Design For Dummies®

My overall rating of this book: ❏ Very good [1] ❏ Good [2] ❏ Satisfactory [3] ❏ Fair [4] ❏ Poor [5]

How I first heard about this book:

❏ Found in bookstore; name: [6]

❏ Advertisement: [8]

❏ Word of mouth; heard about book from friend, co-worker, etc.: [10]

❏ Book review: [7]

❏ Catalog: [9]

❏ Other: [11]

What I liked most about this book:

What I would change, add, delete, etc., in future editions of this book:

Other comments:

Number of computer books I purchase in a year: ❏ 1 [12] ❏ 2-5 [13] ❏ 6-10 [14] ❏ More than 10 [15]

I would characterize my computer skills as: ❏ Beginner [16] ❏ Intermediate [17] ❏ Advanced [18] ❏ Professional [19]

I use ❏ DOS [20] ❏ Windows [21] ❏ OS/2 [22] ❏ Unix [23] ❏ Macintosh [24] ❏ Other: [25]_____
(please specify)

I would be interested in new books on the following subjects:
(please check all that apply, and use the spaces provided to identify specific software)

❏ Word processing: [26]

❏ Data bases: [28]

❏ File Utilities: [30]

❏ Networking: [32]

❏ Other: [34]

❏ Spreadsheets: [27]

❏ Desktop publishing: [29]

❏ Money management: [31]

❏ Programming languages: [33]

I use a PC at (please check all that apply): ❏ home [35] ❏ work [36] ❏ school [37] ❏ other: [38] _____

The disks I prefer to use are ❏ 5.25 [39] ❏ 3.5 [40] ❏ other: [41]_____

I have a CD ROM: ❏ yes [42] ❏ no [43]

I plan to buy or upgrade computer hardware this year: ❏ yes [44] ❏ no [45]

I plan to buy or upgrade computer software this year: ❏ yes [46] ❏ no [47]

Name: _____ Business title: [48] _____ Type of Business: [49] _____

Address (❏ home [50] ❏ work [51] /Company name: _____)

Street/Suite#

City [52] /State [53] /Zipcode [54]: _____ Country [55] _____

❏ **I liked this book!** You may quote me by name in future
IDG Books Worldwide promotional materials.

My daytime phone number is _____

IDG BOOKS

THE WORLD OF
COMPUTER
KNOWLEDGE

☐ **YES!**

Please keep me informed about IDG's World of Computer Knowledge.
Send me the latest IDG Books catalog.